C000003658

COMMENTING ON COMMENTARIES

COMMENTING
ON COMMENTARIES

Wise Counsel on Buying the Best Books

CHARLES HADDON SPURGEON

SOLID GROUND CHRISTIAN BOOKS
BIRMINGHAM, ALABAMA USA

Solid Ground Christian Books
2090 Columbiana Rd, Suite 2000
Birmingham, AL 35216
205-443-0311
sgcb@charter.net
http://solid-ground-books.com

COMMENTING ON COMMENTARIES
Charles Haddon Spurgeon (1834-1892)

Solid Ground Classic Reprints

First printing of new edition February 2006

Cover work by Borgo Design, Tuscaloosa, AL
Contact them at nelbrown@comcast.net

*Cover image is a picture of Spurgeon sitting in his Study where
he is surrounded by thousands of his friends, many of whom are
discussed in this volume.*

ISBN: 1-59925-053-5

Preface

Commenting and Commentaries is a guide for buying and using Bible commentaries of many kinds, made entertaining by the pungent good humor of the author, Charles Haddon Spurgeon. It is an invaluable resource for ministers and theological students, as well as all Bible students, introducing them to the riches of the best of what has been written about the Bible in past generations.

Even for those who have been reading for decades, *Commenting and Commentaries* continues to be a reliable guide for older, minor titles that may escape one's memory. Spurgeon's helpful placement of the author's name in boldface type, when connected with the most important commentaries, as well as placing the less important entries in two sizes of lightface type, to indicate lesser levels of importance, helps us see at a glance the approximate value of each book.

If there is any danger involved in using *Commenting and Commentaries,* I suppose it is that of treating Spurgeon's assessments as incontrovertible. Publishers may be prone to do this most of all, for few publishers will take on a reprinting project of an old commentary disparaged by Spurgeon. If Spurgeon had rated *The Dutch Annotations,* translated by Theodore Haak, for example, according to its just deserts, perhaps it would have been reprinted several times during the twentieth century! Spurgeon himself, no doubt, would have written *Commenting and Commentaries* a bit more carefully at places had he known how scrupulously many publishers and ministers would use his book to guide them in publishing and purchasing books.

That said, we do marvel at Spurgeon's overall reliability of assessment and his ability to say so much in so few words, and with such flair. This book reflects a master student of Scripture at work, and confirms what others have said as to how much reading went into Spurgeon's preparation of sermons.

The opening lectures in this book should not be passed by. "A Chat about Commentaries" is by far the most valuable, succinct treatment of sets of commentaries ever written. "On Commenting" is a powerful chapter promoting a brief exposition of a Bible chapter as an important aspect of pulpit ministry. Most of what Spurgeon says in this chapter can be applied to full-length sermons as well. A minister of the gospel would do well to read this chapter every year and examine his preaching in light of it.

Let *Commenting and Commentaries* be your key to unlock the world of pre-twentieth-century evangelical Bible commentaries. You will find the key tried and true!

Joel R. Beeke
Puritan Reformed Theological Seminary
Grand Rapids, Michigan

TABLE OF CONTENTS

LECTURE I.

A Chat about Commentaries.

In order to be able to expound the Scriptures, and as an aid to your pulpit studies, you will need to be familiar with the commentators: a glorious army, let me tell you, whose acquaintance will be your delight and profit. Of course, you are not such wiseacres as to think or say that you can expound Scripture without assistance from the works of divines and learned men who have laboured before you in the field of exposition. If you are of that opinion, pray remain so, for you are not worth the trouble of conversion, and like a little coterie who think with you, would resent the attempt as an insult to your infallibility. It seems odd, that certain men who talk so much of what the Holy Spirit reveals to themselves, should think so little of what he has revealed to others. My chat this afternoon is not for these great originals, but for you who are content to learn of holy men, taught of God, and mighty in the Scriptures. It has been the fashion of late years to speak against the use of commentaries. If there were any fear that the expositions of Matthew Henry, Gill, Scott, and others, would be exalted into Christian Targums, we would join the chorus of objectors, but the existence or approach of such a danger we do not suspect. The temptations of our times lie rather in empty pretensions to novelty of sentiment, than in a slavish following of accepted guides. A respectable acquaintance with the opinions of the giants of the past, might have saved many an erratic thinker from wild interpretations and outrageous inferences. Usually, we have found the despisers of commentaries to be men who have no sort of acquaintance with them; in their case, it is the opposite of familiarity which has bred contempt. It is true there are a number of expositions of the whole Bible which are hardly worth shelfroom; they aim at too much and fail altogether; the authors have spread a little learning over a vast surface, and have badly attempted for the entire Scriptures what they might have accomplished for one book with tolerable success; but who will deny the pre-eminent value of such expositions as those of Calvin, Ness, Henry, Trapp, Poole, and Bengel, which are as deep as they are broad? and yet further, who can pretend to biblical learning who has not made himself familiar with the great writers who spent a life in explaining some one sacred book? Caryl on Job will not exhaust the patience of a student who loves every letter of the Word; even Collinges, with his nine hundred and nine pages upon one chapter of the Song, will not be too full for the preacher's use; nor will Manton's long—metre edition of the hundred and nineteenth Psalm be too profuse. No stranger could imagine the vast amount of real learning to be found in old commentaries like the following:—Durham on Solomon's Song, Wilcocks on Psalms and Proverbs, Jermin on Ecclesiastes and Proverbs, Greenhill on Ezekiel, Burroughs on Hosea, Ainsworth on the Pentateuch, King on Jonah, Hutcheson on John, Peter Martyr on Romans, &c., and in Willett, Sibbes, Bayne, Elton, Byfield, Daillé, Adams, Taylor, Barlow, Goodwin, and others on the various epistles. Without attempting to give in detail the names of all, I intend in a familiar talk to mention the more notable, who wrote upon the whole Bible, or on either Testament, and I especially direct your attention to the titles, which in Puritan writers generally give in brief the run of the work.

First among the mighty for general usefulness we are bound to mention the man whose name is a household word, MATTHEW HENRY.* He is most pious and pithy, sound and sensible, suggestive and sober, terse and trustworthy. You will find him to be glittering with metaphors, rich in analogies, overflowing with illustrations, superabundant in reflections. He delights in apposition and alliteration; he is usually plain, quaint, and full of pith; he sees right through a text directly; apparently he is not critical, but he quietly gives the result of an accurate critical knowledge of the original fully up to the best critics of his time. He is not versed in the manners and customs of the East, for the Holy Land was not so accessible as in our day; but he is deeply spiritual, heavenly, and profitable; finding good matter in every text, and from all deducing most practical and judicious lessons. His is a kind of

---

* An Exposition of all the Books of the Old and New Testaments. By MATTHEW HENRY, late minister of the gospel in Chester. 6 volumes $24.50. Revell.

commentary to be placed where I saw it, in the old meeting-house at Chester—chained in the vestry for anybody and everybody to read. It is the poor man's commentary, the old Christian's companion, suitable to everybody, instructive to all. His own account of how he was led to write his exposition, affords us an example of delighting in the law of the Lord. "If any desire to know how so mean and obscure a person as I am, who in learning, judgment, felicity of expression, and all advantages for such a service, am less than the least of all my Master's servants, came to venture upon so great a work, I can give no other account of it but this. It has long been my practice, what little time I had to spare in my study from my constant preparations for the pulpit, to spend it in drawing up expositions upon some parts of the New Testament, not so much for my own use, as purely for my own entertainment, because I know not how to employ my thoughts and time more to my satisfaction. *Trahit sua quemque voluptas;* every man that studies hath some beloved study, which is his delight above any other; and this is mine. It is that learning which it was my happiness from a child to be trained up in by my ever honoured father, whose memory must always be very dear and precious to me. He often minded me, that a good textuary is a good divine; and that I should read other books with this in my eye, that I might be the better able to understand and apply the Scripture." You are aware, perhaps, that the latter part of the New Testament was completed by other hands, the good man having gone the way of all flesh. The writers were Messrs. Evans, Brown, Mayo, Bays, Rosewell, Harriss, Atkinson, Smith, Tong, Wright, Merrell, Hill, Reynolds, and Billingsley—all Dissenting ministers. They have executed their work exceedingly well, have worked in much of the matter which Henry had collected, and have done their best to follow his methods, but their combined production is far inferior to Matthew Henry himself, and any reader will soon detect the difference. Every minister ought to read Matthew Henry entirely and carefully through once at least. I should recommend you to get through it in the next twelve months after you leave college. Begin at the beginning, and resolve that you will traverse the goodly land from Dan to Beersheba. You will acquire a vast store of sermons if you read with your note-book close at hand; and as for thoughts, they will swarm around you like twittering swallows around an old gable towards the close of autumn. If you publicly expound the chapter you have just been reading, your people will wonder at the novelty of your remarks and the depth of your thoughts, and then you may tell them what a treasure Henry is. Mr. Jay's sermons bear indubitable evidence of his having studied Matthew Henry almost daily. Many of the quaint things in Jay's sermons are either directly traceable to Matthew Henry or to his familiarity with that writer. I have thought that the style of Jay was founded upon Matthew Henry: Matthew Henry is Jay writing, Jay is Matthew Henry preaching. What more could I say in commendation either of the preacher or the author?

It would not be possible for me too earnestly to press upon you the importance of reading the expositions of that prince among men, JOHN CALVIN!* I am afraid that scant purses may debar you from their purchase, but if it be possible procure them, and meanwhile, since they are in the College library, use them diligently. I have often felt inclined to cry out with Father Simon, a Roman Catholic, " Calvin possessed a sublime genius," and with Scaliger, " Oh! how well has Calvin reached the meaning of the prophets— no one better." You will find forty-two or more goodly volumes worth their weight in gold. Of all commentators I believe John Calvin to be the most candid. In his expositions he is not always what moderns would call Calvinistic; that is to say, where Scripture maintains the doctrine of predestination and grace he flinches in no degree, but inasmuch as some Scriptures bear the impress of human free action and responsibility, he does not shun to expound their meaning in all fairness and integrity. He was no trimmer and pruner of texts. He gave their meaning as far as he knew it. His honest intention was to translate the Hebrew and the Greek originals as accurately as he possibly could, and then to give the meaning which would naturally be conveyed by such Greek and Hebrew words: he laboured, in fact, to declare, not his own mind upon the Spirit's words, but the mind of the Spirit as couched in those words. Dr. King very truly says of him, " No writer ever dealt more fairly and honestly by the Word of God. He is scrupulously careful to let it speak for itself, and to guard against every tendency of his own mind to put upon it a questionable meaning for the sake of establishing some doctrine which he

---

* Calvin's Commentary. (Reprint of Calvin Translation Society edition) 45 volumes complete $150.00. Eerdmans. Old Testament only 30 volumes $100.00; New Testament only 15 volumes $50.00. Institutes of the Christian Religion, translated by Henry Beveridge, 2 volumes $7.50. Eerdmans.

feels to be important, or some theory which he is anxious to uphold. This is one of his prime excellences. He will not maintain any doctrine, however orthodox and essential, by a text of Scripture which to him appears of doubtful application, or of inadequate force. For instance, firmly as he believed the doctrine of the Trinity, he refuses to derive an argument in its favour from the plural form of the name of God in the first chapter of Genesis. It were easy to multiply examples of this kind, which, whether we agree in his conclusion or not, cannot fail to produce the conviction that he is at least an honest commentator, and will not make any passage of Scripture speak more or less than, according to his view, its divine Author intended it to speak."

The edition of John Calvin's works which was issued by the Calvin Translation Society, is greatly enriched by the remarks of the editors, consisting not merely of notes on the Latin of Calvin, and the French translation, or on the text of the original Scriptures, but also of weighty opinions of eminent critics, illustrative manners and customs, and observations of travellers. By the way, gentlemen, what a pity it is that people do not, as a rule, read the notes in the old Puritan books! If you purchase old copies of such writers as Brooks, you will find that the notes in the margin are almost as rich as the books themselves. They are dust of gold, of the same metal as the ingots in the centre of the page. But to return to Calvin. If you needed any confirmatory evidence as to the value of his writings, I might summon a cloud of witnesses, but it will suffice to quote one or two. Here is the opinion of one who is looked upon as his great enemy, namely, Arminius: "Next to the perusal of the Scriptures, which I earnestly inculcate, I exhort my pupils to peruse CALVIN'S commentaries, which I extol in loftier terms than *Helmich** himself; for I affirm that *he excels beyond comparison in the interpretation of Scripture, and that his commentaries ought to be more highly valued than all that is handed down to us by the Library of the Fathers;* so that I acknowledge him to have possessed above most others, or rather above all other men, what may be called an eminent gift of prophecy."

Quaint Robert Robinson said of him, "There is no abridging this sententious commentator, and the more I read him, the more does he become a favourite expositor with me." Holy Baxter wrote, "I know no man since the apostles' days, whom I value and honour more than Calvin, and whose judgment in all things, one with another, I more esteem and come nearer to."

---

* Werner Helmich, a Dutch Protestant divine, A.D. 1551—1608.

If you are well enough versed in Latin, you will find in POOLE's
SYNOPSIS,* a marvellous collection of all the wisdom and folly of
the critics. It is a large cyclopædia worthy of the days when
theologians could be cyclopean, and had not shrunk from folios to
octavos. Query—a query for which I will not demand an answer—
has one of you ever beaten the dust from the venerable copy of
Poole which loads our library shelves? Yet as Poole spent no less
than ten years in compiling it, it should be worthy of your frequent notice—ten years, let me add, spent in Amsterdam in exile
for the truth's sake from his native land.

His work was based upon an earlier compilation entitled *Critici
Sacri*, containing the concentrated light of a constellation of learned
men who have never been excelled in any age or country.

MATTHEW POOLE also wrote ANNOTATIONS† upon the Word of
God, in English, which are mentioned by Matthew Henry as
having passed through many impressions in his day, and he not
only highly praises them, but declares that he has in his own work
all along been brief upon that which Mr. Poole has more largely
discussed, and has industriously declined what is to be found there.
The three volumes, tolerably cheap, and easily to be got at, are
necessaries for your libraries. On the whole, if I must have only
one commentary, and had read Matthew Henry as I have, I do
not know but what I should choose Poole. He is a very prudent
and judicious commentator; and one of the few who could honestly
say, "We have not willingly balked any obvious difficulty, and
have designed a just satisfaction to all our readers; and if any
knot remains yet untied, we have told our readers what hath been
most probably said for their satisfaction in the untying of it."
Poole is not so pithy and witty by far as Matthew Henry, but he is
perhaps more accurate, less a commentator, and more an expositor.
You meet with no ostentation of learning in Matthew Poole, and
that for the simple reason that he was so profoundly learned as to
be able to give results without a display of his intellectual crockery.
A pedant who is for ever quoting Ambrose and Jerome, Piscator
and Œcolampadius, in order to show what a copious reader he has
been, is usually a dealer in small wares, and quotes only what others

---

* Synopsis Criticorum aliorumque S. Scripturæ Interpretum. Operâ Matthæi
Poli. *Londinensis*, MDCLXIX.

† Annotations upon the Holy Bible. Wherein the sacred text is inserted, and
various readings annexed, together with the parallel Scriptures. The more difficult
terms in each verse explained; seeming contradictions reconciled; questions and
doubts resolved; and the whole text opened. By the late Rev. and learned divine,
Mr. MATTHEW POOLE. 1700.

have quoted before him, but he who can give you the result and outcome of very extensive reading without sounding a trumpet before him is the really learned man. Mind you do not confound the Annotations with the Synopsis; the English work is not a translation of the Latin one, but an entirely distinct performance. Strange to say, like the other great Matthew he did not live to complete his work beyond Isaiah lviii.; other hands united to finish the design.

Would it be possible to eulogise too much the incomparably sententious and suggestive folios of JOHN TRAPP?* Since Mr. Dickinson has rendered them accessible,† I trust most of you have bought them. Trapp will be most valuable to men of discernment, to thoughtful men, to men who only want a start in a line of thought, and are then able to run alone. Trapp excels in witty stories on the one hand, and learned allusions on the other. You will not *thoroughly* enjoy him unless you can turn to the original, and yet a mere dunce at classics will prize him. His writings remind me of himself: he was a pastor, hence his holy practical remarks; he was the head of a public school, and everywhere we see his profound scholarship; he was for some time amid the guns and drums of a parliamentary garrison, and he gossips and tells queer anecdotes like a man used to soldier-life; yet withal, he comments as if he had been nothing else but a commentator all his days. Some of his remarks are far-fetched, and like the far-fetched rarities of Solomon's Tarshish, there is much gold and silver, but there are also apes and peacocks. His criticisms would some of them be the cause of amusement in these days of greater scholarship; but for all that, he who shall excel Trapp had need rise very early in the morning. Trapp is my especial companion and treasure; I can read him when I am too weary for anything else. Trapp is salt, pepper, mustard, vinegar, and all the other condiments. Put him

---

* Annotations upon the Old and New Testament, in five distinct volumes. Whereof the first is upon the five Books of Moses, and upon the following Books, of Joshua, Judges, Ruth, Samuel, Kings, and Chronicles. The second is upon Ezra, Nehemiah, Esther, Job, and Psalms. The third is upon Proverbs, Ecclesiastes, Solomon's Song, and the four major prophets, with a treatise called, "The righteous Man's Recompense." The fourth is upon the twelve minor prophets, the fifth and last is upon the whole New Testament, with a Decade of Divine Discourses, or Common-places, thereunto annexed. By JOHN TRAPP, M.A., pastor and preacher of the word of God at Weston-upon-Avon, in Gloucestershire. 1662.

† The reprint by Mr. R. D. Dickinson is edited by Rev. W. WEBSTER, and Rev. HUGH MARTIN, with a Memoir of the Author, by Rev. A. B. GROSART, 5 vols., super royal 8vo., cloth

on the table when you study, and when you have your dish ready, use him by way of spicing the whole thing. Yes, gentlemen, read Trapp certainly, and if you catch the infection of his consecrated humour, so much the better for your hearers.

A very distinguished place is due to DR. GILL.* Beyond all controversy, Gill was one of the most able Hebraists of his day, and in other matters no mean proficient. When an opponent in controversy had ventured to call him " a botcher in divinity," the good doctor, being compelled to become a fool in glorying, gave such a list of his attainments as must have covered his accuser with confusion. His great work on the Holy Scriptures is greatly prized at the present day by the best authorities, which is conclusive evidence of its value, since the set of the current of theological thought is quite contrary to that of Dr. Gill. No one in these days is likely to be censured for his Arminianism, but most modern divines affect to sneer at anything a little too highly Calvinistic: however, amid the decadence of his own rigid system, and the disrepute of even more moderate Calvinism, Gill's laurels as an expositor are still green. His ultraism is discarded, but his learning is respected : the world and the church take leave to question his dogmatism, but they both bow before his erudition. Probably no man since Gill's days has at all equalled him in the matter of Rabbinical learning. Say what you will about that lore, it has its value : of course, a man has to rake among perfect dunghills and dustheaps, but there are a few jewels which the world could not afford to miss. Gill was a master cinder-sifter among the Targums, the Talmuds, the Mishna, and the Gemara. Richly did he deserve the

---

* An Exposition of the Old Testament, in which are recorded the origin of mankind, of the several nations of the world, and of the Jewish nation in particular ; the lives of the patriarchs of Israel; the journey of that people from Egypt to the land of Canaan, and their settlement in that land : their laws, moral, ceremonial, and judicial; their government and state under judges and kings ; their several captivities, and their sacred books of devotion : in the exposition of which, it is attempted to give an account of their several books and the writers of them ; a summary of each chapter, and the genuine sense of each verse, and, throughout the whole, the original text and the versions of it, are inspected and compared ; interpretation of the best note, both Jewish and Christian, consulted ; difficult places at large explained, seeming contradictions reconciled, and various passages illustrated and confirmed by testimonies of writers as well Gentile as Jewish. By JOHN GILL, D.D.

An Exposition of the New Testament, in which the sense of the sacred text is taken; doctrinal and practical truths are set in a plain and easy light, difficult passages explained ; seeming contradictions reconciled ; and whatever is material in the various readings and several Oriental versions is observed. The whole illustrated with notes taken from the most ancient Jewish writings. By JOHN GILL, D.D.

Reprint edition complete in 6 volumes under consideration at press time by Kregel Publications.

degree of which he said, "I never bought it, nor thought it, nor sought it."

He was always at work; it is difficult to say when he slept, for he wrote 10,000 folio pages of theology. The portrait of him which belongs to this church, and hangs in my private vestry, and from which all the published portraits have been engraved, represents him after an interview with an Arminian gentleman, turning up his nose in a most expressive manner, as if he could not endure even the smell of free-will. In some such a vein he wrote his commentary. He hunts Arminianism throughout the whole of it. He is far from being so interesting and readable as Matthew Henry. He delivered his comments to his people from Sabbath to Sabbath, hence their peculiar mannerism. His frequent method of animadversion is, "This text does not mean this," nobody ever thought it did; "It does not mean that," only two or three heretics ever imagined it did; and again it does not mean a third thing, or a fourth, or a fifth, or a sixth absurdity; but at last he thinks it does mean so-and-so, and tells you so in a methodical, sermon-like manner. This is an easy method, gentlemen, of filling up the time, if you are ever short of heads for a sermon. Show your people firstly, secondly, and thirdly, what the text does not mean, and then afterwards you can go back and show them what it does mean. It may be thought, however, that one such a teacher is enough, and that what was tolerated from a learned doctor would be scouted in a student fresh from college. For good, sound, massive, sober sense in commenting, who can excel Gill? Very seldom does he allow himself to be run away with by imagination, except now and then when he tries to open up a parable, and finds a meaning in every circumstance and minute detail; or when he falls upon a text which is not congenial with his creed, and hacks and hews terribly to bring the word of God into a more systematic shape. Gill is the Coryphæus of hyper-Calvinism, but if his followers never went beyond their master, they would not go very far astray.

I have placed next to Gill in my library ADAM CLARKE,* but as I have no desire to have my rest broken by wars among the authors, I have placed Doddridge between them. If the spirits of

---

* The Holy Bible, containing the Old and New Testaments. The text carefully printed from the most correct copies of the present Authorised Translation, including the Margin l Readings and Parallel Texts. With a Commentary and Critical Notes: designed as a help to a better understanding of the Sacred Writings. By ADAM CLARKE, LL.D., F.S.A., &c. A new edition with the Author's final corrections. 6 volumes $24.50. Abingdon.

the two worthies could descend to the earth in the same mood in which they departed, no one house would be able to hold them. Adam Clarke is the great annotator of our Wesleyan friends; and they have no reason to be ashamed of him, for he takes rank among the chief of expositors. His mind was evidently fascinated by the singularities of learning, and hence his commentary is rather too much of an old curiosity shop, but it is filled with valuable rarities, such as none but a great man could have collected. Like Gill, he is one-sided, only in the opposite direction to our friend the Baptist. The use of the two authors may help to preserve the balance of your judgments. If you consider Clarke wanting in unction, *do not read him for savour but for criticism,* and then you will not be disappointed.

The author thought that lengthy reflections were rather for the preacher than the commentator, and hence it was not a part of his plan to write such observations as those which endear Matthew Henry to the million. If you have a copy of Adam Clarke, and exercise discretion in reading it, you will derive immense advantage from it, for frequently by a sort of side-light he brings out the meaning of the text in an astonishingly novel manner. I do not wonder that Adam Clarke still stands, notwithstanding his peculiarities, a prince among commentators. I do not find him so helpful as Gill, but still from his side of the question, with which I have personally no sympathy, he is an important writer, and deserves to be studied by every reader of the Scriptures. He very judiciously says of Dr. Gill, " He was a very learned and good man, but has often lost sight of his better judgment in spiritualising the text ;" this is the very verdict which we pass upon himself, only altering the last sentence a word or two ; " He has often lost sight of his better judgment in following learned singularities ;" the monkey, instead of the serpent, tempting Eve, is a notable instance.

As I am paying no sort of attention to chronological order, I shall now wander back to old MASTER MAYER,* a rare and

---

* A Commentary upon the whole " Old Testament," added to that of the same author upon the whole " New Testament," published many years before, to make a complete work upon the whole *Bible.* Wherein the divers Translations and Expositions, *Literall* and *Mysticall*, of all the most famous Commentators, both Ancient and Modern, are propounded, examined, and judged of, for the more full satisfaction of the studious reader in all things, and many most genuine notions inserted for edification in the grace of our Lord Jesus Christ. A work, the like unto which hath never yet been published by any man, yet very necessary, not only for students in divinity, but also for every Christian that loveth the knowledge of divine things, or humane, whereof this comment is also full, &c. By JOHN MAYER, Doctor of Divinity. London. MDCLIII.

valuable author. I have been in London a long time now, but I
have only of late been able to complete my set. The first volume
especially is rare in the extreme. The six volumes, folio, are a
most judicious and able digest of former commentators, enriched
with the author's own notes, forming altogether one of the fullest
and best of learned English commentaries; not meant for popular
use, but invaluable to the student. He is a link between the
modern school, at the head of which I put Poole and Henry, and
the older school who mostly wrote in Latin, and were tinctured
with the conceits of those schoolmen who gathered like flies around
the corpse of Aristotle. He appears to have written before
Diodati and Trapp, but lacked opportunity to publish. I fear he
will be forgotten, as there is but little prospect of the republication
of so diffuse, and perhaps heavy, an author. He is a very Alp of
learning, but cold and lacking in spirituality, hence his lack of
popularity.

In 1653, ARTHUR JACKSON,* Preacher of God's Word in
Wood Street, London, issued four volumes upon the Old Testament, which appear to have been the result of his pulpit expositions to his people. Valuable his works would be if there were
no better, but they are not comparable to others already and afterwards mentioned. You can do without him, but he is a reputable
author. Far more useful is NESS'S HISTORY AND MYSTERY of the
Old and New Testament,† a grand repository of quaint remarks
upon the historical books of Scripture. You will find it contained
in four thin folio volumes, and you will have a treasure if you
procure it.

Need I commend BISHOP HALL'S CONTEMPLATIONS‡ to your

---

* A help for the understanding of the Holy Scripture. Intended chiefly for the
assistance and information of those that use constantly every day to read some part of
the Bible, and would gladly always understand what they read if they had some man
to help them. *The first part.* Containing certain short notes of exposition upon the
five books of Moses, &c. By ARTHUR JACKSON, preacher of God's Word in Wood Street,.
London. Anno Dom. MDCDLII.

† A Complete History and Mystery of the Old and New Testament, logically discussed, and theologically improved. In three distinct volumes. The first beginning
at the Creation of the World, and ending at *Moses.* The second continuing the
History from *Joshua* till the Birth of Christ. The third from the Birth of Christ, to
the Death of the last and longest living Apostle, *John* the Divine. The like undertaking (in such a manner and method) being never attempted before. By Mr.
CHRISTOPHER NESS, minister of the gospel in London. 1690. 3 vols., thin folio.

‡ Contemplations on the historical passages of the Old and New Testament. By
the right Rev. JOSEPH HALL, D.D., Bishop of Norwich. Numerous editions; the one
before us has "a memoir of the author, by JAMES HAMILTON, M.B.S.," and was
published by Mr. Nelson of Edinburgh.

affectionate attention? What wit! What sound sense! What concealed learning! His style is as pithy and witty as that of Thomas Fuller, and it has a sacred unction about it to which Fuller has no pretension.

HAAK'S ANNOTATIONS* come to us as the offspring of the famous Synod of Dort, and the WESTMINSTER ANNOTATIONS† as the production of a still more venerable assembly; but if, with my hat off, bowing profoundly to those august conclaves of master minds, I may venture to say so, I would observe that they furnish another instance that committees seldom equal the labours of individuals. The notes are too short and fragmentary to be of any great value. The volumes are a heavy investment.

Among entire commentators of modern date, a high place is usually awarded to THOMAS SCOTT,‡ and I shall not dispute his right to it. He is the expositor of evangelical Episcopalians, even as Adam Clarke is the prophet of the Wesleyans, but to me he has seldom given a thought, and I have almost discontinued consulting him. The very first money I ever received for pulpit services in London was invested in Thomas Scott, and I neither regretted the investment nor became exhilarated thereby. His work has always been popular, is very judicious, thoroughly sound and gracious; but for suggestiveness and pith is not comparable to Matthew Henry. I know I am talking heresy, but I cannot help saying that for a minister's use, Scott is mere milk and water—good and trustworthy, but not solid enough in matter for full-grown men.

---

* The Dutch Annotations upon the whole Bible ; or, all the Holy Canonical Scriptures of the Old and New Testament, together with, and according to, their own translation of all the text: as both the one and the other were ordered and appointed by the Synod of Dort, 1618, and published by authority, 1637. Now faithfully communicated to the use of Great Britain, in English, &c. By THEODORE HAAK, Esq. London, 1657. 2 volumes folio.

† Annotations upon all the Books of the Old and New Testaments. This third, above the first and second, edition so enlarged, as they make an entire commentary on the sacred Scriptures, the like never before published in English. Wherein the text is explained, doubts resolved, Scriptures paralleled, and various readings observed. By the labour of certain learned divines, thereunto appointed, and therein employed, as is expressed in the preface. London, 1657.

‡ The Holy Bible, containing the Old and New Testaments, according to the authorised version, with explanatory notes, practical observations, and copious marginal references. By THOMAS SCOTT, rector of Ashton Sandford, Bucks. A new edition, with the author's last corrections and improvements, with ten maps. London: L. B. Seeley and Son. 1827.

In the family, Scott will hold his place, but in the study you want condensed thought, and this you must look for elsewhere.

To all young men of light purses let me recommend THE TRACT SOCIETY'S COMMENTARY,* in six volumes, which contains the marrow of Henry and Scott, with notes from a hundred other authors. It is well executed, and for poor men a great Godsend. I believe the Society has some special arrangement for poor students, that they may have these volumes at the cheapest rate.

Gentlemen, if you want something full of marrow and fatness, cheering to your own hearts by way of comment, and likely to help you in giving to your hearers rich expositions, buy DR. HAWKER'S POOR MAN'S COMMENTARY.† Dr. Hawker was the very least of commentators in the matter of criticism; he had no critical capacity, and no ability whatever as an interpreter of the letter; but *he sees Jesus*, and that is a sacred gift which is most precious whether the owner be a critic or no. It is to be confessed that he occasionally sees Jesus where Jesus is not legitimately to be seen. He allows his reason to be mastered by his affections, which, vice as it is, is not the worst fault in the world. There is always such a savour of the Lord Jesus Christ in Dr. Hawker that you cannot read him without profit. He has the peculiar idea that Christ is in every Psalm, and this often leads him totally astray, because he attributes expressions to the Saviour which really shock the holy mind to imagine our Lord's using. However, not as a substantial dish, but as a condiment, place the Plymouth vicar's work on the table. His writing is all sugar, and you will know how to use it, not devouring it in lumps, but using it to flavour other things.

"ALBERT BARNES," say you, "what do you think of Albert Barnes?" Albert Barnes is a learned and able divine, but his productions are unequal in value, the gospels are of comparatively little worth, but his other comments are extremely useful for Sunday-school teachers and persons with a narrow range of reading,

---

* The Holy Bible; the text according to the authorised version; and a Commentary from Henry and Scott, with numerous Observations and Notes from other Authors; also, the Marginal References, Maps of the Countries mentioned in Scripture, and various useful Tables. London: The Religious Tract Society. (6 volumes.)

† The Poor Man's Commentary on the Bible. By ROBERT HAWKER, D.D., Vicar of Charles, Plymouth, 1822. (3 vols. folio, or 10 vols. 8vo.)

endowed with enough good sense to discriminate between good and evil. If a controversial eye had been turned upon Barnes's Notes years ago, and his inaccuracies shown up by some unsparing hand, he would never have had the popularity which at one time set rival publishers advertising him in every direction. His Old Testament volumes are to be greatly commended as learned and laborious, and the epistles are useful as a valuable collection of the various opinions of learned men. Placed by the side of the great masters, Barnes is a lesser light, but taking his work for what it is and professes to be, no minister can afford to be without it, and this is no small praise for works which were only intended for Sunday-school teachers.*

Upon the New Testament DODDRIDGE'S EXPOSITOR† is worthy of a far more extensive reading than is nowadays accorded to it. It is all in the form of a paraphrase, with the text in italics; a mode of treatment far from satisfactory as a rule, but exceedingly well carried out in this instance. The notes are very good, and reveal the thorough scholar. Our authorised version is placed in the margin, and a new translation in the paraphrase. The four evangelists are thrown into a harmony, a plan which has its advantages but is not without its evils. The practical improvements at the end of each chapter generally consist of pressing exhortations and devout meditations, suggested by the matter under discussion. It is sadly indicative of the Socinianism of the age in which this good man lived, that he feels called upon to apologise for the evangelical strain in which he has written. He appears to have barely finished this work in shorthand at the time of his death, and the later books were transcribed under the care of Job Orton. No Life Insurance Society should accept the proposals of a commentator on the whole of either Testament, for

---

* Barnes, Albert—Notes on the New Testament. Enlarged type edition, edited by Robert Frew. 11 volumes $35.00 Baker; Notes on the Old Testament, edited by Robert Frew. Job, 2 vols.; Psalms, 3 vols.; Isaiah, 2 vols.; Daniel, 2 vols., total 9 volumes. $31.50. $3.50 per volume. Baker.

† The Family Expositor; or a Paraphrase and Version of the New Testament; with Critical Notes, and a Practical Improvement of each Section. By P. DODDRIDGE, D.D. To which is prefixed a Life of the Author, By Andrew Kippis, D.D., F.R.S., and S.A. London: Longman, Orme, and Co., 1840. (4 vols. 8vo.)

it seems to be the rule that such students of the Word should be taken up to their reward before their task is quite completed.

Then, of course, gentlemen, you will economise rigidly until you have accumulated funds to purchase KITTO'S PICTORIAL BIBLE. You mean to take that goodly freight on board before you launch upon the sea of married life. As you cannot visit the Holy Land, it is well for you that there is a work like the Pictorial Bible, in which the notes of the most observant travellers are arranged under the texts which they illustrate. For the geography, zoology, botany, and manners and customs of Palestine, this will be your counsellor and guide. Add to this noble comment, which is sold at a surprisingly low price, the eight volumes of KITTO'S DAILY READINGS.* They are not exactly a commentary, but what marvellous expositions you have there! You have reading more interesting than any novel that was ever written, and as instructive as the heaviest theology. The matter is quite attractive and fascinating, and yet so weighty, that the man who shall study those eight volumes thoroughly, will not fail to read his Bible intelligently and with growing interest.

THE GNOMON OF THE NEW TESTAMENT, BY JOHN ALBERT BENGEL,† is the scholar's delight. He selected the title as modest and appropriate, intending it in the sense of a pointer or indicator, like the sun-dial; his aim being to point out or indicate the full force and meaning of the words and sentences of the New Testament. He endeavours to let the text itself cast its shadow on his page, believing with Luther that "the science of theology is nothing else but grammar exercised on the words of the Holy Spirit." The editor of the translation published by Messrs. Clarke, says in his preface, "It is quite superfluous to write in praise of the Gnomon of Bengel. Ever since the year in which it was first published, A.D. 1742, up to the present time, it has been growing in estimation, and has been more and more widely circulated among the scholars of all countries. Though modern criticism has furnished many valuable additions to our materials for New

* Daily Bible Illustrations, being Original Readings for a Year, on subjects from Sacred History, Biography, Antiquities, and Theology. Especially designed for the family circle. By JOHN KITTO, D.D., F.S.A. 8 volumes, small 8vo. (A New Annotated edition has just been brought out by Messrs. Oliphant of Edinburgh.)
† Gnomon of the New Testament, by JOHN ALBERT BENGEL. Now first translated into English, with original notes explanatory and illustrative. Revised and edited by Rev. Andrew R. Fausset, M.A., of Trinity College, Dublin. Edinburgh: T. & T. Clarke, 38, George-street, 1863. Five vols. demy 8vo.

Testament exegesis, yet, in some respects, Bengel stands out still
'*facile princeps*' among all who have laboured, or who as yet
labour in that important field.   He is unrivalled in felicitous
brevity, combined with what seldom accompanies that excellence,
namely, perspicuity.   Terse, weighty, and suggestive, he often, as a
modern writer observes, 'condenses more matter into a line, than
can be extracted from pages of other writers.'" . . . . . "In the
passages which form the subject of controversy between Calvinists
and Arminians, Bengel takes the view adopted by the latter, and
in this respect I do not concur with him.   But whilst he thus gives
an undue prominence, as it would seem to me, to the responsibility
and freedom of man in these passages, yet, in the general tenor of
his work, there breathe such a holy reverence for God's sovereignty,
and such spiritual unction, that the most extreme Calvinist would,
for the most part, be unable to discover to what section of opinions
he attached himself, and as to the controverted passages would
feel inclined to say, '*Quum talis sis, utinam noster esses.*'"
.Men with a dislike for thinking had better not purchase the five
precious volumes, for they will be of little use to them; but men
who love brain-work will find fine exercise in spelling out the deep
meaning of Bengel's excessively terse sentences.   His principles of
interpretation stated in his "Essay on the Right Way of Handling
Divine Subjects," are such as will make the lover of God's word
feel safe in his hands: "Put nothing *into* the Scriptures, but draw
everything *from* them, and suffer nothing to remain hidden, that is
really *in* them."   "Though each inspired writer has his own manner
and style, one and the same Spirit breathes through all, one grand
idea pervades all."   "Every divine communication carries (like the
diamond) its own light with it, thus showing whence it comes; no
touchstone is required to discriminate it."   "The true commentator
will fasten his primary attention on the *letter* (literal meaning),
but never forget that the *Spirit* must equally accompany him; at
the same time we must never devise a more spiritual meaning for
Scripture passages than the Holy Spirit intended."   "The *historical*
matters of Scripture, both narrative and prophecy, constitute as it
were the *bones* of its system, whereas the *spiritual* matters are as
its muscles, blood-vessels, and nerves.   As the *bones* are necessary
to the human system, so Scripture *must* have its *historical* matters.
The expositor who nullifies the *historical* ground-work of Scripture
for the sake of finding only spiritual truths everywhere, brings
death on all correct interpretations.   Those expositions are the
safest which keep closest to the text."

His idea of the true mode of dying touched me much when I first saw it. He declared that he would make no spiritual parade of his last hours, but if possible continue at his usual works, and depart this life as a person in the midst of business leaves the room to attend to a knock at the door. Accordingly he was occupied with the correction of his proof-sheets as at other times, and the last messenger summoned him to his rest while his hands were full. This reveals a calm, well-balanced mind, and unveils many of those singular characteristics which enabled him to become the laborious recensor of the various MSS., and the pioneer of true Biblical criticism.

THE CRITICAL ENGLISH TESTAMENT.*—" A Critical New Testament, so compiled as to enable a reader, unacquainted with Greek, to ascertain the exact English force and meaning of the language of the New Testament, and to appreciate the latest results of modern criticism." Such is the professed aim of this commentary, and the compilers have very fairly carried out their intentions. The whole of Bengel's Gnomon is bodily transferred into the work, and as one hundred and twenty years have elapsed since the first issue of that book, it may be supposed that much has since been added to the wealth of Scripture exposition; the substance of this has been incorporated in brackets, so as to bring it down to the present advanced state of knowledge. We strongly advise the purchase of this book, as it is *multum in parvo*, and will well repay an attentive perusal. Tischendorf and Alford have contributed largely, with other German and English critics, to make this one of the most lucid and concise commentaries on the text and teachings of the New Testament.

ALFORD'S GREEK TESTAMENT,† " for the use of Theological Students and Ministers," is an invaluable aid to the critical study of the text of the New Testament. You will find in it the ripened results of a matured scholarship, the harvesting of a judgment, generally highly impartial, always worthy of respect, which has gleaned from the most important fields of Biblical research, both

---

* THE CRITICAL ENGLISH TESTAMENT.—Being an adaption of Bengel's Gnomon, with numerous Notes, showing Precise Results of Modern Criticism and Exegesis. Edited by Rev. W. L. Blackley, M.A., and Rev. James Hawes, M.A. Published by Messrs. Isbister and Co, Ludgate Hill, London. Three vols.

† The Greek Testament: with a Critically Revised Text; a Digest of various Readings; Marginal References to Verbal and Idiomatic Usage; Prolegomena; and a Critical and Exegetical Commentary. For the use of Theological Students and Ministers. By HENRY ALFORD, D.D., Dean of Canterbury. In four volumes. London: Rivingtons, Waterloo Place; and Deighton, Bell, and Co., Cambridge. 1861.

modern and ancient, at home and abroad. You will not look here
for any spirituality of thought or tenderness of feeling; you will
find the learned Dean does not forget to do full justice to his own
views, and is quite able to express himself vigorously against his
opponents; but for what it professes to be, it is an exceedingly
able and successful work. The later issues are by far the most
desirable, as the author has considerably revised the work in the
fourth edition.

What I have said of his Greek Testament applies equally to
ALFORD'S NEW TESTAMENT FOR ENGLISH READERS,* which is
also a standard work.

I must confess also a very tender side towards BLOOMFIELD'S
GREEK TESTAMENT,† and I am singular enough to prefer it in
some respects to Alford; at least, I have got more out of it on
some passages, and I think it does not deserve to be regarded as
superseded.

The Commentary by PATRICK, LOWTH, ARNALD, WHITBY,
and LOWMAN,‡ is said by Darling to be of standard authority,
but you may do without it with less loss than in the case of
several others I have mentioned. The authors were men of great
learning, their association in one commentary is remarkable, and
their joint production has a place in all complete libraries.

DR. WORDSWORTH'S HOLY BIBLE, WITH NOTES AND INTRO-
DUCTIONS,‖ is a valuable addition to our stores, but it is rendered
much more bulky and expensive than it needed to be by the printing
of the text at large. It gives many precious hints, and much of
the choicest thought of mediæval writers, besides suggesting
catch-words and showing connections between various passages.

---

* The New Testament for English Readers ; containing the Authorized Version,
with a revised English Text ; Marginal References ; and a Critical and Explanatory
Commentary ; By HENRY ALFORD, D.D., late Dean of Canterbury. New edition. 4
vols. 8vo.   London, Oxford, and Cambridge. Rivingtons, and G. Bell and
Sons, 1872.

† The Greek Testament, with English Notes, Critical, Philological, and Explanatory ; partly selected and arranged from the best Commentators, ancient and modern,
but chiefly original. Fourth edition, revised. 2 vols. 8vo. London. 1841.

‡ A Critical Commentary and Paraphrase on the Old and New Testament, and the
Apocrypha. By PATRICK, LOWTH, ARNALD, WHITBY, and LOWMAN. A new edition,
&c., in 4 vols. William Tegg and Co.

‖ The Holy Bible ; with Notes and Introductions [Old Testament only]. 6 vols.
imp. 8vo.   —The New Testament in the original Greek ; with Notes, Introductions,
and Indexes. By CHR. WORDSWORTH, D.D., Bishop of Lincoln. 2 vols. imp. 8vo.
London, Oxford, and Cambridge. Rivingtons. 1872, etc.

although it is occasionally marred by the characteristic weaknesses of the Bishop, and has here and there foolishnesses at which one cannot but smile, it is a great work, such as only an eminent scholar could have produced.

I am not so enamoured of the German writers as certain of my brethren appear to be, for they are generally cold and hard, and unspiritual. As Dr. Graham says, "there are about twenty or thirty names in the literary world who have gained a conspicuous place in theological circles; and in German commentaries these are perpetually introduced. In some of them the bulk of the work is made up of these authoritative names, and quotations from their works. This gives their writings the appearance of prodigious learning and research. Every page is bristling with hard words and strange languages, and the eye of the common reader is terrified at the very appearance, as the peaceful citizen is at the pointed cannon of a fortress." I do, however, greatly prize the series lately produced under the presidency of Dr. Lange.* These volumes are not all of equal value, but, as a whole, they are a grand addition to our stores. The American translators have added considerably to the German work, and in some cases these additions are more valuable than the original matter. For homiletical purposes these volumes are so many hills of gold, but, alas, there is dross also, for Baptismal Regeneration and other grave errors occur.

The Speaker's Commentary † is issued (August, 1875) as far as the Lamentations. It is costly, too costly for your pockets, and I am therefore somewhat the less sorry to add that it is not what I hoped it would be. Of course it is a great work, and contains much which tends to illustrate the text; but if you had it you would not turn to it for spiritual food, or for fruitful suggestion, or if you did so, you would be disappointed. The object of the

---

* A Commentary on the Holy Scriptures, Critical, Doctrinal, and Homiletical, with special reference to Ministers and Students, by John Peter Lange, D.D., in connection with a number of eminent European divines. Translated from the German, and edited, with additions, by Phillip Schaff, D.D., in connection with American scholars of various Evangelical denominations. Imperial 8vo. 24 volumes $97.80. Zondervan.

† The Holy Bible, according to the Authorized Version (A.D. 1611), with an Explanatory and Critical Commentary, and a Revision of the Translation by Bishops and other Clergy of the Anglican Church. Edited by F. C. Cook, M.A., Canon of Exeter, Preacher at Lincoln's Inn, and Chaplain in Ordinary to the Queen. Medium 8vo. London, John Murray. 1871, etc. 13 volumes including 2 volumes of Apocrypha.

work is to help the general reader to know what the Scriptures really say and mean, and to remove some of the difficulties. It keeps to its design and in a measure accomplishes it.

I must also add to the list A COMMENTARY, CRITICAL, EX-PERIMENTAL, AND PRACTICAL, ON THE OLD AND NEW TESTA-MENTS.* Of this I have a very high opinion. It is the joint work of Dr. Jamieson, A. R. Fausset, and Dr. David Brown. It is to some extent a compilation and condensation of other men's thoughts, but it is sufficiently original to claim a place in every minister's library: indeed it contains so great a variety of information that if a man had no other exposition he would find himself at no great loss if he possessed this and used it diligently.

Several other works I omit, not because they are worthless, or unknown to me, but because for scant purses the best will be best. I must not omit upon the New Testament the goodly volume of BURKITT.† If you can get him cheap, buy him. He is the cele-brated " Rector" whom Keach " rectified" in the matter of infant baptism. Burkitt is somewhat pithy, and for a modern rather rich and racy, but he is far from deep, and is frequently common-place. I liked him well enough till I had read abler works and grown older. Some books grow upon us as we read and re-read them, but Burkitt does not. Yet so far from depreciating the good man, I should be sorry to have missed his acquaintance, and would bespeak for him your attentive perusal.

The best commentators, after all, are those who have written upon only one book. Few men can comment eminently well upon the whole Bible, there are sure to be some weak points in colossal works; prolixity in so vast an undertaking is natural, and dulness follows at its heels—but a life devoted to one of the inspired volumes of our priceless Bible must surely yield a noble result. If I find myself able to do so, at some future time I will introduce you to a selection of the great one-book writers. For the present this much must suffice.

---

* A Commentary, Critical, Experimental, and Practical, on the Old and New Testaments. By the Rev. ROBERT JAMIESON, D.D., St. Paul's, Glasgow ; Rev. A. R. FAUSSET, A.M., St. Cuthbert's, York ; and the Rev. DAVID BROWN, D.D., Professor of Theology, Aberdeen. 6 vols. $25.00. Eerdmans. One volume abridgement. $7.95. Zondervan.

† Expository Notes, with Practical Observations, on the New Testament of our Lord and Saviour Jesus Christ, wherein, &c. Endeavoured by WILLIAM BURKITT, M.A. Late Vicar and Lecturer of Dedham, in Essex. (Numerous editions, folio and quarto.)

LECTURE II.

On Commenting.

HAVING introduced you to the commentators, I must now press
upon you one of the most practical uses of them, namely, your
own public commenting upon the Scriptures read during divine
service. Preaching in the olden time consisted very much more
of exposition than it does now. I suppose that the sermons of the
primitive Christians were for the most part expositions of lengthy
passages of the Old Testament; and when copies of the gospels, and
the epistles of Paul, had become accessible to the churches, the chief
work of the preacher would be to press home the apostolical
teachings by delivering an address, the back-bone of which would
be a complete passage of Scripture : there would probably be but
faint traces of divisions, heads and points, such as we employ in
modern discoursing, but the teacher would follow the run of the
passage which was open before him, commenting as he read. I
suppose this to have been the case, because some of the early
Christian modes of worship were founded very much upon that of
the synagogue. I say some of the modes, since I suppose that as
the Lord Jesus left his disciples free from rubrics and liturgies,
each church worshipped according to the working of the free
Spirit among them; one with the open meeting of the Corinthians,
and another with a presiding minister, and a third with a mixture
of the two methods. In the synagogue, it was the rule of the
Rabbis that never less than twenty-two verses of the law should
be read at one time, and the preaching consisted of notes upon a
passage of that length. Such a rule would be a mere superstition
if we were slavishly bound by it, but I could almost wish that the
custom were re-established, for the present plan of preaching from
short texts, together with the great neglect of commenting publicly

upon the word is very unsatisfactory. We cannot expect to deliver much of the teaching of Holy Scripture by picking out verse by verse, and holding these up at random. The process resembles that of showing a house by exhibiting separate bricks. It would be an astounding absurdity if our friends used our private letters in this fashion, and interpreted them by short sentences disconnected and taken away from the context. Such expositors would make us out to say in every letter all we ever thought of, and a great many things besides far enough from our minds; while the real intent of our epistles would probably escape attention. Nowadays since expository preaching is not so common as it ought to be, there is the more necessity for our commenting during the time of our reading the Scriptures. Since topical preaching, hortatory preaching, experimental preaching, and so on—all exceedingly useful in their way—have almost pushed proper expository preaching out of place, there is the more need that we should, when we read passages of Holy Writ, habitually give running comments upon them.

I support my opinion with this reason, that *the public reading of the abstruser parts of Scripture is of exceedingly little use to the majority of the people listening.* I can recollect hearing in my younger days long passages out of Daniel, which might have been exceedingly instructive to me if I had obtained the remotest conception of what they meant. Take again, parts of the prophecy of Ezekiel, and ask yourselves what profit can arise from their perusal by the illiterate, "unless some man shall guide them"? What more edification can come from a chapter in English which is not understood than from the same passage in Hebrew or Greek? The same argument which enforces translation demands exposition. If but a few explanatory words are thrown in by a judicious reader, it is wonderful how luminous obscure portions may be made. Two or three sentences will often reveal the drift of a whole chapter; the key of a great difficulty may be presented to the hearer in half-a-score words, and thus the public reading may be made abundantly profitable. I once saw a school of blind children among the charming ruins of York Abbey, and could not help pitying their incapacity to enjoy so much beauty: how willingly would I have opened their eyes! Are ignorant people wandering among the glories of Scripture much less to be pitied? Who will refuse them the light?

Abundant evidence has come before me that *brief comments upon Scripture in our ordinary services are most acceptable and instructive to our people.* I have often heard from working men, and their wives, and from merchants and their families, that my own expositions have been most helpful to them. They testify that when they read the Bible at home in the family, the exposition makes it doubly precious to them; and the chapter which they had unprofitably read in course at family prayers, when they peruse it the next time, recollecting what their minister has said upon it, becomes a real delight to them. The mass of our hearers, in London at least, do not, to any appreciable extent, read commentaries or any other books which throw a light upon the Scriptures. They have neither the money nor the time to do so, and if they are to be instructed in the Word of God in things which they cannot find out by mere experience, and are not likely to have explained to them by their associates, they must get that instruction from us, or nowhere else; nor do I see how we are to give them such spiritual assistance except through the regular practice of exposition.

Besides, if you are in the habit of commenting, *it will give you an opportunity of saying many things which are not of sufficient importance to become the theme of a whole sermon*, and therefore would probably remain unnoticed, to the great loss of the Lord's people and others. It is astounding what a range of truth, doctrinal, practical, and experimental, Holy Scripture brings before us; and equally worthy of admiration is the forcible manner in which that truth is advanced. Hints given in the way in which the word of God offers them are always wise and opportune; as, for instance, the rebukes which the word administers might have seemed too severe had they been made by the pastor, unsustained by the word and unsuggested by it, but arising out of the chapter they cannot be resented. You can both censure sins and encourage virtues by dilating upon the histories which you read in the inspired records, whereas you might never have touched upon them had not the chapter read brought the matter before you. If you want to make full proof of your ministry, and to leave no single point of revelation untouched, your easiest mode will be to comment upon Scripture habitually. Without this much of the word will be utterly unknown to many of your people. It is a very sad fact that they do not read so much as they should at home; the ungodly, in England, scarcely read the Bible at all; and if only that part which we preach upon be expounded to them, how little of the Bible can they ever know! If you will mark your Bibles with lines under the texts from which you have spoken, as I have always done with an old copy which I keep in my study, you will discover that in twelve or fourteen years very little of the book has been gone through; a very large proportion of it remains unmarked, like a field unploughed. Try, then, by exposition to give your people a fair view of the entire compass of revelation; take them as it were to the top of Nebo, and show them the whole land from Dan to Beersheba, and prove to them that everywhere it floweth with milk and honey.

Earnestly do I advocate commenting. It is unfashionable in England, though somewhat more usual beyond the Tweed. The practice was hardly followed up anywhere in England a few years ago, and it is very uncommon still. It may be pressed upon you for one other reason, namely, that *in order to execute it well, the commenting minister will at first have to study twice as much as the mere preacher*, because he will be called upon to prepare both his sermons and his expositions. As a rule, I spend much more time over the exposition than over the discourse. Once start a sermon with a great idea, and from that moment the discourse forms itself without much labour to the preacher, for truth naturally consolidates and crystallises itself around the main subject like sweet crystals around a string hung up in syrup; but as for the exposition, you must keep to the text, you must face the difficult points, and must search into the mind of the Spirit rather than your own. You will soon reveal your ignorance as an expositor if you do not study; therefore diligent reading will be forced upon you. Anything which compels the preacher to search the grand old Book is of immense service to him. If any are jealous lest the labour should injure their constitutions, let them remember that mental work up to a certain point is most refreshing, and where the Bible is the theme toil is delight. It is only when mental labour passes beyond the bounds of common sense that the mind becomes enfeebled by it, and this is not usually reached except by injudicious persons, or men engaged on topics which are unrefreshing and disagreeable; but our subject is a recreative one, and to young men like ourselves the vigorous use of our faculties is a most healthy exercise. Classics and mathematics may exhaust us, but not the volume of our Father's grace, the charter of our joys, the treasure of our wealth.

A man to comment well should be able to *read the Bible in the original*. Every minister should aim at a tolerable proficiency both in the Hebrew and the Greek. These two languages will give him a library at a small expense, an inexhaustible thesaurus, a mine of spiritual wealth. Really, the effort of acquiring a language is not so prodigious that brethren of moderate abilities should so frequently shrink from the attempt. A minister ought to attain enough of these tongues to be at least able to make out a passage by the aid of a lexicon, so as to be sure that he is not misrepresenting the Spirit of God in his discoursings, but is, as nearly as he can judge, giving forth what the Lord intended to reveal by the language employed. Such knowledge would prevent his founding doctrines upon expressions in our version when nothing at all analagous is to be found in the inspired original. This has been done by preachers time out of mind, and they have shouted over an inference drawn from a *shall*, or an *if* gathered out of the translation, with as much assurance of infallibility and sense of importance as if the same language had occurred in the words which the Holy Ghost used. At such times, we have been reminded of the story told by the late beloved Henry Craik, in his book on the Hebrew language. At one time, the Latin Vulgate was so constantly spoken of as the very word of God, that a Roman Catholic theologian thus commented upon Genesis i. 10:—"The gathering together of the waters called he seas." The Latin term for seas is *Maria*. On this ground, the writer asks, "What is the gathering together of waters but the accumulation of all the graces into one place, that is, into the Virgin Mary (*Maria*)? But there is this distinction, that *Maria* (*the seas*) has the (i) short, because that which the seas contain is only of a transitory nature, while the gifts and graces of the blessed Virgin (*Maria*) shall endure for ever." Such superlative nonsense may be indulged in if we forget that translations cannot be verbally inspired, and that to the original is the last appeal.

Fail not to be expert in the use of your *Concordance*. Every day I live I thank God more and more for that poor half-crazy Alexander Cruden.* Of course you have read his life, which is prefixed to the concordance; it exhibits him as a man of diseased mind, once or twice the inmate of a lunatic asylum, but yet for all that successfully devoting his energies to producing a work of absolutely priceless value, which never has been improved upon, and probably never will be; a volume which must ever yield the greatest possible assistance to a Christian minister, being as necessary to him as a plane to the carpenter, or a plough to the husbandman. Be sure you buy a genuine unabridged Cruden, and none of the modern substitutes; good as they may be at the price, they are a delusion and a snare to ministers, and should never be tolerated in the manse library. To consider cheapness in purchasing

---

* Cruden, Alexander—Unabridged Concordance with Notes and Comments. $5.95. Baker.

a concordance is folly. You need only one : have none but the
best. At the head of each notable word, Cruden gives you its
meaning, and very often all its particular shades of meaning, so
that he even helps you in sermonising. When you have read his
headings, by following out the concordance, you will observe connections in which the word occurs, which most advantageously and
correctly fix its meaning. Thus will the word of God be its own
key. A good textuary is a good theologian; be then well skilled
in using Cruden.

I make but small account of most *reference Bibles;* they would
be very useful if they were good for anything ; but it is extremely
easy to bring out a reference Bible which has verbal and apparent
references, and nothing more. You will often turn to a reference,
and will have to say, " Well, it is a reference, certainly, in a way,
for it contains the same word, but there is no reference in the
sense that the one text will explain the other." The useful reference cuts the diamond with a diamond, comparing spiritual
things with spiritual; it is a thought-reference, and not a word-
reference. If you meet with a really valuable reference Bible, it
will be to you what I once heard a countryman call " a reverence
Bible," for it will lead you to prize more and more the sacred
volume. The best reference Bible is a thoroughly good concordance. Get the best, keep it always on the table, use it hourly,
and you will have found your best companion.

Need I after my previous lectures commend to you the judicious
reading of *commentaries !* These are called " dead men's brains"
by certain knowing people, who claim to give us nothing in their
sermons but what they pretend the Lord reveals direct to themselves.
Yet these men are by no means original, and often their supposed
inspiration is but borrowed wit. They get a peep at Gill on the sly.
The remarks which they give forth as the Spirit's mind are very
inferior in all respects to what they affect to despise, namely, the
mind of good and learned men. A batch of poems was sent me
some time ago for *The Sword and the Trowel,* which were written
by a person claiming to be under the immediate influence of the
Holy Spirit. He informed me that he was passive, and that what
was enclosed was written under the direct physical and mental
influence of the Spirit upon his mind and hand. My bookshelves
can show many poems as much superior to these pretended inspir-
ations as angels are to blue-bottles ; the miserable doggrel bore on
its face the evidence of imposture. So when I listen to the senseless twaddle of certain wise gentlemen who are always boasting

that they alone are ministers of the Spirit, I am ashamed of their pretensions and of them. No, my dear friends, you may take it as a rule that the Spirit of God does not usually do for us what we can do for ourselves, and that if religious knowledge is printed in a book, and we can read it, there is no necessity for the Holy Ghost to make a fresh revelation of it to us in order to screen our laziness. Read, then, the admirable commentaries which I have already introduced to you. Yet be sure you use your own minds too, or the expounding will lack interest. Here I call to mind two wells in the courtyard of the Doge's palace at Venice, upon which I looked with much interest. One is filled artificially by water brought in barges from a distance, and few care for its insipid contents; the other is a refreshing natural well, cool and delicious, and the people contend for every drop of it. Freshness, naturalness, life, will always attract, whereas mere borrowed learning is flat and insipid. Mr. Cecil says his plan was, when he laid a hold of a Scripture, to pray over it, and get his own thoughts on it, and then, after he had so done, to take up the ablest divines who wrote upon the subject, and see what their thoughts were. If you do not think and think much, you will become slaves and mere copyists. The exercise of your own mind is most healthful to you, and by perseverance, with divine help, you may expect to get at the meaning of every understandable passage. So to rely upon your own abilities as to be unwilling to learn from others is clearly folly; so to study others as not to judge for yourself is imbecility.

What should be the manner of your public commenting? One rule should be always to *point out very carefully wherever a word bears a special sense;* for rest assured in Holy Scripture the same word does not always mean the same thing. The Bible is a book meant for human beings, and therefore it is written in human language; and in human language the same word may signify two or three things. For instance, "a pear fell from the tree;" "a man fell into drunken habits." There the meaning of the second word, "fell," is evidently different from the first, since it is not literal, but metaphorical. Again, "the cabman mounted the box;" "the child was pleased with his Christmas box;" "his lordship is staying at his shooting box." In each case there is the same word, but who does not see that there is a great difference of meaning? So it is in the word of God. You must explain the difference between a word used in a peculiar sense, and the ordinary meaning of the word, and thus you will prevent your people falling into mistakes. If people will say that the same word in Scripture always means the same thing, as I have heard some assert publicly, they will make nonsense of the word of God, and fall into error through their own irrational maxims. To set up canons of interpretation for the Book of God which would be absurd if applied to other writings is egregious folly: it has a show of accuracy, but inevitably leads to confusion.

The obvious literal meaning of a Scripture is not always the true one, and ignorant persons are apt enough to fall into the most singular misconceptions—a judicious remark from the pulpit will be of signal service. Many persons have accustomed themselves to misunderstand certain texts; they have heard wrong interpretations in their youth, and will never know better unless the correct meaning be indicated to them.

We must make sure in our public expositions that *obscure and involved sentences are explained.* To overleap difficulties, and only expound what is already clear, is to make commenting ridiculous. When we speak of obscure sentences, we mean such as are mostly to be found in the prophets, and are rendered dark through the translation, or the Orientalism of their structure, or through their intrinsic weight of meaning. Involved sentences most abound in the writings of Paul, whose luxuriant mind was not to be restrained to any one line of argument. He begins a sentence, and does not finish it perhaps until eight verses further on, and all the interstices between the commencement and the end of the sentence are packed full of compressed truth, which it is not always easy to separate from the general argument. Hints consisting of but two or three words will let your hearers know where the reasoning breaks off, and where it is taken up again. In many poetical parts of the Old Testament the speakers change; as in Solomon's Song, which is mostly a dialogue. Here perfect nonsense is often made by reading the passage as if it were all spoken by the same person. In Isaiah the strain often varies most suddenly, and while one verse is addressed to the Jews, the next may be spoken to the Messiah or to the Gentiles. Is it not always well to notify this to the congregation? If the chapters and verses had been divided with a little common sense, this might be of less importance, but as our version is so clumsily chopped into fragments, the preacher must insert the proper paragraphs and divisions as he reads aloud. In fine, your business is to make the word plain. In Lombardy I observed great heaps of huge stones in the fields, which had been gathered out from the soil by diligent hands to make room for the crops; your duty is to " gather out the stones," and leave the fruitful field of Scripture for your people to till. There are Orientalisms, metaphors, peculiar expressions, idioms, and other verbal memorabilia which arise from the Bible having been written in the East; all these you will do well to explain. To this end be diligent students of Oriental life. Let the geography of Palestine, its natural history, its fauna and its flora, be as familiar to you as those of your own native village. Then as you read you will interpret the word, and your flock will be fed thereby.*

The chief part of your commenting, however, *should consist in applying the truth to the hearts of your hearers,* for he who merely comprehends the meaning of the letter without understanding how it bears upon the hearts and consciences of men, is like a man who causes the bellows of an organ to be blown, and then fails to place his fingers on the keys; it is of little service to supply men with information unless we urge upon them the practical inferences therefrom. Look, my brethren, straight down into the secret chambers of the human soul, and let fall the divine teaching through the window, and thus light will be carried to the heart and conscience. Make remarks suitable to the occasion, and applicable to the cases of those present. Show how a truth which was first heard in the days of David is still forcible and pertinent in these modern times, and you will thus endear the Scriptures to the minds of your people, who prize your remarks much more than you imagine. Clean the grand old pictures of the divine masters; hang them up in new frames; fix them on the walls of your people's memories, and their well-instructed hearts shall bless you.

Is a caution needed amongst intelligent men? Yes, it must be given. Be sure *to avoid prosiness.* Avoid it everywhere, but especially in this. Do not be long in your notes. If you are supremely gifted do not be long; people do not appreciate too much of a good thing; and if your comments are only second-rate, why, then be shorter still, for men soon weary of inferior talking. Very little time in the service can be afforded for reading the lessons; do not rob the prayer and the sermon for the sake of commenting. This robbing Peter to pay Paul is senseless. Do not repeat commonplace things which must have occurred even to a Sunday-school

---

* For suggestions as to interpretation the student is referred to the Bible Handbook by Dr. Joseph Angus. From page 150 of that work and onwards the most valuable hints will be met with. Much that we would otherwise have inserted in this volume is admirably stated by our learned friend. Edition Revised by Samuel Green. $5.95. Zondervan.

child.   Do not remind your hearers of what they could not
possibly have forgotten.   Give them something weighty if not
new, so that an intelligent listener may feel when the service is
over that he has learned at least a little.

Again, *avoid all pedantry.*   As a general rule, it may be observed
that those gentlemen who know the least Greek are the most sure
to air their rags of learning in the pulpit; they miss no chance of
saying, "The Greek is so-and-so."   It makes a man an inch and
a-half taller by a foolometer, if he .everlastingly lets fall bits
of Greek and Hebrew, and even tells the people the tense of the
verb and the case of the noun, as I have known some do.   Those
who have no learning usually make a point of displaying the pegs
on which learning ought to hang.   Brethren, the whole process of
interpretation is to be carried on in your study; you are not to
show your congregation the process, but to give them the result;
like a good cook who would never think of bringing up dishes, and
pans, and rolling pin, and spice box into the dining hall, but without ostentation sends up the feast.

Never strain passages when you are expounding.   Be thoroughly
honest with the word: even if the Scriptures were the writing of mere
men, conscience would demand fairness of you; but when it is the
Lord's own word, be careful not to pervert it even in the smallest
degree. Let it be said of you, as I have heard a venerable hearer of
Mr. Simeon say of him, " Sir, he was very Calvinistic when the text
was so, and people thought him an Arminian when the text was
that way, for he always stuck to its plain sense."   A very sound
neighbour of ours once said, by way of depreciating the grand old
reformer, "John Calvin was not half a Calvinist," and the remark
was correct as to his expositions, for in them, as we have seen, he
always gave his Lord's mind and not his own.   In the church
of St. Zeno, in Verona, I saw ancient frescoes which had been
plastered over, and then covered with other designs; I fear many
do this with Scripture, daubing the text with their own glosses,
and laying on their own conceits.   There are enough of these
plasterers abroad, let us leave the evil trade to them and follow an
honest calling.   Remember Cowper's lines—

> "A critic on the sacred text should be
> Candid and learn'd, dispassionate and free;
> Free from the wayward bias bigots feel,
> From fancy's influence and intemperate zeal;
> For of all arts sagacious dupes invent,
> To cheat themselves and gain the world's assent,
> The worst is—Scripture warped from its intent."

Use your judgment more than your fancy. Flowers are well enough, but hungry souls prefer bread. To allegorize with Origen may make men stare at you, but your work is to fill men's mouths with truth, not to open them with wonder.

Do not be carried away with new meanings. Plymouth Brethren delight to fish up some hitherto undiscovered tadpole of interpretation, and cry it round the town as a rare dainty; let us be content with more ordinary and more wholesome fishery. No one text is to be exalted above the plain analogy of faith; and no solitary expression is to shape our theology for us. Other men and wiser men have expounded before us, and anything undiscovered by them it were well to put to test and trial before we boast too loudly of the treasure-trove.

Do not needlessly amend our authorized version. It is faulty in many places, but still it is a grand work taking it for all in all, and it is unwise to be making every old lady distrust the only Bible she can get at, or what is more likely, mistrust you for falling out with her cherished treasure. Correct where correction must be for truth's sake, but never for the vainglorious display of your critical ability. When reading short psalms, or connected passages of the other books, *do not split up the author's utterances by interjecting your notes.* Read the paragraph through, and then go over it again with your explanations; breaking it up as you may think fit at the second reading. No one would dream of dividing a stanza of a poet with an explanatory remark; it would be treason to common sense to do so: sound judgment will forbid your thus marring the word of God. Better far never to comment than to cut and carve the utterances of inspiration, and obscure their meaning by impertinently thrusting in untimely remarks of your own. Upon many passages comments would be gross folly: never think of painting the lily or gilding refined gold; leave the sublime sentences alone in their glory. I speak as unto wise men; prove your wisdom in this thing also.

If I were bound to deliver a sermon upon the subject in hand, I could not desire a better text than Nehemiah viii. 8: "So they read in the book in the law 'of God distinctly, and gave the sense, and caused them to understand the reading." Here is a hint for the reader as to his *reading.* Let it always be distinct. Aim to be good readers, and be the more anxious about it because few men are so, and all preachers ought to be so. It is as good as a sermon to hear our best men read the Scriptures; they bring out the meaning by their correct emphasis and tone.

Never fall into the idea that the mere utterance of the words before you is all that is required of you in reading; good reading is a high, but rare attainment. Even if you do not comment, yet read the chapter previously, and become familiar with it; it is inexcusable for a man to betray the fact that he is out of his latitude in the reading, traversing untrodden ground, floundering and picking his way across country, like a huntsman who has lost his bearings. Never open the Bible in the pulpit to read the chapter for the first time, but go to the familiar page after many rehearsals. You will be doubly useful if in addition to this you "*give the sense.*" You will then, by God's blessing, be the pastor of an intelligent, Bible-loving people. You will hear in your meeting-house that delightful rustle of Bible leaves which is so dear to the lover of the Word; your people will open their Bibles, looking for a feast. The Word will become increasingly precious to yourself, your knowledge will enlarge, and your aptness to teach will become every day more apparent. Try it, my brethren, for even if you should see cause to discontinue it, at least no harm will come of the attempt.

In all that I have said I have given you another reason for seeking the aid of the Holy Spirit. If you do not understand a book by a departed writer you are unable to ask him his meaning, but the Spirit, who inspired Holy Scripture, lives for ever, and he delights to open up the Word to those who seek his instruction. He is always accessible: " he dwelleth with you and shall be in you." Go to him for yourselves and cry, " Open thou mine eyes that I may behold wondrous things out of thy law"; and, this being granted you, entreat him to send forth his light and power with the Word when you expound it, that your hearers also may be led into all truth. Commentaries, expositions, interpretations, are all mere scaffolding; the Holy Ghost himself must edify you and help you to build up the church of the living God.

Remarks upon the Catalogue of Commentaries.

THIS Catalogue is compiled for the use of ministers of average attainments, and the brief reviews are written from that standpoint. Other useful lists have been published, specially those by Darling, Orme, and Hartwell Horne, but these are not easily procurable, and are not quite what is needed; and therefore as the furnishing of the Pastors' College Library necessitated a Catalogue, and afforded an opportunity for purchasing books, the present work has been produced. Few can conceive the amount of toil which this compilation has involved, both to myself and my industrious amanuensis, Mr. J. L. Keys. In almost every case the books have been actually examined by myself, and my opinion, whatever it may be worth, is an original one. A complete list of all comments has not been attempted. Numbers of volumes have been left out because they were not easily procurable, or were judged to be worthless, although some of both these classes have been admitted as specimens, or as warnings.

The reader will please observe that the books most heartily recommended are printed in the largest type with the remarks in italics. Good, but more ordinary, works are in medium type, and the least desirable are in the smallest letter. Thus we hope the eye will be caught at once by volumes best worthy of attention.

Latin authors are not inserted, because few can procure them, and fewer still can read them with ease. We are not, however, ignorant of their value. Hosts of family Bibles, discourses, and paraphrases are omitted, because they would have wasted our limited space, and we could only have admitted them by raising the price of our book, which we resolved not to do, lest it should be out of the reach of men of slender incomes. The first volume of this series* has had so excellent a circulation that we are able to issue this second one, although we know from the nature of the work that its sale will, in all probability, never cover the cost of production. We *give* the labour to our brethren freely, only wishing that we could with it confer upon our poorer friends the means of purchasing the choicest of the comments here mentioned.

It is to be specially noted, that *in no case do we endorse all that any author has written in his commentary.*   We could not read the works through, it would have needed a Methuselah to do that; nor have we thought it needful to omit a book because it contains a measure of error, provided it is useful in its own way; for this catalogue is for thoughtful, discerning men, and not for children. We have not, however, knowingly mentioned works whose main drift is sceptical, or Socinian, except with a purpose; and where we have admitted comments by writers of doubtful doctrine, because of their superior scholarship and the correctness of their criticisms we have given hints which will be enough for the wise. It is sometimes very useful to know what our opponents have to say.

The writers on the Prophetical Books have completely mastered us, and after almost completing a full list we could not in our conscience believe that a tithe of them would yield anything to the student but bewilderment, and therefore we reduced the number to small dimensions.   We reverence the teaching of the prophets, and the Apocalypse, but for many of the professed expounders of those inspired books we entertain another feeling.

May God bless this laborious endeavour to aid his ministers in searching the Scriptures.   If Biblical studies shall be in any measure promoted, we shall be more than repaid.

---

* Lectures to my Students: a Selection from Addresses delivered to the Students of the Pastors' College, Metropolitan Tabernacle.   By C. H. Spurgeon, President. Abridged edition by D. O. Fuller, D. D., $3.50.   Zondervan.

CATALOGUE

OF

𝕭𝖎𝖇𝖑𝖎𝖈𝖆𝖑 𝕮𝖔𝖒𝖒𝖊𝖓𝖙𝖆𝖗𝖎𝖊𝖘 & 𝕰𝖝𝖕𝖔𝖘𝖎𝖙𝖎𝖔𝖓𝖘.

COMMENTARIES ON THE WHOLE BIBLE.

1 ALLEN (JOHN).—A Spiritual Exposition of the Old and New Testaments; or, The Christian's Gospel Treasure. Three vols. 8vo. 1816.
Spiritual reflections after the High Calvinistic School. Some preachers cannot see Christ where he is, but Allen finds him where he is not. There is in these reflections much godly savour, but very little exposition.

2 ASSEMBLY OF DIVINES, Westminster.—Annotations. Two vols. Folio. *Lond.*, 1657.
Contain valuable remarks, but are somewhat out of date. The work is probably less esteemed than it should be. (See page 12).

3 **BARTH** *(Dr. C. G., of Calw, Wurtemberg).* — Practical Commentary on the Books of Holy Scripture, arranged in Chronological Order ; being a *Bible Manual* for the use of Students of the Word of God. Translated from the German. Imp. 8vo. *Lond.*, Nisbet & Co.
Helpful in showing the historical position of the books, and in assisting to illustrate them by the circumstances under which they were written. We have referred to it with benefit.

4 BENSON (JOSEPH, 1748—1821. *An eminent Methodist Preacher*). Notes, Critical, Explanatory, and Practical. Six vols. Imp. 8vo. *Lond.*, Wesleyan Conference Office.
Adopted by the Wesleyan Conference as a standard work, and characterized by that body as marked by " solid learning, soundness of theological opinion, and an edifying attention to experimental and practical religion." Necessary to Methodist Students.

5 **BIBLICAL MUSEUM.** (James Comper Gray).
Revised edition reissued as Gray and Adams' Bible
Commentary. 6 volumes $24.75. Zondervan.

*We can only speak of the New Testament; it is surpassingly
useful, sententious and sensible. Buy the work at once.*

6 **BONAR** (Horatius, D.D.)—Light and Truth: or, Bible
Thoughts and Themes. Vol. I., Old Testament.
Vol. II., Gospels. Vol. III., Acts and Larger Epistles.
Vol. IV., Lesser Epistles. Vol. V., Revelation of
St. John. Crown 8vo.   *Lond.,* Nisbet.
*One volume is rather short space in which to bring out the
" light and truth" of the Old Testament. If Dr. Bonar required
four volumes for the New, we wish he had felt the same need
for the Old. The passages selected are popularly expounded,
but the thought is not deep. The volumes will be more prized by
the ordinary reader than by the minister.*

7 BOOTHROYD (Benjamin, D.D., 1768—1836.—*A learned Independent Minister and eminent Hebrew scholar.*)—Family Bible.
Improved Version. Notes, and reflections on each chapter;
introduction on the authenticity and inspiration of the sacred
books, and a complete view of the Mosaic laws, &c. Three
vols. Royal 4to, 1824, or one vol., thick 8vo., 1853,
Good, but may be dispensed with, now that the East has been more
fully explored.

8 BROWN (John, 1722—1787).—Self-Interpreting Bible.
Useful in its day, and still popular. Notes on New Testament
an undisguised plagiarism from Guyse. Not a Student's book.

9 BURDER (Samuel, A.M.) The Scripture Expositor; a New
Commentary, Critical and Practical. Four vols., 4to. 1811.
Well selected notes. Those upon Eastern manners, geography, &c.,
are collected very judiciously.

10 **CALVIN** (John, 1509—1564). In the works of Calvin,
published by the Calvin Translation Society, are the
Commentaries, in 45 volumes.   Old copies of
Calvin's comments are to be met with at second-hand
book stores. We have entered most of them in their
proper places, but cannot afford space for separate
mention of the volumes of the C. T. Society.
Reprint of Calvin Translation Society edition $150.00.

Eerdmans.
Of priceless value. (See pages 4 and 5 of this work)

11 **CHALMERS** (THOMAS, D.D., LL.D., 1780—1847). Daily Scripture Readings (3 vols.) and Sabbath Scripture Readings (2 vols.) being vols. I. to V. of the "Posthumous Works" of Dr. Chalmers, edited by Rev. W. Hanna, D.D. *Lond.*, Hamilton, Adams & Co. ; *Edinb.*, Edmonston & Douglas, in whose catalogue they are priced as follows : D. S. Readings, 3 vols., crown 8vo.,

Those acquainted with the writings of Chalmers will know what to expect from his pen when guided by fervent devotion.

12 **CLARKE** (ADAM, LL.D., 1760—1832).—A New Edition, with the Author's final corrections. Six vols., Imp. 8vo. $24.50. Abingdon.

Despite some few oddities, this is one of the most learned of English expositions. (See page 9.)

13 CLARKE (SAMUEL. Died 1701).—The Old and New Testament, with Annotations and Parallel Scriptures. Folio. *Lond.*, 1690.

Notes very brief, but judicious. Author one of the ejected ministers, an exceedingly learned man. This work was highly commended by Owen, Baxter, Howe, and others, but is now superseded.

14 **CLASS AND THE DESK, The.**—By J. COMPER GRAY, of Halifax; and C. STOKES CAREY, of London. Four vols. Crown 8vo. *Lond.*, J. Sangster & Co.
Condensed thought. Suited for Teachers and Local Preachers.

15 COBBIN, (INGRAM).—Evangelical Synopsis. The Holy Bible, with Notes Explanatory and Practical, selected from the writings of the most esteemed divines and Biblical critics. Three vols. Imp. 4to. *Lond.*, George Berger.
An admirable collection of notes. Men with small means will find it a miniature library. We have heard brethren who have had no commentary but Cobbin's speak of the work with much enthusiasm.

16 COBBIN (INGRAM). A condensed Commentary on the Bible. Second edition. Imp. 8vo. *Lond.*, 1839.
An excellent makeshift for a poor man.

17 COKE (THOMAS, LL.D. *Wesleyan Methodist Minister. Died* 1814.) A Commentary on the Old and New Testament. 6 vols. 4to. *Lond.*, 1803.
A Wesleyan comment. Too big : ought to have been put in half the space. Moreover, it is next door to a fraud, for it is "in the main a reprint of the work of Dr. Dodd," without that author's name. Ah, Dr. Coke, this is a burning shame !

18 COMMENTARY, WHOLLY BIBLICAL, The: An Exposition in the very words of Scripture. 3 vols., 4to. *Lond.*, S. Bagster and Sons.

It is very handy to have explanatory passages thus presented to the eye. In general the work is excellently done ; but ministers with scanty purses can make a Biblical exposition for themselves.

19 COMPREHENSIVE BIBLE, The. (Edited by W. Greenfield, M.R.A.S.). The Old and New Testaments, with the various readings and marginal notes, parallel passages systematically arranged, numerous philological and explanatory notes, &c., &c. Medium 4to., pica type, in cloth ; crown 4to., small pica type, cloth. *Lond.*, S. Bagster & Sons.

Generally used as a Pulpit Bible. Said to contain 4,000 notes and 500,000 parallel passages, being all those of Blayney, Scott, Clarke, and others. The tables, notes, introductions, &c., are of standard value.

20 DIODATI (JOHN, 1576—1649). Annotations plainly expounding the most difficult places. Third edition. Folio. *Lond.* 1651. [Quarto editions exist, but the folio is best.

Bickersteth says : " The spiritual and evangelical remarks are of much value." Diodati's notes are short and worth consulting.

21 DODD (WILLIAM, D.D.) A Commentary on the Books of the Old and New Testament ; in which are inserted the notes and collections of John Locke, Esq. ; Daniel Waterland, D.D. ; the Earl of Clarendon, and other learned persons ; with practical improvements, &c. 3 vols. Folio. *Lond.*, 1770.

An almost forgotten production of the unhappy Dodd. It is founded on the manuscript collections of Cudworth, Waterland, Clarendon, and others. Not very likely to quicken piety, or inspire spiritual thought ; yet, as Adam Clarke thought very highly of it, and Dr. Coke appropriated it, it must have some value.

22 D'OYLY AND MANT. Notes, taken principally from the Church of England writers. Published by the S.P.C.K. Prepared by the Rev. Geo. D'Oyly, D.D., and the Rev. R. Mant, D.D. 3 vols. Royal 8vo., with the text, or in 1 vol., without the text, 1845, &c.

Of moderate value. More fitted for the family than the study. A compilation most appreciated among Episcopalians.

23 DUTCH ANNOTATIONS upon the whole Bible, as ordered by the Synod of Dort, 1618, and published in English, by *Theodore Haak, Esq.* 2 vols. Folio. *Lond.*, 1657.

Similar to the Westminster Assembly's Annotations. (See page 12).

24 **FAUSSET** (A.R., A.M.—See JAMIESON, and page 20.)

25 **FOURFOLD UNION COMMENTARY, The.** Containing, I. Parallel Texts, in full. II. Commentary of Matthew Henry, &c. III. Scott's Commentary condensed. IV. Commentary by Jamieson, Fausset, and Brown. To which is added the Biblical Cyclopædia, by

Dr. John Eadie, a Biblical Atlas, &c. Two handsome volumes. Royal 4to. *Lond.*, Wesley. 1872.

A Christian man wishing for the cream of expository writers could not make a better purchase. Ministers, as a rule, should not buy condensations, but get the works themselves.

26 **FRASER** (DONALD, D.D.) Synoptical Lectures on the Books of Holy Scripture. First Series—Genesis to Canticles. Second Series—Isaiah to Acts. Post 8vo. *Lond.*, Nisbet and Co.

Dr. Fraser has observed, like many others of us, the mischief which results from cutting the Bible into fragments, and using it piecemeal. In these volumes he discourses of the Bible at large, indicates the scope of each book, and furnishes a brief digest of its contents. He has compressed rigorously. The design was in itself most laudable, and it has been well carried out.

27 **GILL** (JOHN, D.D. 1697—1771). An Exposition of the Old and New Testament. Reprint edition complete in 6 volumes under consideration at press time by Kregel Publications.

Invaluable in its own line of things. (For full title and extended remarks see pages 8 and 9.)

28 HAAK (THEODORE). See under " *Dutch Annotations.*"

29 **HALL** (JOSEPH, D.D. *Bishop of Norwich.* 1574—1656). Contemplations. Several editions ; the one published by T. Nelson, *Edinb.*, 1844, has a memoir of the good Bishop by the late Dr. James Hamilton.

The work can be readily procured ; but if its price were raised in proportion to its real value, it would become one of the most costly books extant. (See page 11.)

30 HALL (JOSEPH) A Plain and Familiar Explication, by way of Paraphrase, of all the *Hard Texts* of the whole Divine Scriptures. Small Folio, 1633. Also forming Vols. III. and IV. of the 8vo. edition of Hall's works in 12 vols. *Oxford*, 1837.

Not so pithy as the Contemplations ; nor, indeed, could it be expected to be so. It is not necessary to the Student, but might be useful.

31 HAWEIS (THOMAS. 1734—1820). The Evangelical Expositor. 2 vols. Folio. 1765-6.
Partakes of the author's character ; for of him it has been said, that "he was rather useful than eminent." The work is mainly an abridgment of Henry.

32 HAWKER (ROBERT, D.D. 1753—1827). The Poor Man's Commentary. 9 vols. 8vo., and 3 vols. 4to. 1843.
Full of devotion and sweetness. (*See page* 13.)

33 HENRY (MATTHEW. 1662—1714). A Commentary of the Whole Bible, New Biographical Edition, 6 volumes $24.50. Revell.

(For title and remarks see pages 2, 3, 4)

34 HOLDEN (GEORGE, M.A.) Christian Expositor. 2 vols., 8vo. 1837.
Notes highly spoken of ; we consider them the most ordinary of platitudes.

35 JAMIESON (REV. DR., *Glasgow*). **FAUSSET** (REV. A.R. *York*), and **BROWN** (REV. DR. D., *Aberdeen*). **THE LIBRARY COMMENTARY**, Critical, Experimental, and Practical. 6 vols. $25.00. Eerdmans ; One volume abridgement. $7.95 . Zondervan.

A really standard work. We consult it continually, and with growing interest. Mr. Fausset's portion strikes us as being of the highest order. (See page 20.)

The following are different forms or abridgments of the same work, each of which we can highly recommend :—

36 JAMIESON. The Complete Commentary. 2 vols., Royal 4to., with maps, Much the same as the Fourfold Commentary. *Edinb.*, W. Collins. (See No. 25.)

37 „ The Student's Commentary. 4 vols., foolscap 8vo. W. Collins.

38 „ The Portable Commentary. 2 vols., post 8vo. W. Collins, Sons, & Co.

39 KITTO (JOHN, D.D., F.S.A., 1804—1850). The Pictorial Bible. 4 vols., Imp. 8vo., 1855. *Lond.* and *Edinb.*, Chambers.

A work of art as well as learning. (See page 15.)

40 KITTO. The Illustrated Commentary of the Old and New Testaments. A reproduction of the Notes, &c., of the Pictorial Bible. 5 vols., 8vo. 1840.

The omission of the text renders the work cheaper.

41 KITTO'S Daily Bible Illustrations: being Original Readings for a Year, on subjects relating to Sacred History, Biography, Geography, Antiquities, and Theology. New edition, edited and revised by *J. L. Porter, D.D.* 8 vols., *Edinb.*, Oliphant & Co.

May always be obtained, both new and second-hand. (See page 15.)

42 **LANGE** (J. P., D.D.) Translations of the Commentaries of *Dr. Lange*, and his Collaborateurs. Edited by *Dr. Schaff.*

Complete unabridged Edition, 24 volumes $97.80. Zondervan. These volumes may be purchased either in single volumes or as a complete set. Single volume price — $3.95 per volume with the exception of Psalms, Isaiah, Ezekiel-Daniel—$4.95.

The volumes greatly differ in excellence, yet none could be spared. We have nothing equal to them as a series. (See page 19.)

43 LEES (FRED. R., Ph.D.) and BURNS (DAWSON, M.A.). The Temperance Bible Commentary. Demy 8vo., *Lond.*, S. W. Partridge & Co. 1872.

Readers will probably estimate the value of this work according to their views upon Total Abstinence. This question appears to be one which renders both advocates and opponents too warm either to give or accept a cool, impartial verdict ; we shall not therefore offer one.

44 LEIGH (SIR EDWARD. 1602-3—1671). Annotations from Job to Canticles. Folio. *Lond.*, 1657.

Annotations upon all the New Testament. Philological and Theological. Folio. *Lond.*, 1650. Frequently associated with *Richardson* on the Old Testament. (See No. 71.)

Good, brief notes. Antique, but still prized.

Critica Sacra. In two parts : I. Observations on all the primitive Hebrew words of the Old Testament. II. Philological and Theological Observations on all the Greek words of the New Testament. Folio. *Lond.*, 1662.

Horne says this is "a very valuable help to the understanding of the original languages." Parkhurst valued it.

45 MANT. (See D'Oyly).

46 MAYER (JOHN, D.D.) Commentary. 6 vols. folio, and 1 vol. 4to. *Lond.*, 1653. [The seventh volume, containing the Catholic Epistles and Revelation, was published in 4to. only] (For full title and remarks see pages 10 and 11.)

Laborious writing and heavy reading.

47 MILLINGTON (THOMAS S.) The Testimony of the Heathen to the Truths of Holy Writ. Compiled almost exclusively from Greek and Latin Authors of the Classical Ages of Antiquity. 4to. *Lond.*, Seeley, Jackson, & Halliday. 1863.

It was a capital idea to lay the heathen under contribution. The author is at home in the Classics, and has performed his work well.

48 **NESS** (CHRISTOPHER. 1621—1705). History and Mystery. 4 vols., Folio. *Lond.*, 1690—96.
Quaint, pithy, suggestive. Full of remarks such as are to be found in Thomas Fuller and Bishop Hall. (See page 11.)

49 NEW BIBLE COMMENTARY, The. [Sometimes spoken of as "*The Speaker's Commentary.*"] In progress. *Lond.*, Murray. 1871, etc. (For full title see page 19)
The proverb concerning too many cooks applies also to Commentators. The work is good, but it might have been better.

50 **PATRICK & LOWTH.** A Critical Commentary. Corrected by the *Rev. J. R. Pitman.* 6 vols., Royal 4to. 1822. [There are other editions, but some of them do not contain the whole of the Commentary ; the above is one of the best. Good edition in smaller type, 4 vols., Imp. *Lond.*, W. Tegg.]   (*See page* 18.)

51 **POOLE** (MATTHEW. 1624—1679). Annotations. Our copy is dated 1853. *Lond.*, Nisbet & Co.
See title and remarks on pages 6 *and* 7.

52 PURVER (ANTHONY. 1702—1777). A New and Literal Translation, with Notes. 2 vols., Folio. *Lond.*, 1764.
A Quaker Translation. Often ungrammatical and unintelligible. Not without its good points, but much more curious than useful.

53 RELIGIOUS TRACT SOCIETY'S COMMENTARY. From *Henry* and *Scott*, with numerous observations from other writers. With the text and maps, 6 vols., Super-royal 8vo., *Without the text*, 6 vols., 12mo.,

The abridgements are carefully executed.

54 **SCOTT** (THOMAS. 1747—1821). The Holy Bible. A New Edition. 6 vols., 4to. *Lond.*, Nisbet & Co. (For title and remarks see page 12.)
J. M. Neale says of Scott's practical observations, " They are such as some men would not take the trouble of even thinking, many would not be at the pains of speaking, and—one should have imagined, were not the fact as it is—such as no man would have condescended to write down." This judgment is far too severe, and reveals the High Churchman : it raises Scott in our esteem.

55 SIMEON (CHARLES, M.A. 1759—1836). Horæ Homileticæ ; or, Discourses digested into one continued series, and forming a Comment upon every book of the Old and New Testament ; Reissued as Expository Outlines on the Whole Bible in 21 volumes. $103.95. Volumes being reprinted bi-monthly beginning January 1955. Individual volumes $4.95. Zondervan.

Not Commentaries, but we could not exclude them. They have been called " a valley of dry bones " : be a prophet and they will live.

56 SPEAKER'S COMMENTARY,The. (See *New Bible Commentary*).

57 SUTCLIFFE (JOSEPH, M.A. *Wesleyan Minister*). A Commentary; containing Copious Notes. Imp. 8vo., 12/6. *Lond.*, 66, Paternoster Row, E.C.

To comprise the whole Bible in one volume necessitated notes few and brief. *Sutcliffe*, though an Arminian, is in general so good that we wish we had more of him; his style is vivacious and forcible.

58 TEMPERANCE BIBLE COMMENTARY, (The). (See *Lees R.*)

59 **TRAPP** (JOHN. 1611—1669). Commentary. 5 vols., Folio. 1654, etc. There are also 4to. editions of parts of the Commentary. Reprinted by Mr. R. D. Dickinson, Farringdon Street, E.C., in 5 vols., Super-royal 8vo.,

Oh, rare John Trapp! (See pages 7 and 8.)

60 WALL (WILLIAM, D.D. 1646—1720). Critical Notes on the Old and New Testament. 3 vols., 8vo. *Lond.*, 1730-34.

Dr. Wall was the great champion of infant baptism against the learned Gale. His notes are good, but out of date.

61 WELLS (EDWARD, D.D., *Died* 1724). Help for the more easy and clear understanding of the Holy Scriptures. 6 vols., 4to. *Oxford*, 1724, etc.

Seldom to be met with complete, but this need not be regretted, for though somewhat useful, it is not of primary importance.

62 WESLEY (JOHN, A.M. 1703—1791). Notes on Old and New Testament. 4 vols., 4to. *Lond.*, 1764. Explanatory Notes on the New Testament, 1 volume $2.75. Allenson.

The Notes on the New Testament are esteemed, but Dr. Clark says that those on the Old are meagre and unsatisfactory. He is quite right.

63 WILSON (THOMAS, D.D. 1663—1755. *Bishop of Sodor and Man*). The Holy Bible, with Notes and various renderings. By the Rev. C. Crutwell. 3 vols., 4to. *Lond.*, 1785.

The good Bishop's notes are brief hints, only intended for the explanation or practical improvement of certain passages; their value to Biblical Students is inconsiderable. Crutwell's various readings are numerous. We gave no less than £3 3s. for the copy by which we have been able to form this estimate; but for our own use we should be sorry to give half-a-guinea for it.

64 **WORDSWORTH** (CHRISTOPHER, D.D. *Bishop of Lincoln*). See page 18.

65 YOUNG (ROBERT, LL.D.) Commentary on the Bible, as Literally and Idiomatically Translated. Crown 8vo. *Lond.*, Fullarton & Co.

Too small to be of any use. You cannot put the sea into a tea cup.

OLD TESTAMENT, OR CONSIDERABLE PORTIONS THEREOF.

66 **AINSWORTH** (HENRY, *Died* 1622). Annotations upon the Five Bookes of Moses, the Booke of Psalmes, and the Song of Songs : wherein the Hebrew words and sentences are compared with the Greeke and Chaldee versions. Folio. *Lond.*, 1627 and 1639.

" Ainsworth was a celebrated scholar and an excellent divine. His uncommon skill in Hebrew learning, and his excellent Commentaries on the Scriptures are held in high reputation to this day."—Brook's Lives of the Puritans.

67 HENGSTENBERG (E. W. D.D.), Christology of the Old Testament : a Commentary on the Messianic Predictions. 4 vols., *Edinb.*, T. & T. Clark. 1858. ᛙ

This great work deals with a most vital theme in a masterly manner ; it has always been held in high esteem. We confess, however, that we can only read it as a task, for the dry scholastic style repels us, and it seems to us that in answering a number of sceptical doctors, whose opinions are ridiculous, the author has made much ado about nothing.

68 HORSLEY (SAMUEL, LL.D., F.R.S., and F.A.S. *Bishop of St. Asaph.* 1733—1806). Biblical Criticism on the first fourteen Historical Books of the Old Testament ; also on the first nine Prophetical Books. Second edition. 2 vols., 8vo. *Lona.*, 1844.

These criticisms will be of more interest to the scholar than of value to the minister. *Horsley* was far too ready to invent new readings; yet he was a master in his own line. He writes very dogmatically and with a violent bias toward a theory of interpretation which, with all its excellencies, cannot be everywhere maintained. Numbers of other writers have followed in his track, but none with equal footsteps.

69 JACKSON (ARTHUR, M.A. 1593—1666). A Help for the Understanding of the Holy Scriptures (Genesis to Isaiah). 4 vols. 4to. 1643, etc.

Rather tame, but will well repay quiet reading. His works are now somewhat rare. (See page 11.)

70 ORTON (JOB, D.D. 1717—1783). Exposition of the Old Testament, with Devotional and Practical Reflections, Published from the Author's Manuscripts, by Robert Gentleman. 6 vols. 8vo. *Shrewsbury*, 1788. Reprinted, 1822.

A sort of paraphrase, after the manner of *Doddridge's Family Expositor*, which it was intended to accompany. Not a very able production.

71 RICHARDSON (JOHN, *Bishop of Ardagh. Died* 1654). Choice Observations and Explanations upon the Old Testament, containing in them many remarkable matters, additional to the large Annotations made by some of the Assembly of Divines. Folio, 1655.

Of secondary importance, and very short; yet good. Frequently bound up with *Leigh* (No. 44).

PENTATEUCH AND OTHER HISTORICAL BOOKS OF THE OLD TESTAMENT.

72 **AINSWORTH** (HENRY), Annotations on the Pentateuch (See also No. 66). 4to. 1616.

Thoroughly learned. Though old, not out of date.

73 ALEXANDER (WILLIAM). The Pentateuch, with Notes.

A book of no importance.

74 BABINGTON (GERVASE, *Bishop of Worcester.* Died 1610). In *Babington's Works*, folio, 1622, there are " Certaine plain, brief, and comfortable notes " upon the five books of Moses.

Our copy is in the old Black Letter. It contains little to repay the student for toiling through the old-fashioned expressions.

75 BARRETT (R. A. F., M.A.). A Synopsis of Criticisms upon those passages of the Old Testament in which modern commentators have differed from the Authorized Version. 2 vols. in 2 parts each, and vol. III. part 1, large 8vo., 1847. [Only extends from Genesis to Esther.]

The object of this work is to lay before the reader the principal alterations which modern critics have proposed in the Authorized Version, together with the reasons for or against such emendations. Many of the notes are in Latin. Of small use to the average minister.

76 BATE (JULIUS, M.A. 1711—1771). New Literal Translation of the Pentateuch and Historical Books to end of 2 Kings. With Notes. 4to. *Lond.,* 1773.

Paper spoiled. We greatly grudge the four shillings which we gave for it.

77 BIBLE TEACHINGS; or, Remarks on Genesis, Exodus, and Leviticus. With Recommendatory Preface by Rev. W. B. Mackenzie. 8vo. *Lond.,* 1855.

This book was written by the *Three Misses Bird*, of *Taplow.* The Remarks are very plain and practical, and a spirit of earnest piety and fervent prayer pervades them throughout.

78 BLUNT (HENRY, A.M. *Died* 1843). Family Exposition of Pentateuch. 1844. 3 vols., 12mo.

See remarks under each separate volume.

79 BRIGHTWELL (T.) Notes selected from the exegetical parts of *Rosenmüller's Scholia,* and of *Dathe's Notes* to his Latin version ; also from *Schrank, Michaelis, Le Clerc, Ainsworth, Poole,* and other authors. 8vo. *Lond.,* 1840.

This writer worked very industriously at the almost impossible task of condensing the twenty-eight volumes of *Rosenmüller's Notes.* Besides the remarks from authors mentioned in the text, there are observations from the manuscripts of *Joseph Kinghorn,* of Norwich. It is not a didactic or spiritual work, but almost entirely explanatory and illustrative.

80 CHRIST IN THE LAW; or the Gospel foreshadowed in the Pentateuch.
    Compiled by a Priest of the Church of England.   CHRIST IN THE
    PROPHETS.—Joshua to Kings.   2 vols., Foolscap 8vo.   *Lond.*
    Masters, 1872 and 1873.
Of the High Church order, and praised by the *Saturday Review.* What worse
need be said ? Yet will we add that the savour of Christ in these books saves them
from unqualified condemnation.

81 DELGADO (ISAAC. *Jewish Teacher*). New Translation. 4to. *Lond.*, 1789.
    The author modestly says, that his work is *highly useful.* This is another instance
of paternal partiality, and of "great cry and little wool."

82 ETHERIDGE (J. W., M.A.). The Targums of Onkelos and Jonathan Ben
    Uzziel on the Pentateuch, with the Fragments of the Jerusalem Targum.
    Leviticus, Numbers, and Deuteronomy.   8vo.   *Lond.*, Longmans, 1865.

Comparatively few of our readers will set much store by the Targums of *Onkelos*
and *Jonathan Ben Uzziel;* but those who desire to read them will find here a good
literal version.

83 GEDDES (ALEXANDER, LL.D.—*A Roman Catholic divine.*—1737—1802.)—
    Translation from corrected texts with various Readings and Notes. [Genesis
    to Ruth only published.] 3 vols, 4to., 1792—1800.
The author was a Hebraist of considerable repute, but treated the inspired word far
too flippantly.   His style of criticism is essentially sceptical.

84 GERLACH (OTTO VON. 1801—1849). Pentateuch. Translated
    by the Rev. Henry Downing. Demy 8vo.,   *Edinb.*,
    T. & T. Clark.

Very different from other German authors. Plain, clear, and instructive.
Not choked up with metaphysical bewilderments and long lists of
sceptical authors whose names defile the pages which bear them.

85 HÄVERNICK (Dr. H. A. Ch.) Historico-Critical Introduction to the Penta-
    teuch.   Translated by A. Thomson, A.M.   *Edinb.*, Clark. 1850.
Almost entirely occupied with a discussion upon the genuineness of the Pentateuch.
A check to the rationalistic and infidel spirit.   Those who have never taken the
poison do not need the antidote.

86 HENGSTENBERG (E.W., D.D.) Genuineness of the Pentateuch.
    Translated by J. E. Ryland. 2 vols., 8vo. *Edinb.*, 1847.

This great author contends ably for the Pentateuch, but the perusal
of his book reminds us of the king who
               "Fought all his battles o'er again,
        And thrice he routed all his foes, and thrice he slew the slain."

87   „   Egypt and the Books of Moses ; or, the Books of Moses
        Illustrated by the Monuments of Egypt. 8vo.   *Edinb.*,
        1845. T. & T. Clark.
Dr. Hengstenberg, as Professor at Berlin, had access to the rich
collection of Egyptian antiquities in the Museum, and he has made
noble use of his advantages.

88 HOWARD (The Hon. E. J., D.D.. *Dean of Lichfield.*) 1. Genesis according
    to the LXX. Translated into English, with Notes on the Passages in
    which it differs from our Authorized Version. Cr. 8vo.   2. Exodus
    and Leviticus,   3. Numbers and Deuteronomy,   *Camb.*,
    Macmillan, 1857, etc.
Of no particular use to preachers ; but the *Guardian* says, "It is an excellent
introduction to the comparative study of God's word, in those three languages with
which an ordinary English student is mainly concerned."

89 JAMIESON (J., LL.D.) The Pentateuch, with Notes, &c. [Anon.] Folio, *Lond.*, 1748.
Published anonymously. Mainly a compilation, in which more industry was shown in the collection than discretion in the selection.

90 KALISCH (M.M., Ph.D.) Historical and Critical Commentary on the Old Testament ; with a New Translation. 8vo. Vol. I. Genesis, Vol. II. Exodus, Vol. III. Leviticus, part 1, Vol. IV. Leviticus, part 2, *Lond.*, Longmans. 1858.
Contains a large amount of historical illustration, shedding new light upon the letter of the Word. The author has used the fresh information which has come to us from the Euphrates and the Nile. At the same time he sows scepticisms broadcast, and we cannot recommend him.

91 KEIL (CARL FRIEDRICH, D.D., Ph.D.) Pentateuch. 3 vols., $10.50. Eerdmans.
A work for the learned. It has received the highest commendations from competent scholars. But it is somewhat dull and formal.

92 KELLY (WILLIAM). Introductory. Lectures. Cr. 8vo., *Lond.*, W. H. Broom.
By a leading writer of the exclusive Plymouth school. Not to our mind.

93 KIDDER (RICHARD, D.D., *Bp. of Bath and Wells.*—Died 1703). Five Books of Moses. 2 vols., 8vo. *Lond.*, 1694.
Of no importance : a chip in the porridge : mild as a modern bishop.

94 KINGSLEY (CHARLES, M.A., *Canon of Westminster. Died* 1875). The Gospel of the Pentateuch. [18 sermons]. Foolscap 8vo. *Lond.*, Macmillan.
A small volume of *Kingsley's* usual sort. Not over-freighted with what is usually known as the Gospel; but plain and practical, with common-sense remarks for common people.

95 LAW (HENRY, M.A., *Dean of Gloucester*). " Christ is All." The Gospel.of the Old Testament. Several editions ; a recent one is published by the Religious Tract Society, in 4 vols., Cr. 8vo.
Deservedly popular. Simple, instructive, full of Christ. Law *abounds in gospel.*

96 MACDONALD (DONALD, M.A.) Introduction, and an enquiry into the genuineness, authority and design of the Mosaic writings. 2 vols., demy 8vo. *Edinb.*, Clark. 1861.
" A full review of the evidence, external and internal, for the genuineness, authenticity, and Divine character of the Pentateuch. Its special attention is devoted to the connection between the Pentateuch and the great scheme of revelation, of which it forms the basis."—*Guardian.*

97 MORISON (JAMES, 1762—1809). Introductory Key to the first four Books of Moses ; being an attempt to show that the great design of the things recorded therein was the sufferings of Christ and the following glory. 8vo. *Perth*, 1810.
Plain, forcible, and instructive remarks, realizing the title—an Introductory Key.

98 PARKER (Samuel, *son of Bp. Samuel Parker*). Bibliotheca Biblica ; a Commentary gathered out of the writings of fathers and ecclesiastical historians, &c. [Anonymous.] 5 vols., 4to. *Oxf.*, 1720, etc. [Genesis to Deuteronomy only completed.]

Darling says, that this is " a commentary of profound learning and research;" but it seems to us to be mainly filled with that archaic learning which is now out of date.

99 PIERCE (Samuel Eyles). Discourses on the several Revelations of the Lord Jesus, from the Fall, to Moses, &c. 8vo. *Lond.*, 1815.

Dr. Hawker says, that "these Discourses carry with them testimonies of being written under Divine teaching." Sweet, but not very expository.

100 PYLE (Thomas, M.A. 1674—1756). Paraphrase, with Notes. 4 vols., 8vo. 1717—28. [Genesis to Esther only.]

A pile of paper, valuable to housemaids for lighting fires.

101 ROBERTSON (James, A.M.) Clavis Pentateuchi. Analysis of the Hebrew words in the Pentateuch, with Notes. Reprinted, edited by *Kinghorn*, at Norwich, 1824. 8vo.

Almost entirely in Latin, and therefore useful only to those who can readily read that language. The work was in good repute in its day.

102 SAURIN (James. 1677—1730). Dissertations on the most memorable events of the Bible. [Vol. I., The Books of Moses, was all ever published in English. Folio. *Lond.*, 1723].

More eloquent than accurate. Florid rather than solid.

103 SHEPHEARD (H., M.A.) Traditions of Eden ; or, Proofs of the Historical Truth of the Pentateuch, from existing facts, and from the Customs and Monuments of all Nations. Demy 8vo. *Lond.*, Nisbet & Co.

A very interesting and curious work. Good lectures might be gathered from it for week-night instruction. Not a Commentary.

104 STANLEY (Arthur Penrhyn, D.D., *Dean of Westminster*). Lectures on the History of the Jewish Church. Part I. Abraham to Samuel. Part II. Samuel to the Captivity. 2 vols., 8vo. *Lond.*, 1870.

A fascinating book, which no one can read without being the better able to realize the scenes of Scripture history. The author's broad views are known and deplored : that he has equal breadth of learning we cheerfully admit.

105 THISTLEWAITE (W., M.A.) Expository Sermons. 4 vols., 12mo. *Lond.*, 1837-8.

Sermons as good as these are plentiful as blackberries. Why were they printed ?

106 TOWNSEND (George, D.D., *Canon of Durham*). The Pentateuch and the Book of Job, arranged in Chronological Order, with Prayers and Notes. 2 vols., 8vo. *Lond.*, 1849.

A singular combination of family prayers, essays and notes, by an able but singular writer.

107 WRIGHT (Abraham). A Practical Commentary, wherein the Text of every Chapter is Practically expounded, in a way not usually trod by Commentators. Folio. 1662.

An extremely rare book. The style and matter are after the manner of *Christopher Ness*. *Wright* does not comment upon every verse, but after indicating the run of the chapter gives little sermons upon the more salient points. He is very quaint and pithy.

GENESIS.

108 **ALFORD** (HENRY, *Dean of Canterbury.* 1810—1871). The Book of Genesis and part of the Book of Exodus [Ch. I.—XXV.] : a revised version, with Commentary. Demy 8vo. *Lond.,* W. Isbister & Co. 1872.
The works of this eminent scholar are too well known and appreciated to need even a word from us.

109 BLUNT (HENRY, M.A.) Genesis [Vol. I. of a Family Exposition of the Pentateuch. 12mo. *Lond.,* Hatchards. 1841].
Simple Expositions for family reading. Good, but not brilliant.

110 BURROUGHS (W. K., M.A.) Lectures on Genesis. 8vo. *Dub.,* 1848.
Useful to grocers and buttermen. Worth nothing to students.

111 BUSH (GEORGE. *Prof. of Heb. and Orient. Lit., New York*). Notes on Genesis. 2 vols., small 8vo. *New York,* 1852. Reprinted in *London* in 1 vol., 8vo.

Bush has in the most barefaced manner taken copious verbatim extracts from *Andrew Fuller,* without acknowledgment, and he has also plagiarized *Lawson* on *Joseph* by wholesale, without even mentioning his name. For such a scholar to be guilty of wholesale plunder is inexcusable. It is one of the worst cases of robbery we have ever met with, and deserves a far stronger denunciation than our gentle pen and slender space will permit.

112 **CALVIN** (JOHN). Genesis   Reprint of C.T.S. edition, Volume 1, $4.50. Volume 2, $3.50. Eerdmans.
Participates in the general excellencies of Calvin's works.

113 **CANDLISH** (ROBERT S., D.D.) Lectures. New edition. 2 volumes in one. $9.95. Zondervan.
We venture to characterize this as THE *work upon Genesis, so far as lectures can make up an exposition ; we have greatly profited by its perusal. It should be in every Biblical library.*

114 CLOSE (FRANCIS, D.D., A.M., *Dean of Carlisle*). Historical Discourses. 12mo. *Lond.,* 1828.
A course of smoothly-flowing, respectable, quiet, evangelical sermons. Nobody could be so wicked as to call them sensational.

115 COGHLAN (C. L.) Genesis and St. Matthew. 2 vols., 8vo. 1832.
Consists entirely of parallel and illustrative passages of Scripture printed in full; it is superseded by the *Commentary Wholly Biblical.*

116 CUMMING (JOHN, D.D., F.R.S.E.) Scripture Readings on Genesis. Small 8vo. *Lond.,* J. F. Shaw. 1853.
Dr. Cumming's works are not very original, but his style is flowing, his teachings are always evangelical, and he puts other men's thoughts into pleasing language.

117   DAWSON (ABRAHAM).   New Translation of Genesis [I.—XVII.], with
        Notes.   4to.   *Lond.*, 1763.
   Tainted with infidelity.   A writer of the Geddes school.

118   DIMOCK (HENRY).   Notes.   4to.   *Gloucester*, 1804.
   Chiefly taken up with the various readings of Hebrew MSS.   The young student
will not value it.   The same author has written on Exodus and the Prophets.

119   FRANKS (JAMES, A.M.)   Sacred Literature; or, Remarks on Genesis.   8vo.
        Halifax, 1802.
   This writer collected notes from various authors.   As the sources from which he
drew his extracts are within reach, we can select for ourselves.

120   **FULLER** (ANDREW, 1754—1815).   Expository Discourses
        on Genesis.   One small vol.,   (Also in *Fuller's*
        Works.)
   Weighty, judicious, and full of Gospel truth.   One of the very
best series of discourses extant upon Genesis, as Bush also thought.

121   GIBBENS (NICHOLAS).   Questions and Disputations concerning Holy Scrip-
        ture.   Genesis.   4to.   1602.
   In his own fashion this antique writer tries to answer curious questions which are
suggested by Genesis.   His day is over.

122   GREENFIELD (WILLIAM, M.R.A.S.   *Editor of the Comprehen-*
        sive Bible).   Genesis in English and Hebrew, with an Inter-
        linear Translation, Notes, and Grammatical Introduction.   8vo.
        Lond., 1862.
   This work will not only enable the Student to get at the literal
meaning of the text, but may be used as an introduction to the Hebrew
language.   The plan is most admirable, and we earnestly commend it
to the attention of those uninstructed in the sacred tongue.

123   GROVES (HENRY CHARLES, M.A.)   Commentary on Genesis,
        for readers of the English version.   Small 8vo.   *Lond.* and *Camb.*,
        Macmillan & Co.   1861.
   Physical science, the discoveries of travellers, and the results of
criticism, so far as they bear upon Genesis, are here brought within the
reach of the general reader.

124   HARWOOD (T.)   Annotations.   8vo.   *Lond.*, 1789.
   The author professed to offer his work with great diffidence, and he had just cause
to do so : he had better have burned his manuscript.

125   HAWKER (JOHN, M.A.)   Bible Thoughts in Quiet Hours.
        Genesis.   Small Cr. 8vo.   *Lond.*, Yapp.   1873.
   Deeply spiritual reflections, not without learning and critical power.
The preacher will find here many hints for sermons.

126   HEAD (F. A.)   The World and its Creator.   Cr. 8vo.   *Lond.*, 1847.
   One of the many *good* books which from lack of vigour are only "born to die."

127   **HUGHES** (GEORGE, B.D., *Puritan*, 1603—1667).   Analy-
        tical Exposition of Genesis, and of XXIII. chapters of
        Exodus.   Folio.   1672.
   The deductions which Hughes draws from the text are of the
nature of homiletical hints, and for this reason he will be a treasure
to the minister.   He belongs to the noble army of Puritans.

128 **JACOBUS** (MELANCTHON W., *Professor of Biblical Literature, Alleghany, U. S.*). Notes. 2 vols. sm. 8vo. *New York*, 1866.

A very valuable work, in which Colenso is boldly met and answered. It contains much Gospel teaching, and aids the preacher greatly. Not easily to be obtained. It ought to be reprinted.

129 JERVIS-WHITE-JERVIS (JOHN) Genesis : a New Translation collated with the Samaritan, Septuagint, and Syriac, with Notes, 8vo. *Lond.*, Bagsters. 1852.

Brings out very vividly the oriental character of Genesis, and although we cannot reconcile ourselves to *Abh-rauhaum, Is'hauk, and Y'aakobh,* and find it hard to believe in *Saurauh* and *Haughaur,* we have been glad of the light which the East and its languages have here afforded.

130 JUKES (ANDREW). Types of Genesis. 8vo. *Lond.*, Long-mans. 1858.

In many places far too forced, and therefore to be read with caution ; but in its own spiritualizing way very masterly. Jukes dives deep.

131 **LANGE'S COMMENTARY** edited by Dr. Schaff. Vol. I. Commentary on Genesis. $3.95. Zondervan.

The best of the series, and in all respects beyond price.

132 **M[ACKINTOSH]** (C. H.). Notes on Genesis. By *C. H. M.* $2.00. Loizeaux ; $2.00. Revell.

Precious and edifying reflections marred by peculiarities.

133 MACGREGOR (SIR C., BART., M.A.) Notes for Students in Divinity. Part I. [Chap. i.-xi.] 8vo. *Lond.*, Parker. 1853.

Contains a great deal of learning, of small use to the preacher. Many curious and knotty points which arise in the first eleven chapters of Genesis are discussed with considerable ability.

134 **MURPHY** (JAMES G., LL.D., *Professor of Hebrew, Belfast*). Commentary on Genesis, with a New Translation. 8vo. *Edinb.*, T. & T. Clark. 1863.

"A work of massive scholarship, abounding in rich and noble thought, and remarkably fresh and suggestive."—Evangelical Mag.

135 OSBURN (WILLIAM). Israel in Egypt ; or, the Books of Genesis and Exodus illustrated by existing Monuments. Small 8vo. *Lond.*, Seeleys. 1856.

Not a Commentary ; but a volume full of interest, which should be studied by all who would understand this portion of history.

136 PAUL (WILLIAM, A.M.) Analysis and Critical Interpretation of the Hebrew Text, preceded by a Hebrew Grammar. 8vo. *Edinb.* and *Lond.* W. Blackwood & Sons. 1852.

Designed to promote the study of Hebrew. Not a comment, but rather a grammatical exercise. Useful to students of the sacred tongue.

137   PRESTON (THEODORE, M.A.) Phraseological Notes on the Hebrew Text.
8vo.   *Lond.*, 1853.
Intended to explain and illustrate the most remarkable peculiarities and anomalies of matter, style, and phrase in the Book of Genesis. It may interest Hebraists, but can little aid the preacher.

138   SIBTHORPE (RICHARD WALDO, B.D.) Genesis, with Brief Observations.
Imp. 8vo.   *Lond.*, 1835.
Mere platitudes. Paper spoiled.

139   TURNER (SAMUEL H., D.D., *Prof. Columbia Coll., New York*).
A companion to Genesis. 8vo.   *New York*, 1851.
In *Horne's Introduction* we read :—" Though not designed to be a Commentary, this valuable work furnishes the Biblical student with abundant aid for the exact and literal interpretation of the Book of Genesis."

140   WARNER (RICHARD). Exposition. 12mo. *Lond.*, Longmans. 1840.
Common-place remarks; intended to be used at family worship. Likely to send the servants to sleep.

141   WHATELEY (WILLIAM). Prototypes; or, the Primarie Precedent Presidents out of the Booke of Genesis. Shewing the Good and Bad Things they Did and Had. Practically adapted to our Information and Reformation. Folio. *Lond.*, 1640.
A queer old book. The oddity of the title is borne out by the singularity of the matter. It does not expound each verse ; but certain incidents are dwelt upon.

142   WILLET (ANDREW. 1562—1621). Hexapla. A sixfold Exposition of Genesis. Folio. 1605.
This work is called by its author a *Hexapla,* because he treats his subject under six heads, giving "a sixfold use of every chapter, showing, 1. The method, or argument. 2. The divers readings. 3. The explanation of difficult questions and doubtful places. 4. The places of doctrine. 5. Places of confutation. 6. Moral observations." *Willet* is tedious reading ; his method hampers him. In all his Commentaries he lumbers along in his six-wheeled wagon.

143   WRIGHT (C. H. H.) Book of Genesis in Hebrew, with various Readings, Notes, etc. 8vo.   *Lond.*, Williams & Norgate.
Intended to assist the student who has mastered the elements of Hebrew Grammar to acquire a better knowledge of that language. Rather a class-book than a Commentary.

GENESIS—EARLY CHAPTERS, AND PATRIARCHS.

144 BONAR (HORATIUS, D.D.) Earth's Morning; or, Thoughts on Genesis. 12mo.   *Lond.*, Nisbet & Co. 1875.
An exposition of the first six chapters only. The author endeavours " to investigate the meaning of each verse and word ; that, having done so, the exact revelation of God in these may be brought out, and the spiritual truth evolved." He has in a great measure attained his object. What more could be said in his praise?

145 BUNYAN (John). Ten first chapters of Genesis, and part of the eleventh. [In *Bunyan's Works*.] Complete works,
Allegorical and spiritual. *Bunyan's* characteristics are very prominently manifest.

146 EDERSHEIM (Alfred, D.D.) World before the Flood, and History of the Patriarchs.   Included in Bible History-Old Testament by Edersheim, 2 volumes $10.00. Eerdmans.
The author has mainly aimed at giving instruction to the Sunday School Teacher, and the Bible Class Student. He may be read with profit by students of a higher grade. The work is not a Commentary, but is full of instruction.

147 HENRY (Philip, M.A. 1631—1696). Exposition of the first eleven chapters of Genesis. 18mo. *Lond.*, 1839.
Interesting as the exposition of *Matthew Henry's* father, taken down from his lips at family prayer by *Matthew*, his son. This probably suggested the famous Commentary.

148 HURDIS (James). Select Critical Remarks upon the English version of the first ten chapters of Genesis. 8vo. *Lond.*, 1793.
"Judicious observations"; but it is so easy to be *judicious*. Unimportant.

149 LUTHER (Martin). On the first five chapters of Genesis, translated by Dr. Henry Cole. 8vo. *Edinb.*, 1858.
Cole made a choice selection. Luther left four volumes upon Genesis in Latin. How these Reformers worked !

150 MACDONALD (D.) Creation and the Fall. The first three chapters of Genesis. 8vo. *Edinb.*, T. & T. Clark.
" We do not hesitate to designate this volume as the most complete examination of the literature and the exegesis of the Creation and the Fall which has appeared in England."—*Journal of Sacred Literature.*

151 NEEDLER (Benjamin). Expository Notes, with Observations, towards the opening of the five first chapters of Genesis. Small 8vo. *Lond.*,1655.
Needler was one of the eminent divines who took part in the famous Morning Exercises. The little work is a curiosity, but nothing more.

152 ROSSE (Alexander). Exposition of the fourteen first chapters of Genesis. 8vo. *Lond.*, 1626.
A very scarce catechism by that Scotch divine who is mentioned in *Hudibras* in the lines—
" There was an ancient sound philosopher
That had read Alexander Ross over."

153 WHITE (John, M.A. *A Puritan Divine, called " The Patriarch of Dorchester.*" *Died* 1648.) The Three First Chapters of Genesis. Folio. 1656.
A folio upon three chapters ! There were giants in those days. *Manton* says, " To speak of the worth of the author is needless, his praise being already in all the churches," and he adds that he had been greatly refreshed by the perusal of this book.

154 WILLIAMS (Isaac, B.D.) Beginning of Genesis, with Notes. Sm. 8vo.   *Lond.*, Rivingtons. 1861.
A very remarkable work by a high churchman, opening up in a masterly manner the mystical teachings of the early chapters of Genesis. To be read cum grano salis.

[The following works are placed in chronological order.]

155 BONNET (L.)   The Exile from Eden; Meditations on the Third Chapter of Genesis, translated from the French, by Rev. W. Hare. Small 8vo. *Lond.*, 1839.

After the French manner. In nine meditations the salient points in the all-important story of the Fall are touched upon. One of the best separate treatises upon the subject.

156 OLMSTEAD (J., *American*.)   Noah and his Times.   *Edinb.*, Collins.
One of the dreariest works ever written. We have often wondered why it was reprinted, or even printed at all. It is as dry as Noah in the ark.

157 BLUNT (HENRY, A.M.)   Twelve Lectures on the History of Abraham. 12mo.   Eight Lectures on the History of Jacob.   *Lond.*, Hatchards. 1842.

Like the rest of this author's lectures. Good, plain addresses.

158 SHUTE (JOSIAS, B.D. "*Above three-and-thirty years Rector of St. Mary, Woolnoth.*")   Sarah and Hagar ; or, Genesis xvi. opened in Twenty Sermons. Folio. 1649.

In shape, the editor tells us, " this book is somewhat slender, like the encouragements of learning."   He informs us that the author was " one of the five famous brother-preachers, somewhat like the five fingers on the right hand of fellowship ; " and that *Chrysostom* did so much lie in his bosom that he became like him in his flowing style and golden eloquence. He writes like a learned man, and treats the Scriptures as if " each book were a course, each chapter a Benjamin's mess, and every verse a morsel of the food of angels."

159 BOUCHIER (BARTON, M.A.)   History of Isaac. 12mo. *Lond.*, Houlston.

A charming book, in *Bouchier's* gracious style.

160 ROLLINSON (FRANCIS, B.D.)   Twelve Prophetical Legacies ; or, Twelve Sermons upon Jacob's Last Will, recorded in the 45th chapt. of Genesis. 4to., *Lond.*, 1612. Scarce.
Old-fashioned learning, and singular remarks ; its rarity is no great calamity.

161 CUMMING (JOHN, D.D., F.R.S.E.)   The Last of the Patriarchs; or, Lessons from Life of Joseph. Sm. 8vo. 1856.

Fitted for popular reading : ministers need more thought.

162 GIBSON (T.) Lectures on Joseph. 8vo. *Lond.*, 1848.
Very respectable sermons, bringing out the gospel of Joseph's history.

163 LAWSON (GEORGE, D.D., 1749—1820). Lectures on Joseph. 2 vols., 12mo. *Edinb.*, 1807 & 1812.

Dr. Lawson had a fertile mind, and a heart alive both to the human and divine side of truth. He writes with pleasing simplicity of style. One of the highest compliments to this book is found in the fact that a distinguished American scholar issued much of it as his own.

164 **SMITH** (THORNLEY). History of Joseph viewed in connection with the Antiquities of Egypt, and the times in which he lived. Cr. 8vo. *Edinb.*, W. Oliphant. 1875.

" *Written under the full light of the most recent archæological discoveries, modern scholarship, and theological science, it is* THE *book on the subject. Now we have it, we cannot dispense with it."—Homilist.*

165 WARDLAW (RALPH, D.D.) Life of Joseph and the Last Years of Jacob. 12mo. 1845.

Wardlaw, though rather wordy, is always instructive.

EXODUS.

166 BIRKS (T. R., M.A.) The Exodus of Israel; its Difficulties explained and its Truth confirmed. 8vo. 1863.

A reply to *Dr. Colenso's* famous assault upon the Pentateuch. The great abilities of the author are known to all.

167 BLUNT (HENRY, M.A.) Exodus and Leviticus. Vol. 2 of A Family Exposition of the Pentateuch. 12mo. *Lond.*, Hatchards. 1842.

Profitable for household and private reading : not very striking.

168 BUSH (GEORGE). Notes on Exodus. 2 vols., sm. 8vo. *New York*, 1856, etc.

Of considerable value. We do not know that it is a plagiarism.

169 COTTAGE READINGS on the Book of Exodus. [Anon.] Sm. cr. 8vo. *Lond.*, Nisbet & Co.

Not at all a student's book ; yet many preachers might learn from it how to put things plainly. There is a similar volume on Genesis.

170 CUMMING (JOHN, D.D.) Sabbath Morning Readings on Exodus. Sm. 8vo. *Lond.*, J. F. Shaw. 1853.

Dr. Cumming's style is a model, but his matter seldom verges upon originality. He always gives you the gospel when he is not prophesying.

171 EXELL (JOSEPH S.) Homiletic Commentary on Exodus. Included in The Preacher's Homiletic Commentary. 32 volumes $67.50. Eerdmans. Funk & Wagnalls.

It excels, so far as we have seen.

172 HUGHES (GEORGE). See No. 127.

173 JACKSON (THOMAS, D.D., *Dean of Peterborough.*—1579—1640). Paraphrase on the eleven first chapters of Exodus, with Annotations, &c. *Works*, 8vo., IX., 384. Folio, III., 191. 3 vols. folio 12 vols. 8vo.

George Herbert set great store by *Dr. Jackson's* writings, for he said,—" I bless God for the confirmation *Dr. Jackson* has given me in the Christian religion, against the Atheist, Jew, and Socinian, and in the Protestant against Rome." It would hardly repay a student to purchase three folio volumes to obtain the small portion allotted to his Paraphrase. · So far as commenting is concerned it is not important.

174 **M[ACKINTOSH]** C.H.) Notes. By C. H. M. 12mo.
$2.00. Loizeaux ; $2.00. Revell.
Not free from Plymouth errors, yet remarkably suggestive.

175 **MILLINGTON** (THOMAS S.) Signs and Wonders in the
Land of Ham. A Description of the Ten Plagues of
Egypt. Post 8vo.   *Lond.*, Murray. 1873.
*It has been an intellectual treat to read this interesting work.
On the same subject there is an old work by James Bryant,
1794 ; but Millington is enough.*

176 **MURPHY** (JAMES G., LL.D.)   Commentary on Exodus.
New Translation. 8vo. *Edinb.*, Clark. 1866.
The result of laborious study by a scholar of ripe learning.

177 WILLET (ANDREW). Hexapla ; or, Sixfold Commentarie upon
Exodus. Folio. *Lond.*, 1608.
See No. 142. Full, exhaustive, and exhausting.

LIVES OF MOSES.

178 **HAMILTON** (JAMES, D.D., F.L.S. 1814—1867). Moses,
the Man of God. Sm. cr. 8vo.   *Lond.*, Nisbet.
*Beautiful as a poem, like everything which fell from Dr. Hamil-
ton's pen. It would be impossible to study it without profit.*

179 OOSTERZEE (J. J. VAN, D.D.) The Life of Moses. *Edinb.*,
T. & T. Clark.

180 **SMITH** (THORNLEY). History of Moses ; viewed in
connection with Egyptian Antiquities, and the times in
which he lived. Cr. 8vo.   *Lond.*, Hamilton. 1862.
Of the same class as Kitto's Daily Readings : well executed.

181 SPONG (JAMES). Moses.—The Hero of the Desert. Cr. 8vo.   *Lond.*,
Partridge & Co.
A book for the public. Not for students.

JOURNEYINGS OF THE CHILDREN OF ISRAEL.

182 BUDDICOM (R. P., M.A., F.A.S.) The Christian Exodus,
in a Series of Discourses. 2 vols., 8vo. *Lond.*, 1826.
Able discourses, using the Exodus spiritually and wisely.

183 CARDALL (WILLIAM, M.A.) Israel's Journeys, illustrative of the **Divine**
Pilgrimage. 8vo. *Lond.*, Hatchards. 1848.
Twenty evangelical lectures manifesting respectable ability.

184 FORSTER (CHARLES, B.D.) "Israel in the Wilderness"; or, Gleanings from the Scenes of the Wanderings. 8vo. *Lond.*, Richard Bentley. 1865.

If the author's renderings of the desert inscriptions are indeed correct, this is a wonderful book. That, however, is a question for the learned, and they have pronounced against him.

185 JOURNEYINGS OF THE CHILDREN OF ISRAEL, and their Settlement in the Promised Land. (ANON.) 18mo.   *Lond.*, Religious Tract Society. 1832.

Useful to the young, but the engravings are of almost Pre-Adamite antiquity, and nearly as ugly as the profoundest master of the ridiculous could have made them.

186 KRUMMACHER (GOTTFRIED DANIEL. 1774—1837). Israel's Wanderings. 2 vols., Sm. 8vo. *Lond.*, Nisbet. 1837.

Written by the uncle of the author of *Elijah the Tishbite*. A good, thought-breeding work.

187 OSBURN (W.) See under Genesis, No. 135.

188 **SEATON** (W.) Church in the Wilderness. 2 vols. 12mo. 2nd edition, *Lond.*, 1821. Enlarged. 2 vols., 8vo.

Of the thoroughly evangelical school, fraught with much experimental truth and sound doctrine soberly discussed.

189 **WAGNER** (GEORGE). The Wanderings of the Children of Israel. Cr. 8vo.   *Lond.*, Nisbet & Co. 1862.

A book which we have read with great pleasure and profit, and very heartily recommend.

THE DECALOGUE.

[This list does not include comments contained in Bodies of Divinity, &c., but those forming separate volumes. In many theological works there are lengthy portions set apart for the Commandments.]

190 **ANDREWES** (LANCELOT, *Bp. of Worcester.* 1555—1626). The Patterne of Catechisticall Doctrine at large; or a Learned and Pious Exposition of the X Commandments. Folio. 1675.

This is a book indeed; it is a joy to read it, for it flashes with thought and illustration, and sparkles with ingenious remarks. Profound learning did not lead the Bishop into the depths of dulness, as it has done many another divine; he manifests the happy quaintness of Latimer side by side with great scholarship. He was highly esteemed by his contemporaries; but we can hardly believe that his death

"Left the dim face of our dull hemisphere
All one great eye all drown'd in one great tear."

Yet so we are informed at the foot of his effigies.

191 BARKER (PETER). A Learned and Familiar Exposition. 4to. 1624.

Old-fashioned, remarkably quaint, and even coarse in places. Barker's work abounds in Scriptural illustrations, but it is almost forgotten.

192 DALE (R. W., M.A., of Birmingham.) The Ten Commandments. Cr. 8vo. *Lond.*, Hodder and Stoughton. 1873.

Written in a clear, bold, and trenchant style. We could not subscribe to all the author's views, but we admire his practical remarks, and their outspoken manner.

193 DOD (JOHN) & CLEAVER (ROBERT). Familiar Exposition. Eighteenth edition. 4to. *Lond.*, 1632.

This work was published by *John Dod* and *Robert Cleaver*, with an intimation that the name of the author was purposely suppressed. Our edition, dated 1632, is the eighteenth, so that the work enjoyed a rare popularity in its own time. It has been frequently reprinted since. The book has been long held in high esteem.

194 DOWNAME, or DOWNHAM (GEORGE, D.D., *Bishop of Derry. Died* 1634). Abstract of the Duties Commanded and Sinnes Forbidden in the Law of God. 8vo. *Lond.*, 1635.

A sort of catalogue of sins, arranged in a tabular form under the Ten Commandments. These are the heads and divisions of a larger treatise, which does not appear to have been published. These mighty men could afford to leave in the oblivion of manuscript works which would cost modern weaklings half a life-time to write.

195 **DURHAM** (JAMES. 1622—1658.) Exposition, with a resolution of several momentous questions, and cases of conscience. 4to. *Lond.*, 1675. 8vo., 1735,

Whatever Durham has written is very precious. He has the pen of a ready writer, and indites good matter.

196 ELTON (EDWARD, B.D.) God's Holy Minde, Touching Matters Morall; which himself uttered in Ten Commandments. 4to. *Lond.*, 1648.

This work discusses the Decalogue in question and answer, in a somewhat dull manner; but touches many cases of conscience, and deals wisely with them. Belief in witchcraft comes out very strongly in some passages.

197 FISHER (EDWARD, A.M. *Born about 1600.*) A plain, pithy, and spiritual Exposition of the Ten Commandments. [*Marrow of Modern Divinity.* Numerous editions.] 12mo.

This exposition is part of the work which occasioned the famous *Marrow Controversy.* One fails to see anything calculated to stir up such a strife. *Fisher* might have said that the lines had fallen to him in troubled waters.

198 HOOPER (JOHN. *Bishop and Martyr.* 1495—1554). A Declaration of the Ten Holy Commandments of Almighty God. 1548, 1550, etc. [Reprinted in *Hooper's Works.*]

After the manner of the English Reformers. The style is harsh to the modern ear, and the matter too much occupied with the controversies raging in the author's times to be very interesting now.

199 HOPKINS (Ezekiel, D.D. *Bp. of London-Derry.* 1633—1690).
An Exposition of the Ten Commandments. 4to. 1692. [Reprinted in *Hopkins' Works.*]

Hopkins in this exposition searches the heart thoroughly, and makes very practical application of the Commandments to the situations and circumstances of daily life. His homely eloquence will always make his works valuable.

200 KNEWSTUB (John). Lectures on Exodus XX. 4to. 1584.
More valuable for its antiquity than for anything else.

201 McCAUL (Joseph B., *Chaplain to the Bp. of Rochester*). The Ten Commandments; the Christian's Rule of Daily Life. 8vo. *Lond.*, Saunders, Otley & Co. 1861.

The author says, "There is nothing deep in the following pages except their subject": a modest estimate.

202 **NEWTON** (Richard, D.D.) The King's Highway. Post 8vo. *Lond.*, Nelson. Also 16mo. Nisbet.

Though intended for children, ministers will find it useful, for it teems with illustration, and brings up little points of conduct worth touching upon. Dr. Newton is the prince of preachers to children.

203 TUDOR (Richard, B.A.) Decalogue viewed as the Christian's Law. Cr. 8vo. 10/6. *Lond.*, Macmillan. 1860.

The author attempts to give the Christian sense of the Decalogue in its application to present needs and questions. With much moderation he discusses many of the disputed points of the day, such as the legislative enforcement of the Sabbath, marriage with a deceased wife's sister, &c. He usually takes the view which is natural to a clergyman; but he says some capital things.

204 WEEMSE (John. *Died about 1636*). The Morall Laws. [In Vol. I. of Weemse's *Works;* 2 vols., 4to. *Lond.*, 1632, &c.]

Solid, sober, weighty. *Orme* says of *Weemse:* "He was well acquainted with the original Scriptures, with Jewish manners and antiquities, and with the best mode of interpreting the Bible. The style is quaint, but always intelligible." (See No. 225.)

205 WHATELEY (William. *Puritan.* 1583—1639). A Pithie, Short, and Methodicall Opening of the Ten Commandments. 12mo. *Lond.*, 1622. (Not often in the market.)

Exceedingly scarce, but as rich as it is rare.

THE TABERNACLE.

[Of works on this subject it is not possible to give more than a selection.]

206 BROWN (W.) The Tabernacle and its Services in relation to Christ and the Church. 8vo. *Edinb.*, Oliphant & Co. 1874.

An instructive interpretation of the types of the Tabernacle.

207 GARRATT (S.) Scripture Symbolism. Sm. 8vo. 1848.
Most unexceptionable in doctrine and style. It deals mainly with the
sacred vessels.

208 KITTO (JOHN, D.D.) Tabernacle and its Furniture. 4to. 1849.
Artistic illustrations with a little letter-press. *Soltau* well supplies the
place of this rare work.

209 MUDGE (WILLIAM). The Tabernacle in the Wilderness. 12mo.
Lond., Simpkin & Marshall. 1861.
The writer, a thoroughly evangelical second-advent clergyman, makes
some very admirable remarks in these Lectures, which were delivered in
his parish church. Our copy is in the third edition. We are not sur-
prised to find the work thus popular.

210 SOLTAU (H. W.) The Holy Vessels and Furniture of the
Tabernacle of Israel. [With Ten Chromo-Lithographic Illustrations.] Imp. oblong 8vo.   *Lond.*, Yapp & Hawkins,
and S. W. Partridge & Co.
A series of sumptuous pictures, executed in the best style of art,
impressing the mind far more vividly than any letter-press could do.

211 **SOLTAU** (H. W.) The Tabernacle, the Priestly Garments,
and the Priesthood. 8vo.   *Lond.*, Morgan & Scott.
*Richly suggestive. Exceedingly well worked out in details; but
not so wire-drawn as to prevent thought on the reader's part.*

212 WHITE (FRANK H.) Christ in the Tabernacle, with some
Remarks on the Offerings. Illustrated by Twelve Chromo-
Lithographs. Cr. 8vo.,   *Lond.*, S. W. Partridge. 1873.
Written for the private Christian. Full of instruction and devotion.

LEVITICUS.

213 **BONAR** (ANDREW A.) Leviticus. With Notes. 8vo.
Lond., Nisbet & Co. 1861.
*Very precious. Mr. Andrew Bonar has a keen eye for a typical
analogy, but he always keeps the rein upon his imagination, and is
therefore safe to follow. He is a master in Israel.*

214 **BUSH** (GEORGE). Notes on Leviticus. Sm. 8vo. *New
York*, 1857.
*The author read extensively to produce this volume. In his later
years he became a Swedenborgian, but there is no trace of that
leaning in this or his other comments. He inserts the notes of the
Pictorial Bible, but handsomely acknowledges them.*

215 CUMMING (JOHN, D.D.) Sabbath Morning Readings on
Leviticus. Sm. 8vo. *Lond.*, J. F. Shaw. 1854.
For popular reading. The author wrote too much to be profound.

216 CUMMING (JOHN, D.D.) The Great Sacrifice; or, the Gospel according to Leviticus.
A companion to the volume last mentioned.

217 JAMES (HORATIO, M.A.) Sermons on the Levitical Types. Sm. 8vo. *Lond.*, 1847.
Very attenuated. These sermons, like the lean kine, have eaten up the fat kine of the types and are never the fatter.

218 **JUKES** (ANDREW). The Law of the Offerings [Leviticus, chap. I-VII]. Cr. 8vo. *Lond.*, Nisbet & Co. 1854.
A very condensed, instructive, refreshing book. It will open up new trains of thought to those unversed in the teaching of the types.

219 M[ACKINTOSH] (C. H.) Notes on Leviticus. By C. H. M. $2.00. Loizeaux; $2.00 Revell.
We do not endorse the Plymouthism which pervades these notes, but they are frequently suggestive. Should be read cautiously.

220 MATHER (SAMUEL. 1626—1671). The Figures or Types of the Old Testament. Second edition. 4to. *Lond.*, 1705.
Though this is a work upon all the types, it contains so much instructive matter upon the Levitical sacrifices that we cannot forbear mentioning it here. It is one of the old standard books of our fathers.

221 KEACH (BENJAMIN, *Baptist Pastor.* 1640—1704). Tropologia. Folio and Roy. 8vo.
This is a vast cyclopædia of types and metaphors of all sorts, and was once very popular. It is a capital book, though too often the figures not only run on all-fours but on as many legs as a centipede. It is not strictly upon Leviticus, but we felt bound to insert it in this place.

222 MICHAELIS (SIR JOHN DAVID. 1717—1791). The Laws of Moses. Translated by Alexander Smith, D.D. 4 vols., 8vo. *Lond.*, 1814.
However much of learning there may be here, we are not prepared to recommend a work which treats so sacred a subject with levity and coarseness.

223 NEWTON (BENJAMIN WILLS). Thoughts on Parts of Leviticus. 12mo. *Lond.*, Houlston. 1857.
This touches only the first six chapters; but it treats of the offerings in a manner deeply spiritual and helpful. This writer has some peculiarities of style and thought; but in matter and spirit he is far removed from the Darby school.

224 SEISS (JOSEPH A., D.D.) The Gospel in Leviticus. 8vo. *Edinb.*, Thomas C. Jack. 1860.
Twenty-one very admirable lectures, founded upon *Bush* and *Bonar*, but containing much original matter. The work deserves attention.

225 WEEMSE (JOHN). Exposition of the Laws of Moses, Moral, Ceremonial, Judicial, &c. 2 vols., 4to. *Lond.*, 1632.
This contains many useful and curious things, together with fancies and rabbinical trifles. *Weemse* may generally be bought very cheap, and we should think his work is very little read or cared for. (See *Orme's* opinion, No. 204.)

226 WILLET (ANDREW). Hexapla ; Leviticus. Folio. 1631.

Plodding along with his six-fold load, *Willet* gives us a comparison of ten versions, "handles well nigh two thousand theological questions," and quotes "above forty authors, old and new." He sums up all preceding commentaries, both Protestant and Romish.

NUMBERS.

[Seaton, Wagner, and other writers whom we have placed under Exodus are equally upon Numbers, and should be referred to.]

227 ATTERSOLL (WILLIAM). A Commentarie upon Numbers. Folio. *Lond.*, 1618.

A stupendous work, well fitted to make a headstone for the author's grave. It is so huge that it might have been the work of a lifetime, and yet the same writer has also given us Philemon. Think of 1271 folio pages on Numbers!

228 BLUNT (HENRY, M.A.) Numbers and Deuteronomy. [Vol. 3 of Pentateuch.] 12mo., *Lond.*, Hatchards. 1843.

Intended for families, but not without value to the preacher.

229 BUSH (GEORGE). Notes on Numbers. Thick small 8vo. *New York*, 1858.

Although Bush is indebted to many authors, he is by no means a mere collector; his remarks repay you for consultation, and we hope that in this case they are his own.

230 CUMMING (JOHN, D.D.) Readings on Numbers. 8vo. *Lond.*, J. F. Shaw. 1855.

Good, as usual.

231 M[ACKINTOSH] (C. H.) Notes on Numbers. By C. H. M. $2.00. Loizeaux ; $2.00. Revell.

Like the other notes of C. H. M., they need filtering. Good as they are, their *Darbyism* gives them an unpleasant and unhealthy savour.

DEUTERONOMY.

[As so few expositions have been written upon Deuteronomy alone, the reader will do well to use the Commentaries upon the Pentateuch and the whole Old Testament.]

232 CALVIN (JOHN). Sermons upon Deuteronomie. Translated out of French by A. Golding. Folio. 1583.

This is not the same as that which is contained in the "Calvin Translation Society's Commentaries." Everything that Calvin wrote by way of exposition is priceless; even those who differ from him in theology admit this.

233 CUMMING (JOHN, D.D.) Readings in Deuteronomy. Sm. 8vo. *Lond.*, J. F. Shaw. 1856.
Pretty, popular, profitable.

JOSHUA.

234 BLACKWOOD (STEVENSON A.) Heavenly Places. Addresses. Sm. cr. 8vo. *Lond.*, Nisbet & Co. 1873.
Mr. Blackwood has illustrated passages from the first five chapters only. He has a beautifully quiet way of saying very sweet things. This little book will be useful if it shows the young preacher how to expound Scripture with unction and power.

235 **BUSH** (GEORGE). Notes. Sm. 8vo. *New York.* 1852.
Bush is a careful illustrator of the Word, and apt at giving the practical lesson. His works are well compiled.

236 **CALVIN** (JOHN). Commentarie upon Joshue. Translated by W. F. Reprint of C.T.S. edition. $3.00. Eerdmans.
We have said enough upon Calvin in general. His expositions are more equal in excellence than those of other men ; other men rise and fall, but he is almost uniformly good.

237 CHRIST IN THE PROPHETS.—Joshua, Judges, Samuel, Kings. [Anon.] Foolscap 8vo. *Lond.*, Masters. 1873.
See Christ in the Law, No. 80. Needs well sifting. There is much rubbish.

238 CUMMING (JOHN, D.D.) Readings on Joshua and Judges. Sm. 8vo. *Lond.*, J. F. Shaw. 1857.
Dr. Cumming keeps up to his average of value.

239 GROSER (W. H.) Joshua and his Successors: an Introduction to Joshua, Judges, Ruth, and Samuel I., with Notes. Parts I. and II. 8vo. *Lond.*, S. S. Union. 1874.
A very useful condensed book for teachers.

240 KEIL (KARL FRIEDRICH, D.D., Ph.D.) Joshua, Judges, and Ruth. $3.50. Eerdmans.
"Let our biblical students not only master the facts and logic, but catch the spirit of these commentaries, and we can have no fear for the issue of that conflict with Rationalism and Popery united, by which Protestantism in this country seems to be threatened."—*Wesleyan Methodist Magazine.*

241 KELLY (WILLIAM). Lectures Introductory to the Study of the earlier Historical Books [Joshua to II Samuel]. 8vo. *Lond.*, Broom. 1874.
After the manner of Plymouth commenting in general ; quite sufficiently taken up with spiritualizing and nice points : but yet, read with half a ton of salt, a book likely to arouse thought, and suggest topics.

242 **LANGE'S COMMENTARY.**—Joshua (by F. R. Fay);
Judges, Ruth (by P. Cassel, D.D.) Edited by Dr. Schaff.
$3.95. Zondervan.

This is a standard work. No minister's library is furnished
without the whole set. Joshua however is inferior to Judges.

243 MARCHANT (F. G.) Commentary on Joshua. [Part III. of
Preacher's Commentary. *Lond.*, Dickinson. 1875.

While writing this we have only one number before us, but it promises
well, and we feel sure its quality will be sustained, for we know the
author's industrious habits.

244 THE GOSPEL IN THE BOOK OF JOSHUA. [Anon.] Cr. 8vo.
Lond., Partridge & Co. 1867.

Pious remarks, such as anyone would make.

245 SEATON (W.) The Church in Canaan; or, heirs in possession
receiving the promises. Vol. I. 12mo. *Lond.*, 1823.

A sequel to No. 188.

246 **SMITH** (THORNLEY). The History of Joshua, viewed in
connection with the Topography of Canaan, and the
Customs of the Times in which he lived. Cr. 8vo.
Edinb., W. Oliphant & Co. 1870.

Although not a commentary, it will answer the same purpose;
for almost every event is fully illustrated. A capital work.

JUDGES.

[See also under *Joshua*.]

247 **BUSH** (GEORGE). Notes on Judges. Sm. 8vo. *New*
York, 1852.

Like other works of this author—of considerable value.

248 DODS (MARCUS, M.A., D.D.) Israel's Iron Age : Sketches from the Period
of the Judges. Crown 8vo. *Lond.*, Hodder & Stoughton. 1874.

Dr. Dods considers that to find in Samson and other judges types of our Lord
Jesus is mere fancy, and he interprets upon "a rational principle" which renders
his book dry and unspiritual; at the same time his sketches are not without value.

249 HENGSTENBERG (E. W.) Time of the Judges. (See No. 86.)

250 **KITTO** (JOHN, D.D.) "The Judges," in *Daily Bible Illus-*
trations. (See No. 41.)

Exceedingly meritorious. Refer to it frequently.

251 MARTYR (PETER. 1500—1562). Most Fruitful and Learned Commentarie
upon the Book of Judges. *Black Letter.* Folio. 1560. Rare.

This would seem to be a profound work. *Rogers* says of *Peter Martyr* :—" Few
private men can understand his works, and few ministers who understand them can
obtain them ; nor if they can will they find in them much that will benefit their
simple hearers." This has not been our experience with *Peter Martyr's* works; on
the contrary, we have read them with interest.

252 NOBLE (SAMUEL). Sermons on the singular histories recorded in the first
eleven chapters. 8vo. 3/6. *Lond.*, J. S. Hodson. 1856.
Swedenborgian mysticism. Exposition in a trance.

253 **ROGERS** (RICHARD. *Puritan.*) The whole Book of
Judges. [103 Sermons.] Folio. *Lond.*, 1615.
This for the Puritan period is THE *work upon Judges. It is
thoroughly plain and eminently practical.*

254 **WISEMAN** (LUKE H., M.A. *Died* 1875). Men of
Faith ; or, Sketches from the Book of Judges. Cr. 8vo.
Lond., Hodder & Stoughton. 1874.
*Mr. Wiseman in this work tells "of Gideon and Barak, of
Samson and of Jephthah", and he does it in a powerful style. He
was one of the best preachers in the Wesleyan body. A man of
fulness, and judiciousness; in fact, a wise man.*

---

255 BRUCE (JOHN, D.D.) The Life of Gideon. Fcap. 8vo.
Edinb., Edmonston & Douglas. 1870.
The author deserves attention, both for matter and style. Note *Hugh
Miller's* high opinion of his "Biography of Samson:" (No. 259).
Gideon is a better work, but both are over-estimated.

256 ELWIN (FOUNTAIN). Sermons on the character of Gideon. 12mo. *Lond.*,
Hatchards. 1844.
Seven sermons, containing nothing remarkable.

257 HOWARD (LADY). Gideon the Mighty Man of Valour. [Anon]. *Lond.*,
Hatchards. 1841.
Of small use to the preacher.

258 **ROGERS** (GEORGE ALBERT, M.A.) The Valour of Faith;
or, the Gospel in the Life of Gideon. 12mo. *Lond.*,
Wertheim, Macintosh & Hunt. 1859.
*A thoroughly lively little book. Each of the eight chapters is
full of thought.*

259 BRUCE (JOHN, D.D.) The Biography of Samson. 18mo.
Edinb., Edmonston & Douglas. 1870.
Hugh Miller said : "There is a poetic richness in the style, which at
one time reminds us of *Chalmers*, and at another of *Jeremy Taylor*, but
which in reality is *Dr. Bruce's* own, that does not seem poor or bald
beside even the blank verse of the great master of English song." We
think this eulogy is greatly overdone.

260 QUARLES (FRANCIS. 1592—1644). The Historie of Samson.
4to. *Lond.*, 1631.
This queer, quaint, odd volume of rhymes is far from despicable.
Kitto frequently quotes *Quarles* upon Samson, and says of him that he
was a poet of no mean order. We are glad to have his testimony to
confirm our own opinion. Refined tastes will be offended, but those
who wish for quaint thought will be gratified. The book is very rare.

RUTH.

[See also under *Joshua*.]

261 BERNARD (RICHARD. *Puritan. Died* 1641). Ruth's Recompense. 4to. 1628.

Mr. Grosart is enthusiastic in his praise of this work, and says "that
it abounds with apophthegms and compressed thoughts." We defer to
so high an authority, but we are not much fascinated by the book.

262 FULLER (THOMAS, D.D. 1608—1661).   A Comment on
Ruth, with two Sermons. 8vo. 1650.

Not one of *Fuller's* best; but still quaint and pithy, and lit up with
flashes of his irrepressible wit.   The above works of *Bernard* and
Fuller have been reprinted in *Nichol's Series of Commentaries,* in one
volume.   Cr. 4to.   *Lond.,* Nisbet & Co.   1865.

Mr. Tegg, Pancras Lane, London, has also published a reprint of
Fuller's Comment on Ruth, and Notes upon Jonah.   Cr. 8vo.

263 BRADEN (WILLIAM).   The Beautiful Gleaner.   Cr. 8vo.
Lond., James Clark & Co.   1874.

Mr. Braden is an able preacher.   His sermons upon Ruth are popular and practical, though not very remarkable.

264 LAVATER (LEWIS. *A Swiss Protestant Divine.* 1527—1586.) Ruth expounded, in 28 Sermons.   Translated from the Latin by E. Pagett.   8vo.
Lond., 1586.

Lavater was a Reformer of high repute, son-in-law of *Bullinger.*   He wrote a
curious work on spectres, and made a catalogue of comets, thus shewing himself to
be both philosopher and divine.   His book is seldom met with.

265 **LAWSON** (GEORGE, D.D.) Lectures on the Book of
Ruth. 12mo. *Edinb.,* 1805.

*By a man of great genius.   Simple, fresh, and gracious.   Nothing
critical or profound may be looked for, but wise and sound
teaching may be gleaned in these pages.*

266 MACARTNEY (H. B.) Observations on Ruth. 12mo. *Lond.,* 1842. 9d.
A nice *little* book, little in all ways.

267 MACGOWAN (JOHN. 1726—1786.)   Discourses on Ruth, and
other important subjects.   8vo.   *Lond.,* 1781.

Macgowan, the author of the Dialogue of Devils, is well known for
originality and force.   In this case his sermons are full of Gospel truth,
but the texts are too much accommodated and spiritualized.   The discourses are good reading.

268 OXENDEN (A. *Bp. of Montreal*). Story of Ruth. 18mo.   Hatchards.
A very tiny affair, of no great moment to the expositor.

269 PHILPOT (B., A.M.) Six Lectures.   Square Fcap.   *Lond.,* Nisbet & Co.
A very small book, containing good, simple lectures—not an exposition.

270   PRICE (AUBREY C., B.A.)   Six Lectures on the Book of Ruth.
      12mo.   *Lond.*, Hatchards.   1869.

Sermons of remarkable power, both of doctrine and diction.   Not so
expository as practical.   *Mr. Price* is an earnest and large-hearted
clergyman of the thoroughly evangelical school.

271   **TOPSELL** (EDWARD).   The Reward of Religion.   Lectures
      upon Ruth.   8vo.   *Lond.*, 1613.

*A very choice old work.   Attersol in his rhyming preface says
of it—*

> " Go little Booke, display thy golden title,
>   (And yet not little though thou little bee) ;
>   Little for price and yet in price not little,
>   Thine was the Paine, the gaine is ours I see :
>   (Although our gaine thou deem'st no paine to thee).
>   If then, O reader, little paine thou take,
>   Thou greatest gaine with smallest paine shall make."

272   TYNG (STEPHEN, D.D., *of New York*).   The Rich Kinsman; or, the History
      of Ruth.   Small 8vo.   *Lond.*, 1856.

Written for young people, and suitable for their reading, though none too lively.

273   WRIGHT (C. H. H., M.A.)   Ruth, in Hebrew; with gramma-
      tical and critical Commentary.   8vo.   *Lond.*, Williams &
      Norgate.   1864.

For Hebraists only.   The author has selected the book of Ruth as a
study for beginners in the Hebrew tongue, because of the simplicity of
the language.

I. & II. SAMUEL.

[Expositions upon these books being few, the student should consult
works on Scripture characters, and also comments on the Old Testament
as a whole.]

274   KEIL (C. F., D.D.) and DELITZSCH (F., D.D.)   The Books
      of Samuel.   Translated from the German by the Rev. James
      Martin, B.A. $3.50.   Eerdmans.

Like most of *Clark's* series, *Keil's* works are valuable helps towards
obtaining the meaning of the text; but for spiritual i..lections and
fruitful hints we must look elsewhere.

275   LINDSAY (HENRY, M.A.)   Lectures on the Historical Books [1 and 2
      Samuel only].   2 vols.   12mo.   *Lond.*, 1828.

Practical sermons on a few of the more prominent events.

276   **WILLET** (ANDREW).   An Harmonie upon the First
      Booke of Samuel, and an Harmonie upon the Seconde
      Booke of Samuel.   Folio.   1614.   [There is
      also a 4to. edition upon 1 Samuel.   1607.]

*The work continues the Hexapla to which we have referred in
Nos. 142 and 177.   It is unusually brief for the age of its composition, and full of variety.   Under every verse, and often clause of*

a verse, the learned author proposes a question, and proceeds to answer it. These are such as the following :—"What a daughter of Belial is ?" "Whether any may be said to sin with the will of God ?" "What doors of the house of Jehovah Samuel opened ?" "What is to be thought of Eli's state before God ?"

277   GUILD (WILLIAM, D.D.   1586—1657).   The Throne of David. An Exposition of the 2nd Samuel, wherein is set down the Pattern of a Pious and Prudent Prince.   *Oxf.*, 1659.

The MSS. of this rare book was sent to *Dr. John Owen* by the widow of the author, with a letter of her own, informing him that her dying husband desired it to be so forwarded.   *Dr. Owen* says, that he found the treatise "written with perspicuity and clearness, handling a subject cf great and delightful variety, with a choice mixture of spiritual, moral, and political observations, tempered by a good and sound judgment unto common capacities."   We do not presume to criticize where *Owen* commends, but we should not have originated such a commendation.

SAMUEL, SAUL, DAVID.

278   **KITTO.**   *Daily Bible Illustrations*, "Samuel, Saul, and David."   (See No. 41.)
Should always be consulted.

279   **PLUMPTRE** (HELEN).   The History of Samuel.   18mo.   *Lond.*, Nisbet and Co.   1842.
A children's book, and childlike men will be thankful for the many very useful hints which it throws out.   We have got more out of it than we have found in huge and learned tomes.

280   **STEEL** (ROBERT).   Samuel the Prophet. 8vo.   *Lond.*, Nelson & Sons.   1861.
The author has done his work well, and has shown an evident desire to excite others to a greater knowledge of the subject than he could impart.   Hence he gives a list of the writers upon Samuel, and such accounts of them as were within his reach.   Young readers will find this book a great help to them.

281   **MILLER** (J. A.)   Saul, The First King of Israel.   Fcap. 8vo.   *Lond.*, Snow & Co.   1866.
Eminently thoughtful, useful, practical sermons.   We do not see how Saul's life-failure could be more profitably set forth.

282   **BLAIKIE** (WILLIAM G., A.M.)   David, King of Israel : the Divine Plan and Lessons of his Life. 8vo.   *Lond.*, Nisbet & Co.   1861.
Dr. Blaikie is a good writer.   This Life of David has supplied a great lack.

283 CHANDLER (SAMUEL, D.D., F.R.S., and F.A.S. 1693—1766).
A Critical History of the Life of David. 2 vols., 8vo. *Lond.*,
1766. 1 vol., 8vo. J. H. & J. Parker. 1853.

This is a masterpiece as a critical history, and the best of *Chandler's*
productions. Many of the Psalms are explained with commendable
learning, but the spiritual element is absent.

284 DELANY (PATRICK, D.D., *Dean of Down.* 1686—1768). An Historical
Account of the Life and Reign of David. [Anon.] 2 vols., 8vo. *Lond.*,
1745.

Delany was a friend of *Swift*, no great recommendation for a commentator. He
defends David in a way which David would have sternly repudiated. *Chandler* is far
preferable to *Delany*, but both are devoid of the evangelical spirit.

285 KINGSLEY (CHARLES, M.A.) David. Four Sermons. Fcap.
8vo. *Lond.*, Macmillan & Co.

In his usual free and easy manner *Kingsley* speaks of David's strength
and his weakness, his anger and his deserts. The character of this
writer is supposed to be well understood, but we question if many have
formed a true estimate of him. For commenting purposes these sermons
are of small value ; they are plain, practical discourses.

286 KRUMMACHER (F. W., D.D.) David, the King of Israel. Cr.
8vo., *Edinb.*, T. & T. Clark.

Anything by *Krummacher* is worthy of patient reading.

287 **LAWSON** (GEORGE, D.D. 1749—1820.) Discourses on
the History of David. 12mo. *Berwick*, 1833.

*Here the life of David is piously turned to practical use.
Delany and Chandler are but bones, and Lawson the marrow.*

288 MARBECK (JOHN). The whole History of King David. 4to. 1579.

This is in English metre, and was written by the famous organist of the Royal
Chapel in Windsor, in the reign of Henry VIII. He narrowly escaped martyrdom.
His work entitled " Booke of Common Praier noted," is the groundwork of the plain-
song used in our Cathedrals from the Reformation to the present day. *Marbeck's*
History of David is very rare. We cannot therefore set a price.

289 [ROGERS (Mrs.)] The Shepherd King. By the Authoress of
" The Folded Lamb." 12mo. *Lond.*, Nisbet. 1856.

This authoress writes well for the young, and her book will be useful
to those who teach them.

290 SMITH (GEORGE, LL.D. and F.A.S.) The Life and Reign of
David. Cr. 8vo., *Lond.*, Longmans. 1867.

David's life is here concisely written, with such of the Psalms inter-
woven as can be referred to special periods. It cannot be read without
ministering instruction.

291 **TAYLOR** (WILLIAM M., D.D. *Of the Broadway Tabernacle, New York*). David : his Life, and its Lessons.
Cr. 8vo. *Lond.*, Sampson Low, Marston & Co. 1875.

A grand work which should be in every library.

292   THOMPSON (HENRY, M.A.) Davidica. Twelve Sermons on the Life and
       Character of David. 8vo. *Lond.*, 1827.
Discourses of the kind which are usually published by subscription; rather pretentious, but with nothing in them. The process of subscribing to print sermons is
one suggested by kindness, but seldom directed by reason.

293   **VINCE** (CHARLES, *Baptist Minister, of Birmingham. Died
       1875*). Lights and Shadows in the Life of King David.
       Cr. 8vo.   *Lond.,* Elliot Stock.   1871.
*Sermons of the highest order upon a few incidents in David's
life. They are models of chaste, subdued, but powerful preaching.*

I. and II. KINGS.

294   GENESTE (MAXIMILIAN, M.A.)   The Parallel Histories of Judah
       and Israel. 2 vols., Roy. 8vo.   *Lond.*, S. Bagster
       & Sons. 1843.
The explanatory notes are mostly from other authors. The work has a
very noble appearance, and may be useful as showing the run of Biblical
history; but *Barth's Bible Manual* (No. 3) would answer every purpose.

295   JUKES (ANDREW).   The Mystery of the Kingdom, traced through
       the Books of Kings. Part I.   *Lond.*, Longmans.   1858.
This author is more mystical than we could wish, but never writes
without being instructive.

296   KEIL (K. F.) and BERTHEAU (E.)   Commentary on the
       Books of Kings.   By K. F. Keil.   Translated by James
       Murphy, LL.D.   Supplemented by a Commentary on the
       Books of Chronicles.   By Ernst Bertheau, Professor in Goettin-
       gen.   Translated by James Martin, B.A.   2 vols.
       Edinb., T. & T. Clark.   1857.
Distinguished by careful investigation of the meaning of the text.
This is a most important help to the expositor.   The student will not,
however, find much in the way of reflections and doctrines.

297   KEIL and DELITZSCH.   The Books of the Kings.   By C. F.
       Keil.   Translated by James Martin, B.A.   1 vol. $3.50. Eerdmans.

This appears to be another form of the work mentioned above.   At
least there can be no necessity for purchasing both.   This is the better.

298   **KITTO.**   *Daily Bible Illustrations,* "Solomon and the
       Kings."   (*See No.* 41.)
Full of deeply interesting matter.

299   **LANGE'S COMMENTARIES.**   Edited by Dr. Schaff.
       Kings. By Dr. Bahr. 1 vol. $3.95. Zondervan.

*It must have cost great effort to make the homiletical part of this
volume as good as it is.   It is a treasury to the preacher, and is all
the more precious because we have next to nothing upon the books of
the Kings.* (See No. 42).

SOLOMON'S TEMPLE.

300 BUNYAN (JOHN).   Solomon's Temple Spiritualized.   *Lond.*,
1688.   [In Bunyan's Works, Offor's edition, III., 460.]
A marvellous display of allegorizing genius: full of Gospel truth.
Bunyan hammers away at each type, but no one may call it tinkering.

301 **EDERSHEIM** (A., D.D.)   The Temple: its Ministry and
Services. $3.50. Eerdmans.
*This will supply the student with all that he needs upon the
subject in hand.*

302 LEE (SAMUEL, M.A.   1625—1691.)   Orbis miraculum; or, the
Temple of Solomon pourtrayed by Scripture light. [Anon.]
Folio. 1659.
Of course, as will be inferred from its date, this work is of the antique
order, but it is profoundly learned, and goes into architectural and
ritualistic details, explaining them spiritually with much sweetness and
suggestiveness.

ELIJAH, ELISHA, &c.

303 ANDERSON (JAMES, S. M., M.A.)   Discourses on Elijah, &c. 8vo. *Lond.*,
1835.
Ordinary sermons by a "Chaplain in Ordinary to the Queen." Rhetorical and
grandiose, but not expository.

304 BAYNE (PETER).   The Days of Jezebel.   An Historical Drama.
12mo.   *Lond.*, Strachan & Co.   1872.
A fine poetic drama, worthy of quotation by preachers; but hardly in
the line of works contemplated by this Catalogue.

305 EDERSHEIM (ALFRED, D.D.)   Elisha the Prophet, a Type of
Christ. Cr. 8vo.   *Lond.*, W. Hunt & Co.   1873.
This author is always interesting, shewing close acquaintance with
Jewish customs, and knowing how to utilize his information.

306 HOWAT (H. T.) Elijah, the Desert Prophet. Cr. 8vo.   *Edinb.*,
Johnstone & Hunter.   1868.
Very picturesque and poetical.   A work to be read for enjoyment.

307 **KRUMMACHER** (F. W., D.D.)   Elijah the Tishbite.
Translated from the German. $2.95. Zondervan.

Too well known and approved to need any commendation from us.

308 **MACDUFF** (J. R., D.D.)   The Prophet of Fire.   Post 8vo.
Lond., James Nisbet & Co.   1863.
*Dr. Macduff writes popularly, yet he is by no means weak or
shallow.   He is to the young minister all the more useful, because
he has worked out the problem of making sound thought intelligible
to the multitude.*

309 M[ACINTOSH] (C. H.) Reflections on the Life and Times of Elijah. By
     C. H. M.   *Lond.*, G. Morrish.
Strongly Plymouthistic. A small affair.

310 BLUNT (HENRY, M.A.) Lectures upon the History of Elisha.
     12mo.   *Lond.*, Hatchards. 1839.
We like *Blunt* better upon Elisha than upon any other portion of
Scripture. He says that, had he known of *Krummacher's* having written
upon the subject, he should not have attempted it himself. A wise
observation. What shall he do that cometh after a King, or after a
Krummacher ?

311 DOTHIE (W. P., M.A.) The History of the Prophet Elisha.
     Cr. 8vo.   *Lond.*, Hodder & Stoughton. 1872.
Sketchy. Not very deep, but interesting.

312 GLYN (GEORGE L., Bart.) Life of Elisha, in eleven plain dis-
     courses. 8vo. *Lond.*, Wertheim & Macintosh. 1857.
Evangelical and simple. Ministers do not need it.

313 **KRUMMACHER** (F. W., D.D.) Elisha. Translated
     from the German. *Lond.*, Nisbet & Co. 1838.
*Of this we may say as we did of the same author's Elijah,—it
needs no commending from us.*

314 BULLOCK (CHARLES). The Syrian Leper. Fcap. 8vo.
     Lond., Wertheim & Macintosh. 1862.
Telling in style, and earnestly evangelical. These chapters are good
specimens of popular expounding.

315 **MACDUFF** (J. R., D.D.) The Healing Waters; or, The
     Story of Naaman. An Old Testament Chapter on Provi-
     dence and Grace. Cr. 8vo.   *Lond.*, Nisbet. 1873.
*In Dr. Macduff's best manner: the story of Naaman is admirably
handled, and made to teach the gospel with much freshness.*

316 **ROGERS** (DANIEL, B.D. *Puritan.* 1573—1652). Naa-
     man the Syrian, his disease and cure; discovering lively
     to the reader the spiritual leprosie of sinne and selfe-love;
     together with the remedies, viz., selfe-denial and faith.
     Folio. *Lond.*, 1642.
*A huge volume of 898 folio pages, almost large enough to have
loaded one of Naaman's mules. It is a work which exhausts the
subject and turns it to earnest evangelical uses.*

317 WOODWARD (HENRY, A.M.) The Shunamite. 8vo.   *Lond.* and
     Camb., Macmillan & Co. 1863.
We scarcely remember a more flagrant case of high-sounding verbiage. Here is
the author's way of describing a hen which has hatched ducklings.—"That much
tried bird, whose hard allotment it has been to hatch and rear a brood of aliens, and
who seems as if melancholy had marked her for her own, when her charge, with
unanimous consent, hurry to some tempting pool of water, and violate her feelings and
shock her instincts, by casting themselves upon that hostile element."

I. and II. CHRONICLES.

318　**BERTHEAU** (E.)　See *Keil* and *Bertheau*, No. 296.

319　KEIL (K. F.)　The Book of the Chronicles.　Translated from the German.　By Andrew Harper, B.D.　$3.50.　Eerdmans.

Without indicating either the spiritual lesson or the moral of the history, *Keil* simply explains the facts, and in so doing aids the reader to realize them.　We confess we should like something more.

EZRA, NEHEMIAH, and ESTHER.

320　KEIL (K. F.)　Commentary on Ezra, Nehemiah, and Esther.　Translated by Sophia Taylor.　$3.50.　Eerdmans.

Just the kind of book in which *Keil's* method of commenting appears to the best advantage.　He gives much needful information, and thus supplements more didactic works.　We cannot read *Keil* with pleasure, for we want spiritual meat, but yet it is most desirable for us to know what the text really means.

321　PILKINGTON (JAMES, B.D.　*Bishop of Durham.* 1520—1575). A Godlie Exposition upon certeine chapters of Nehemiah. 1585.　Reprinted in the *Parker Society's* edition of Pilkington's Works.　8vo.　*Camb.*, 1842.

Very old fashioned and singular, somewhat in the style of Latimer and perhaps a little coarser.　*Pilkington's* downright onslaughts upon the vices and follies of his times are fine instances of personal, faithful preaching; they are, however, so minutely descriptive of the manners which then prevailed that they are the less useful now.　The style is cramped, and even grotesque in places, yet *Pilkington* is a grand old author.　He has only written upon five chapters.

322　RANDALL (J. MONTAGUE, A.K.C.)　Nehemiah, the Tirshatha: his Life and Lessons.　Post 8vo.　*Lond.*, Nisbet.　1874.

The substance of thirteen Sunday evening addresses to a village congregation, "dictated by the author, who is nearly blind, on the following Monday."　These familiar and almost chatty discourses are full of gospel teaching, and while they give a fair idea of Nehemiah and his times, they are also enlivened by anecdote, and made exceedingly interesting.　Students will not learn much from these sermons, but they may see how rustic preaching should be done.

323　SCENES FROM THE LIFE OF NEHEMIAH; or, Chapters for Christian Workers.　[Anon.]　Fcap. 8vo.　*Lond.*, 66, Paternoster Row, E.C.

The heads of these chapters would serve exceedingly well for the keynotes of a series of sermons.

324 STOWELL (HUGH, M.A.) A Model for Men of Business; or, Lectures on the Character of Nehemiah. 8vo. *Lond.*, Hatchards. 1855.

The author does not attempt a full exposition, but aims at furnishing a plain, practical handbook for men of business and others whose time is limited. He gives fourteen good, sensible lectures on the Book.

325 WOODWARD (HENRY, M.A.) Thoughts on the Character and History of Nehemiah. 12mo. *Lond.*, 1849.

Words, and only words.

ESTHER.

326 COOPER (THOMAS). The Churches Deliverance; containing Meditations and short Notes upon the Booke of Hester. 4to. *Lond.*, 1609.

We have not been able to meet with this work.

327 DAVIDSON (ALEXANDER D., D.D.) Lectures on Esther. Cr. 8vo. *Edinb.*, T. & T. Clark. 1859.

Helpful lectures. The Book of Esther is here used for instruction in doctrine and practice. The work is not so much for the study as for the family.

328 HUGHES (JOHN). Esther and her People. Ten Sermons. 18mo. 1842.

Good evangelical discourses, but nothing very special.

329 **LAWSON** (GEORGE, D.D.) Discourses on Esther. 12mo. *Edinb.*, 1804.

Intended for the general reader. The discourses are as spiritual and unaffected as their excellent author. Dr. John Brown, in commending all the Lawson books, says that "he has rendered subjects, apparently barren, full of instruction."

330 **McCRIE** (THOMAS). Lectures on Esther. 12mo. 1838.

Dr. Davidson says of Dr. McCrie: "There is an ancient fable of a king who was gifted with the power of turning everything he touched into gold; and this eminent divine and historian possessed remarkably the gift of rendering every subject he handled so precious, as at least to discourage any one from attempting to follow in his track. In his Lectures upon the book of Esther, he has certainly left little for any to say who may come after him."

331 MORGAN (R. C.) The Book of Esther typical of the Kingdom. Sm. 8vo. 1855.

An allegorical interpretation, which commences with these words: "The true scene of this beautiful book opens in heaven." Is heaven under the dominion of Ahasuerus? Who then is Vashti?

THE POETICAL BOOKS.

332 DURELL (D., D.D.) Critical Remarks on the Books of Job, Prov., Psalms, Eccles., and Canticles. 4to. *Oxf.*, 1772.

A critic who is for ever mending the text, who contends for the modern origin of Job, thinks the Canticles to be a love song, and considers the imprecatory Psalms to be ebullitions of passion, is not one whom our readers need consult.

333 HOLDEN (LAWRENCE). Paraphrase on the Books of Job, Psalms, Proverbs, and Ecclesiastes, with Notes. 4 vols., 8vo. 1763.

An atrocious instance of bombastic verbosity. Job ii. 2 is thus expanded :— " Heaven and earth's great Lord and guardian, the instant Satan appeared observed, and thus demanded of him : ' from what quarter proceedest thou ? or in what district, and to what purpose hast thou lately employed thy perverted, and subtle, wicked abilities and arts ? ' To whom the destroyer answers : ' my last station, or rather, un- settled, wandering motion, has been upon earth ; various districts whereof I have made short visits to, being sometimes with the inhabitants of one region or climate, some- times with those of another.' " Paraphrases generally mean the text padded out with superfluous words, and this is an emphatic instance.

334 **KITTO.** *Daily Bible Illustrations,* " Job and the Poetical Books." (See No. 41.)
Worthy of attentive reading.

335 LEIGH (EDWARD). See under *Whole Bible,* No. 44.

336 WILCOCKS (THOMAS, A.M. *Puritan.* 1549—1908). The Works of that Reverend and Learned Divine, Mr. Thomas Wilcocks, Minister of God's Word : containing an Exposition upon the whole booke of David's Psalmes, Solomon's Proverbs, the Canticles, and part of the eighth chapter of St. Paul's Epistle to the Romans. Folio. *Lond.*, 1589, 1620 and 1624. to 12/-

Very old. The notes are brief, but furnish many hints for sermons.

JOB.

337 ABBOT (GEORGE. *Died* 1648). The whole Book of Job Paraphrased, or made Easie for any to Understand. 4to. *Lond.*, 1640.

This is not by Archbishop Abbot, neither is the work of any value. This *Abbot* was a Member of Parliament, and his paraphrase is better than we could have expected from an M.P. ; but still it is a heavy performance.

338 AMERICAN BIBLE UNION. The Book of Job. A Trans- lation from the Original Hebrew ; on, the Basis of the Common and Earlier English Versions. By Thomas J. Conant, D.D., Professor of Sacred Literature in Rochester Theological Seminary. 4to. New York, 1867. *Lond.*, Trübner.

An excellent translation. The design did not allow of more than slender notes, but those notes are good.

339 **BARNES** (ALBERT. 1798—1870). Notes on Job.
Enlarged Type Edition, edited by Robert Frew, 2 volumes $7.00. Baker.

Exceedingly good. One of the best of this author's generally valuable productions. The student should purchase this work at once, as it is absolutely necessary to his library.

340   BELLAMY (D.) Paraphrase, with observations. 4to. *Lond.*, 1748.
A collection of notes from other authors. Original works are far better.

341   BEZA (THEODORE. 1519—1605.) Job expounded.   8vo.
1590.
Beza was the great friend and assistant of Calvin. As a commentator
he lacked the profound insight and comprehensive grasp of Calvin, but as
a critical scholar he is said to have been his equal if not his superior.
This work on Job is rare.

342   BLACKMORE (SIR R.)   Paraphrase on the Book of Job, the Songs of Moses,
Deborah, and David, four select Psalms, some Chapters of Isaiah, and the
3rd Chapter of Habakkuk. Folio. 1700.
Grandiose poetry. *Pope* speaks of the power of *Blackmore's* numbers "to soothe
the soul in slumbers." The worthy knight is not the worst of the poetical expositors,
but he is bad enough. Miserable paraphrasers are ye all, ye brethren of jingling
rhyme and doubtful measure.

343   **CALVIN** (JOHN). Sermons on the Booke of Job.
LeRoy Nixon translation. $4.50. Eerdmans.
Not the same as the Commentary, but equally rich.

344   CAREY (CATERET PRIAULX, M.A.) Book of Job translated,
explained by Notes, and illustrated by extracts from works on
Antiquities, Science, &c. Roy. 8vo. 1858.
Purely critical and exegetical. The author has grappled manfully
with all difficulties, and has stored up a mass of precious materials with
which to illuminate a book dark from its antiquity.

345   **CARYL** (JOSEPH. 1602—1673). Exposition, with Practical Observations.   12 vols., 4to. 1648—1666.
Also in 2 vols., folio. 1676.
*Caryl must have inherited the patience of Job to have completed
his stupendous task. It would be a mistake to suppose that he is at
all prolix or redundant; he is only full. In the course of his
expounding he has illustrated a very large portion of the whole
Bible with great clearness and power. He is deeply devotional and
spiritual. He gives us much, but none too much. His work can
scarcely be superseded or surpassed.*

346   „   An Abridgment of Caryl's Exposition.
8vo. *Edinb.*, 1836.
*We do not believe in abridgments of a book which is good
throughout. Think of twelve large volumes condensed into one small
one ! An ox in a gallipot is nothing to it.*

347   CHAPPELOW (LEONARD, B.D.) A Commentary, in which is inserted the
Hebrew Text and English Translation. 2 vols., 4to.   *Camb.*, 1752.
Chappelow is great upon Arabic etymologies, but he is dreadfully verbose, and
really says nothing of any consequence. Chappelow and several other authors follow
Schultens in the belief that the Hebrew can only be read by the light of the Arabic ;
they even imagine that the Book of Job was originally composed in Arabic by Job
himself and then translated by someone else into the Hebrew tongue. This opened
a fine field for parading their learning.

348 COLEMAN (J. NOBLE). The Book of Job; from the Hebrew. With Notes. 4to. *Lond.*, Nisbet & Co. 1869.

We do not value this so much as the same author's " Psalms," but it is serviceable in its own way.

349 CONANT (T. J.) See *American Bible Union.* (No. 338.)

350 DAVIDSON (A. B., M.A. *Hebrew Tutor, New Coll., Edinb.*) A Commentary Grammatical and Exegetical; with a Translation. Vol. I. 8vo. *Lond.*, Williams & Norgate. 1862.

Strict grammatical treatment of Scripture is always commendable, and in this case the results are highly valued by advanced scholars.

351 DELITZSCH (FRANZ). Biblical Commentary on Job. 2 vols., $7.00. Eerdmans.

" Unquestionably the most valuable work on this inexhaustibly interesting Scripture that has reached us from Germany."—*Nonconformist.*

352 **DURHAM** (JAMES. 1622—1658). Exposition of Job. 12mo. 1659. Also *Glasgow,* 1759.

This is a small book, and we have been unable to procure it. Orme only mentions it upon the authority of Watt's Bibliotheca. It is certain to be good, for Durham is always admirable.

353 EVANS (ALFRED BOWEN). Lectures on the Book of Job. 8vo. *Lond.*, Bosworth & Harrison. 1856.

Discourses from fourteen single verses from different parts of the patient patriarch's history. They are quite out of the usual run of Church of England preaching, and are full of thought and originality. They would have been all the better for a little gospel, for even if his text does not look that way, we do expect a Christian minister to have something to say about his Master.

354 FENTON (THOMAS, M.A.) Annotations on Job and the Psalms, collected from several Commentators, and methodized and improved. 8vo. *Lond.*, 1732.

All that will be found here is taken from others, but well selected.

355 **FRY** (JOHN). New Translation and Exposition, with Notes, 8vo. *Lond.*, 1827.

Written in a devout, enquiring spirit, with due respect to learned writers, but not with a slavish following of their fancies. Fry's work is somewhat of the same character as Good's (No. 358). We greatly esteem this exposition for its own sake, and also for the evangelical tone which pervades it.

356 GARDEN (CHARLES, D.D.) An Improved Metrical Version, with preliminary dissertation and notes. 8vo. *Oxf.*, 1796.

This author has not attempted a Commentary, but he has consulted a vast array of authors, and from them gathered a large number of notes. His work is of very moderate value.

357 GARNETT (JOHN. *Bishop of Clogher*). A Dissertation on the Book of Job, &c. 4to. *Lond.*, 1749.

Rubbish. This Bishop ascribes the authorship of Job to Ezekiel !

358 GOOD (JOHN MASON, M.D., F.R.S. 1764—1827). The Book of Job literally translated. With Notes, &c. 8vo. *Lond.*,1812.

A very valuable contribution to sacred literature. *Dr. Good's* learning was, however, more extensive than accurate, and it would be dangerous to accept his translations without examination.

359 GREGORY THE GREAT. On the Book of Job. [The MAGNA MORALIA.] Translated, with Notes and Indices. *Library of the Fathers.* 4 vols.
Lond., James Parker & Co.

The Fathers are of course beyond criticism, and contain priceless gems here and there; but they spiritualize at such a rate, and also utter so many crudities and platitudes, that if they were modern writers they would not be so greatly valued as they are. Antiquity lends enchantment.

360 HEATH (THOMAS). Essay toward a New English Version of the Book of Job. With a Commentary. 4to. *Lond.*, 1756.
All that is good in this book is marred by its utterly untenable conjectures. It treats Job with slender reverence. Do not lumber your shelves with it.

361 HODGES (WALTER, D.D.) Elihu: an Enquiry into the Scope and Design of the Book of Job. 4to. *Lond.*, 1750. 12mo., third edition, 1756.
Based upon the absurd supposition that Elihu was the Son of God himself, and Job a type of the Saviour. Poor Job's book has been the subject of trials as numerous as those of its hero, and *Hodges* has given the finishing stroke. The course of dreaming can no further go. *Hodge* the village Methodist could never have raved at the rate of *Dr. Hodge*, Provost of Oriel College, Oxford.

362 HENGSTENBERG (E. W.) See under *Ecclesiastes*.

363 **HULBERT** (CHARLES AUGUSTUS, M.A., *Perpetual Curate of Harthwaite, Yorks.*) The Gospel Revealed to Job. Thirty Lectures, with Notes. 8vo. *Lond.*, Longmans. 1853.
An unusually good book; exceedingly comprehensive and helpful in many ways. The author aimed at usefulness and has succeeded wonderfully. We wonder that his work has not been better known.

364 **HUTCHESON** (GEORGE). An Exposition upon Job, being the sum of 316 Lectures. Folio.
Lond., 1669.
Whenever the student sees a Commentary by Hutcheson let him buy it, for we know of no author who is more thoroughly helpful to the minister of the Word. He distils the text, and gives his readers the quintessence, ready for use.

365 HUTCHINSON (R. E., M.D., M.R.C.S.E., *Surgeon-Major Bengal Army*). Thoughts on the Book of Job. *Lond.*, S. Bagster & Sons.

366 **KITTO** (JOHN, D.D.) "Job and the Poetical Books." In *Daily Bible Illustrations.* (See No. 41.)
Exceedingly instructive. Most charming reading.

367 LANGE'S COMMENTARY. The Book of Job. A Commentary by Otto Zöckler, D.D., Professor of Theology at Greifswald. Translated from the German, with Additions by Prof. L. J. Evans, D.D., Lane Theological Seminary, Cincinnati, Ohio. $3.95. Zondervan.

Contains a large collection of available material, and, if within a minister's means, should be a foundation book in his library. We are very far from endorsing all Zöckler's remarks, but the volume is an important one.

368 LEE (SAMUEL, D.D. 1713—1853). The Book of Job translated; with Introduction and Commentary. 8vo. *Lond.*, 1837.

Barnes says, "This work is not what might have been expected from the learning and reputation of *Prof. Lee.* It abounds with Arabic learning, which is scattered with ostentatious profuseness through the volume, but which often contributes little to the elucidation of the text. It is designed for the critical scholar rather than the general reader."

369 NOYES (G. R., D.D.) A New Translation, with Notes. 12mo. *Boston, U.S.* [N.D.]

We have been informed that *Dr. Noyes* belongs to the Unitarian body, but we fail to see any trace of Arian or Socinian views in this volume. We do not agree with all that he says, but he strikes us as being an honest, able, and accurate translator and commentator, worthy to stand in the foremost rank.

370 PETERS (CHARLES, A.M. *Died* 1777). A Critical Dissertation on the Book of Job. Wherein the Account given in that book by the author of *The Divine Legation of Moses Demonstrated, &c.*, is particularly considered; and a Future State shewn to have been the Popular Belief of the Ancient Hebrews. 4to. *Lond.*, 1751.

Of a controversial character; mainly written against *Warburton* and *Le Clerc*, and as those authors are now almost forgotten, answers to them have lost their interest. *Peters* was an eminently learned man, and well versed in argument; but his work is of very small use for homiletical purposes.

371 QUARLES (FRANCIS). Job Militant, with Meditations, Divine and Moral. 4to. 1624.

A Poem in *Quarles'* usual inflated, but withal instructive, manner.

372 ROBINSON (T., D.D.) A Homiletic Commentary on Job. [In progress. 1875. Being Part IV. of the Preacher's Commentary. *Lond.*, Dickinson.

This we hope will be of use to preachers, but we have hardly enough before us to judge of it.

373 SCOTT (THOMAS). The Book of Job in English Verse, with Remarks. 4to. *Lond.*, 1771. Reprinted, 8vo., 1733.

Here we have Job in rhyme—
"There lived an Arab of distinguish'd fame,
In Idumean Uz; and Job his name.
Of spotless manners, with a soul sincere,
Evil his hate, and God alone his fear."

This will hardly do. To translate Job in metre needed a *Pope* or a *Dryden*, and *Thomas Scott* was neither: he has, however, done his best, the best could have done no more. This is not *Thomas Scott* the great Expositor, but a Dissenting Minister at Ipswich.

374   SENAULT (J. F.)   A Paraphrase.   4to.   *Lond.*, 1648.

Senault was a famous preacher of the Oratory in Paris, who, from the character of his works, would seem to have been almost a Protestant.   His writings were highly esteemed in their day, and translated into English.

375   SMITH (Elizabeth).   The Book of Job translated from the Hebrew, with Annotations.   8vo.   *Lond.*, 1810.

"A good English version of Job, produced chiefly by the aid of *Parkhurst's* Lexicon."—*Orme.*

376   STATHER (Lieut.-Col., W. C.)   The Book of Job, in English Verse; with Notes.   12mo.   *Lond.*, E. Marlborough & Co.   1859.

We do not like Job in rhyme.   We know of no rhyming version of any part of Scripture, except the Psalms, which can be called a success.   Certainly this is not one. The author's *notes* deserve consideration.

377   STOCK (Joseph, D.D.   *Bishop of Killala*).   The Book of Job, Metrically arranged, and newly translated, with Notes.   4to.   1805.

The work of six weeks !   Well may *Magee* say that it is full of " precipitances, mistakes, and mutilations."   This was a bishop and a Doctor of Divinity !   It takes a great man to perpetrate a very great folly.   A metrical translation of Job with Notes in six weeks !   In that time *stocks* bloom to perfection.   Perhaps that fact operated on our author.   Let this blundering haste serve as a warning to young divines.

378   UMBREIT (Friedrich, W. K.   *Prof. of Theol. in Heidelberg.* 1795—1860).   A New Version of the Book of Job; with Notes.   Translated by the Rev. John Hamilton Gray, M.A. 2 vols., 12mo.   *Edinb.*, T. & T. Clark.

Useful philologically ; but *Barnes* would supply far more in that direction, and spiritual exposition besides.

379   VAN HAGEN (Mrs. Henry).   Evenings in the Land of Uz ; a Comment on Job.   Second Edition.   12mo.   1843.

Isaac Taylor commends this volume as one which " disclaiming all purpose of critical exposition, aims only under the guidance of Christian feeling and experience to follow and to unfold the spiritual intention of this rich portion of Holy Scripture."   Such an introduction must have helped to sell the work and carry it speedily to the second edition.

380   WAGNER (George).   Sermons on the Book of Job.   Cr. 8vo. *Lond.*, Nisbet & Co.   1863.

Wagner's sermons are simple and plain, devout and instructive.   We have here nothing very fresh, but everything is sound and good.

381   WEMYSS (Thomas).   Job and his Times.   New Version, with Notes.   8vo.   *Lond.*, 1839.

Barnes says :—" This is designed to be a popular work.   It is not so much of the nature of a Commentary as a collection of fragments and brief essays on various topics referred to in the Book of Job.   It is chiefly valuable for its illustration of the religion of the time of Job, the arts and sciences, the manners and customs, &c."   It lacks lucid arrangement, and furnishes comparatively little illustration of the diffi- culties of the text.

PSALMS.

382 ABBOT (George). Brief Notes. Being a pithie and clear opening of the Scope and Meaning of the Text, to the capacitie of the Weakest. 4to. *Lond.*, 1651.

An experimental exposition by a Member of Parliament under the Commonwealth. Though not of the first order, many of his remarks are good. *Abbot* was nephew to the Archbishop of the same name.

383 **ALEXANDER** (Joseph Addison, D.D., *Professor of Theology, Princeton, U.S.*) The Psalms Translated and Explained. 8vo. *Edinb.*, Andrew Elliot. 1864.

Occupies a first place among expositions. It is a clear and judicious explanation of the text, and cannot be dispensed with.

384 ALEXANDER (William Henry). The Book of Praises. The Psalms, with Notes. Sm. 8vo. *Lond.*, Jackson, Walford & Hodder. 1867.

The Notes are mostly from other authors, and are selected with discretion. They do not appear to have been designed by their collector for use beyond his own family circle, and they were published after his death by his friends. We question the wisdom of the publication.

385 AUGUSTINE. Expositions. Translated, with Notes. 6 vols., 8vo. *Oxf.*, 1847. [In *The Library of the Fathers*, published by Messrs. J. Parker & Co., *Oxf.* and *Lond.*]

As a Father he is beyond ordinary criticism, or we would venture to say that he is too frequently mystical, and confounds plain texts. No theological library is complete without this work, for there are grand thoughts in it like huge nuggets of Australian gold.

386 BAKER (Richard, D.D.) The Psalms Evangelized. 8vo. 1811.

Very pious ; but if the work should ever disappear from literature its absence will not leave a very great gap. *Bishop Horne* and *Dr. Hawker* between them more than cover the space.

387 **BARNES** (Albert). Notes. 3 Enlarged Type Edition, edited by Robert Frew. 3 volumes $10.50. Baker.

Thoroughly good. Using these notes constantly, we are more and more struck with their value. For the general run of preachers this is probably the best commentary extant.

388 BELLARMINE (Robert. *Cardinal.* 1542—1621.) A Commentary. Translated from the Latin, by the Ven. John O'Sullivan, D.D. Sm. 4to. *Lond.*, James Duffy. 1866.

Popish, but marvellously good for a Cardinal. He is frequently as evangelical as a Reformer. He follows the Vulgate text in this comment.

389 BELLET (J. G.) Short Meditations on the Psalms, chiefly in their Prophetic character. *Lond.*, W. H. Broom. 1871.

Mere fragments. in a style which we do not admire, which seems to be peculiar to certain *brethren.* Only the initiated can understand what such writers mean.

390 **BINNIE** (WILLIAM, D.D.) The Psalms : Their History,
      Teachings, and Use. 8vo.   *Lond.*, T. Nelson. 1870.

*A highly valuable work. It is not an exposition, but can
readily be used as such, for it possesses a good index to the
passages treated of.   Dr. Binnie reviews with great skill and
intense devotion the various sacred poems contained in the Book of
Psalms, and gives the general run and character of each one.   His
work is unlike any other, and supplies a great desideratum.*

391 **BONAR** (ANDREW A.)   Christ and his Church in the
      Book of Psalms. Demy 8vo.   *Lond.*, Nisbet. 1859.

*Of the highest order of merit. The author does not strain the
text, but gives its real meaning. His remarks are always weighty,
spiritual, and suggestive ; we only wish there were more of them.
He has cultivated brevity.*

392 BOUCHIER (BARTON, A.M.) Manna in the Heart ; or, Daily
      Comments on the Psalms, for the Use of Families. 2 vols.,
      Sm. 8vo. *Lond.*, J. F. Shaw. 1856.

Among the best books ever written for family reading.   Evangelical,
devotional, and expository.   Preachers will find good thought here.

393 BURTON (JOHN). The Book of Psalms in English Verse. Cr. 8vo.
      Lond., John Shaw & Co. 1871.

↳The Psalms rhymed in a New Testament spirit : they are better in prose.

394 BUSH (G.) A Commentary on the Book of Psalms. With a
      new literal version. 8vo. *New York*, 1838.

Does not appear to have been reprinted in England.

395 **BYTHNER** (VICTOR. *Died* 1670). The Lyre of David;
      or, an Analysis of the Psalms, Critical and Practical ; to
      which is added a Hebrew and Chaldee Grammar. To
      which are added by the Translator a Praxis of the first
      eight Psalms. Translated by the Rev. Thomas Dee,
      A.B. 8vo. 1836.

*We agree with the statement found in the Preface of this work :
" Nearly two centuries have passed away, since Bythner, uncertain
of its reception, first committed his Lyra to public light ; during
which time, instead of sinking, it has advanced in estimation ; being
admitted by all the learned to be the very best work on the Psalms
in Hebrew.   The number of Hebrew radical words is 1867; of
these, 1184 occur in the Psalms ; it follows then, that a thorough
knowledge of the Psalms very nearly amounts to a thorough knowledge of the language, and that Bythner's Lyra, in being the best
work on the Psalms, must be the best work on Hebrew in general."
Our readers will scarcely need us to add that Bythner's work is only
useful to those who study the Hebrew.*

396 **CALVIN** (JOHN). The Psalms of David and others, with Commentaries. Translated by Arthur Golding. 2 vols., 4to. *Lond.*, 1571.

397 „ A Commentary on the Psalms. Translated. Reprint of C. T. S. edition, 5 volumes $18.50. Eerdmans.

Calvin is a tree whose "leaf also shall not wither"; whatever he has written lives on, and is never out of date, because he expounded the word without bias or partiality.

398 CARTER (CHARLES. *Missionary to Ceylon*). The Psalms, newly translated from the Hebrew. 12mo. *Lond.*, J. Snow. 1869.

The emendations are carefully made by the translator, who has been for many years engaged upon the Singalese version. A helpful book.

399 CAYLEY (C.B., B.A.) The Psalms in Metre. [With Notes]. 12mo. *Lond.*, Longmans. 1860.

We do not think much of the metrical rendering, which often jars on the ear. There are a few good notes at the end.

400 CHAMPNEY (H. N., ESQ.) A Textual Commentary on the Psalms. Sq. 16mo. *Lond.*, S. Bagster & Sons. 1852.
Merely a collection of parallel texts. Make one for yourself.

401 CHANDLER (SAMUEL, D.D.) See No. 283.

402 CLAY (WILLIAM KEATINGE, B.D.) Expository Notes on the Prayer Book Version of the Psalms. Sm. 8vo. *Lond.*, John W. Parker. 1839.

Commendable in its way, but not important. Most of its matter is to be found elsewhere.

403 COLEMAN (JOHN NOBLE, M.A.) Psalterium Messianicum Davidis Regis et Prophetæ. A Revision of the Authorized Version, with Notes, original and selected; vindicating the prophetic manifestations of Messiah in the Psalms, &c. Imp. 8vo. *Lond.*, Nisbet & Co. 1865.

Useful for its quotations from the Fathers and ancient writers. The large type swells out a small quantity of material to a needless size, and so puts purchasers to an unnecessary expense.

404 CONANT (THOMAS J.) The Psalms. The Common Version, revised for the American Bible Union. 4to. 1871. *Lond.*, Trübner & Co.

A trustworthy translation with a few notes.

405 CONGLETON (LORD). The Psalms. A New Version, with Notes. Thick 12mo. *Lond.*, James E. Hawkins. 1875.
The translation is mainly that of *Rogers* (No. 464), and the Notes refer the Psalms to historic and prophetic subjects. We see no use whatever in this production.

406 **COWLES** (HENRY, D.D.) The Psalms; with Notes. 8vo. *New York*, 1872.

Always repays for consulting, though it does not contain much that is new, original, or profound. It might be reprinted in England, with the probability of a large sale.

407 CRESSWELL (DANIEL, D.D., F.R.S.) Psalms of David, ac-
     cording to the Book of Common Prayer; with Notes. Sm. 8vo.
     Lond., Rivingtons. 1843.

The explanatory notes are neither prolix nor commonplace, but
show much clear insight. They are deservedly held in esteem.

408 CRITICAL TRANSLATION (A) of the Psalms, in Metre.
     Cr. 8vo.   *Lond.*, S. Bagster & Sons.

The author has laboured hard to arrive at the correct meaning of the
Hebrew, *and to versify it.* The work is very carefully done, but few
preachers can afford to spend their money on a book of this kind.

409 DALLAS (A. R. C., M.A.) The Book of Psalms arranged in Daily Portions
     for Devotional Reading. Cr. 8vo.   *Lond.*, Nisbet & Co. 1860.
A new arrangement : the old one is good enough for us.

410 DARBY (J. N.) Practical Reflections. Cr. 8vo. *Lond.*, R. A. Allen. 1870.
Too mystical for ordinary minds. If the author would write in plain English his
readers would probably discover that there is nothing very valuable in his remarks.

411 DE BURGH (WILLIAM, A.M.) Commentary; Critical, Devo-
     tional, and Prophetical.   2 vols., 8vo.   *Dublin*, Hodges,
     Smith & Co. 1860.

A second-advent interpreter; and one of the best of his class. Highly
esteemed by those who are enthusiastic upon prophetical subjects.

412 DELITZSCH (FRANZ). Commentary on the Psalms. 3 vols.
     $10.50. Eerdmans.

Thoroughly learned, but wants unction. Not adapted for common
readers, but scholars will prize it greatly.
The Princeton Review says of it : "We commend this commentary as
a valuable aid to preachers and exegetes in elucidating the Psalms."

413 **DICKSON** (DAVID. *Professor of Divinity in the University
     of Edinb.* 1583—1662). A brief explanation of the Psalms.
     3 vols., 8vo. *Lond.*, 1655. Reprinted in 2 vols., 12mo.
     Glasg., 1834.

*A rich volume, dropping fatness. Invaluable to the preacher.
Having read and re-read it, we can speak of its holy savour and
suggestiveness.   We commend it with much fervour.*

414 DIMOCK (H.) Notes, Critical and Explanatory, on the Book of Psalms, &c.
     4to. 1791.
The notes mainly concern the various readings, and exhibit considerable learning ;
but we do not think much of a homiletical kind can be got out of them.

415 DUNWELL (F. H., B.A.) Parochial Lectures on the Psalms,
     from the Fathers of the Primitive Church. 8vo. *Lond.*,
     J. H. Parker. 1855.

This author spiritualizes far too much. His metaphors are overdone.

416 EDWARDS (JOSEPH, M.A.) Devotional Exposition. 8vo. *Lond.*, 1850.
A paraphrase of no great value. Even Masters of Arts may fail.

417 EDWARDS (T.) New Translation, with Notes, &c. 8vo. *Lond.*, 1755.
The writer was an able man, but his book is of small worth.

418 EWART (J., A.M.) Lectures on the Psalms. 3 vols., 8vo. *Lond.*, 1826.
The author was a Presbyterian Minister of the time of the Pretender, and we suspect that he was a high and dry Moderate. His comments were given at the public reading of the Scriptures, and although destitute of spirituality and Gospel clearness, they are not without a measure of originality.

419 EXTON (RICHARD BRUDENELL). Sixty Lectures on the Psalms, as appointed to be read in the Services of the Church of England. 8vo. *Lond.*, 1847.
Very poor and prosy. We pity the hearer who sat out these sixty lectures.

420 FENTON (THOMAS, M.A.) Annotations on Job and Psalms, from several Commentators. 8vo. *Lond.*, 1732.
The Annotations are choice, but will be found in easily accessible works.

421 FENWICK (GEORGE, B.D.) Thoughts on the Hebrew Titles of the Psalms, &c. 8vo. *Lond.*, 1749.

422 „ The Psalter in its original form . . . with Arguments and Notes. [Anon.] 8vo. *Lond.*, 1789.
These two works are praiseworthy in design, but they are too fanciful.

423 FORBES (GRANVILLE) The Voice of God in the Psalms. Cr. 8vo. *Lond.*, Macmillan.
Sermons by a Northamptonshire Rector of the Broad School. They do not strike us as being anything very wonderful; certainly "The Voice of God" is not remarkably audible in them.

424 "FOUR FRIENDS." The Psalms of David Chronologically arranged, with Notes. By Four Friends. Cr. 8vo. *Lond.*, Macmillan. 1867.
Here the Psalms are thrust out of their usual order, and treated after the manner of the Broad School of thought. We do not attach any great value to this production. With some persons perversity passes for profundity, and if a man differs from everybody else they are persuaded that he must be an original genius: the "four friends" will stand high in the esteem of such critics. We neither believe in their chronology, their theology, nor their philology.

425 FRENCH (WILLIAM, D.D.) and SKINNER (GEORGE, M.A.) Translation, with Notes. 8vo. *Lond.*, Parker. 1842.
A version held in high esteem. Notes very short.

426 FRY (JOHN, B.A.) A Translation and Exposition of the Psalms; on the principles adopted in the posthumous work of Bishop Horsley; viz., that those sacred oracles have for the most part an immediate reference to Christ and to his first and second advents. 8vo. *Lond.*, Hamilton, Adams & Co. 1842.
Fry follows *Bishop Horsley* and looks much to the second advent. The work is not fair either as a translation, or as an exposition. It is useful in its own direction, as showing how a peculiar theory has been supported by an able man; but it must not be implicitly relied upon.

427 FYSH (FREDERIC, M.A.) A Lyrical, Literal Version [with Notes]. 2 vols., 12mo. *Lond.*, Seeleys. 1851.
A valuable literal version. Notes scant, but scholarly.

428 GEDDES (ALEXANDER, LL.D. *A Roman Catholic divine.* 1737—1802).
New Translation, with Various Readings and Notes. 8vo. *Lond.*, 1807.
This is said to be "a careful rendering, aiming at the primary meaning of the psalmists." *Dr. Henderson* speaks of *Geddes* as flagrantly disfiguring his Biblical labours with profanity. He was a singular mixture of Romanist and free-thinker.

429 **GOOD** (JOHN MASON, M.D., F.R.S.) Historical Outline of the Book of Psalms. Edited by the Rev. John Mason Neale, B.A. *Lond.*, W. H. Dalton. 1842.
This is not a commentary, but may be regarded as an introduction to the work next mentioned, by the same author. Historical light is frequently the very best which can be cast upon a passage, and Dr. Good has known how to apply it. He may sometimes be thought fanciful, but he is never really speculative, and he almost always says something worth noting.

430 **GOOD** (J. M.) The Book of Psalms ; a New Translation, with Notes. Edited by the Rev. E. Henderson, D.D. 8vo. *Lond.*, Seeleys. 1854.
Dr. Good was a medical gentleman with a large practice, and yet he managed to produce this learned volume. "I save every quarter of an hour for it," said he, "for my heart is in it." He was a man of great attainments and genuine piety. The progress made in Hebrew philology and exegesis since his day has been great; but his work has not been altogether superseded. It is of a high class, from a literary point of view, but must not be blindly followed.

431 GREEN (WILLIAM, M.A.) A Translation, with Notes. 8vo. 1762.
A translation with meagre notes.

432 HAMMOND (HENRY, D.D. 1605—1660). Paraphrase and Annotations. Folio. 1659. 2 vols. 8vo. *Oxf.*, 1850. S. 6/-
Much esteemed, and deservedly so. *Hammond's* weighty tome is somewhat dry, and many of his remarks are rather those of a linguist than of a divine, but he touches on many matters which others omit, and is, upon the whole, an expositor of singular merit.

433 HAPSTONE (DALMAN, M.A.) The Psalms in appropriate Metres ; a strictly literal Translation, with Notes. 8vo. *Edinb.*, Oliphant. 1867.
We prefer our own version, and do not think many of *Mr. Hapstone's* stanzas successful as attempts at poetry.

434 HENGSTENBERG (E. W., D.D.) Commentary. 3 vols., 8vo. *Edinb.*, T. & T. Clark. 1845-8.
A masterly work ; but about as dry as Gideon's unwetted fleece.

435 HILLER (O. PRESCOTT. *Minister of the New Jerusalem Church, Cross Street, London.*) Notes on the Psalms [I.—LXXVII.] Explanatory of their Spiritual Sense. 8vo. *Lond.*, James Spiers. 1869.
Swedenborgian, and frequently absurd. The author *con*founds rather than *ex*pounds.

436 **HORNE** (GEORGE, D.D. *Bishop of Norwich.* 1730—1792). Commentary. [Numerous editions : among others a *Glasgow* edition, 3 vols., 12mo., with Introductory

Essay by Edward Irving, M.A., which is one of Irving's best efforts. Tegg's edition. 1 vol., 8vo.

It has been said that this author had no qualification for a commentator except piety. This is not true, for he had natural poetry in his soul; and even if it were true, his work would go far to show how abundantly piety compensates for other deficiencies. He is among the best of our English writers on this part of Scripture, and certainly one of the most popular.

437 HORSLEY (SAMUEL. *Bishop of Norwich*). The Book of Psalms. With Notes Explanatory and Critical. 8vo. *Lond.*, 1833.

Vigorous writing, with a propensity to indulge in new readings, and a persistent twist in one direction. The notes show the hand of a master, and have exerted much influence in directing thoughtful minds to the subject of the Second Advent, as foreshadowed in the Old Testament, but they must be used with extreme caution.

438 JEBB (JOHN). Literal Translation ; with Dissertations on the word *Selah*, and on the Authorship, Order, Titles, and Poetry of the Psalms. 2 vols., 8vo. *Lond.*, Longmans. 1846.

Jebb takes for his motto in translating, that saying of *Hooker :* " I hold it for an infallible rule in expositions of sacred Scripture, that where a literal construction will stand, the farthest from the letter is commonly the worst." His notes are scant, but his dissertations in the second volume are most admirable.

439 JENNINGS (A. C., B.A.) and LOWE (W. H., M.A.) The Psalms, with Introductions and Critical Notes. Books III. and IV. [Psalms LXXIII. to CVI.] Cr. 8vo. *Lond.*, Macmillan & Co. 1874.

Learned, but more occupied with mere verbal criticisms than with any useful suggestions which could be turned to account by a preacher.

440 JONES (JOSEPH, M.A.) The Psalms; with Reflections. 12mo. *Lond.*, 1846.

Pious, but poor.

441 **KAY** (WILLIAM, D.D.) The Psalms translated from the Hebrew. With Notes, chiefly Exegetical. 8vo. *Lond.*, Rivingtons. 1871.

A refreshing book; the notes being out of the ordinary run, and casting much light on many passages. To thoroughly appreciate this author one should be a Hebrew scholar.

442 KEBLE (JOHN, M.A. *Author of "The Christian Year."* 1792— 1869). The Psalter, in English Verse. Fcap. 8vo. *Lond.*, Parker & Co. 1869.

A poet's version of a grand series of poems.

443 LANGE'S COMMENTARY. Edited by Dr. P. Schaff. $4.95. Zondervan.

Comparatively feeble. Not up to the usual standard of this admirable series. Still, it is among the best of modern commentaries.

444 LINTON (HENRY, M.A.) The Psalms of David and Solomon explained. Fcap., 8vo. *Lond.*, Bagsters. 1871.
A small affair in all ways.

445 LUTHER (MARTIN). A Manual of the Book of Psalms ; or the subject-contents of all the Psalms. Translated by Rev. Henry Cole. 8vo. *Lond.*, 1823. [Also a volume of " *The Christian's Family Library.*" 12mo. *Lond.*, Seeleys.]
Fragmentary, a mere table of contents, but truly Lutheran.

446 **MANT** (RICHARD, D.D. *Bishop of Down.* 1776—1849). The Book of Psalms in an English Metrical Version, with Notes. 8vo. *Oxf.*, 1824.
A bold version, with important notes. In this instance we confess that there may be real poetry in a metrical version, and though the flame does not in each composition burn with equal brilliance, yet in some verses it is the true poetic fire. Mant is no mean writer.

447 MARSH (EDWARD GARRARD, M.A.) The Book of Psalms translated into English verse, with Notes. 8vo. *Lond.*, 1832.
Contains nothing of any consequence to an expositor, though the verse is considerably above the average of such productions.

448 MERRICK (JAMES, M.A. 1720—1769). The Psalms Paraphrased in English verse. 12mo. *Reading*, 1766.
      „   Annotations on the Psalms. 4to. *Reading*, 1778.
These two works are scarce. They are rather more suited for the admirers of poetry than for ministers of the Word. It is said that some of the notes are by *Archbishop Secker*, and that *Lowth* also aided in the exposition ; but the combined result is of no great value to the preacher.

449 **MORISON** (JOHN, D.D.) Exposition of the Book of Psalms, explanatory, critical, and devotional. 2 vols., 8vo. 1829. 3 vols., 8vo. 1832.
The first volume is the best. There is nothing very original, but it is an instructive exposition, and ought to be better known.

450 MUDGE (ZACHARY. *Prebendary of Exeter. Died* 1760). An Essay towards a New English Version. 4to. *Lond.*, 1744.
Elegant in taste rather than sound in scholarship. *Mudge* was highly esteemed by *Dr. Johnson*, and he was no doubt a very worthy man ; but his exposition can be dispensed with.

451 **MURPHY** (JAMES G., LL.D.) A Critical and Exegetical Comment. 8vo. *Edinb.*, T. & T. Clark. 1875.
This may be called a volume of compressed thought. The author has aimed at neither being too long nor too short. He has succeeded in producing a very useful and usable work, with many points of unusual value. Dr. Murphy is well known as an accomplished Hebraist and a lucid expositor. We have already noticed his works on Genesis (134) and Exodus (176).

452 NEALE (JOHN MASON, D.D.) and (LITTLEDALE, R. F., LL.D.) A Commentary, from Primitive and Mediæval Writers. 4 vols., post 8vo. *Lond.*, Masters & Co. 1860-74.
Unique, and to very high churchmen most precious. We admire the

learning and research; but the conceits, the twistings, and allegorical interpretations surpass conception. As a collection of mediæval mysticisms it is unrivalled.

453 NICHOLSON (WILLIAM. *Bishop of Gloucester. Died* 1671). David's Harp Strung and Tuned; or, An Easie Analysis of the Whole Book of Psalms. Folio. *Lond.*, 1662. 21/-

"Wholly practical and explanatory. In his explications the author steers between the two extremes of literal and spiritual interpretation. *Dr. Adam Clark* has inserted *Bishop Nicholson's* Analysis in his commentary on the Psalms, omitting his prayers."—*Horne.* This book fetches a high price when complete, and we cannot advise a poor man to lay out so much money upon it, good as it is.

454 NOYES (G. R., D.D.) A New Translation, with Notes. 12mo. *Boston, U. S.*, 1831 and 1846.

Dr. Noyes was the Hebrew Professor in Harvard University. His Introduction is full of information; the new translation is useful, and the notes are brief and pertinent.

455 OXENDEN (ASHTON, D.D. *Bishop of Montreal*). A Simple Exposition. 2 vols., cr. 8vo. *Lond.*, Hatchards.
For reading at family prayers. Alas, poor families! Ye have need of patience.

456 **PEROWNE** (J. J. STEWART, B.D., *Canon Res. of Llandaff*). The Book of Psalms; a New Translation, with Introductions and Notes. 8vo. [Abridged edition for Schools and Private Students. Cr. 8vo. *Lond.*, George Bell & Sons. 1864-68.

A masterpiece of extraordinary learning and critical skill, although not altogether what we would desire. The "Saturday Review" said:—"Mr. Perowne is probably as capable as any one in England of doing all that Hebrew scholarship can do towards a better knowledge of the Psalms. The learning which he has brought together gives a value of its own to his book, and makes it an important contribution to a department of Biblical scholarship in which we are at present rather poorly furnished."

457 PIERCE (SAMUEL EYLES). The Book of Psalms. 2 vols., 8vo. 1817. *Very scarce.*

This author is held in high esteem for the "sound and savoury" character of his works. On the Psalms he writes to comfort and edification. The work is regarded as superexcellent by our extracalvinistic friends, but we do not think it quite worth the fancy price which is now asked.

458 PHILLIPS (GEORGE, B.D.) The Psalms in Hebrew; with Commentary. 2 vols., 8vo. *Lond.*, J. W. Parker, and Williams & Norgate. 1846.

This Commentary will be valued by Hebrew scholars; but it is beyond the general attainments of those for whom this Index is compiled.

459 **PLAIN COMMENTARY** (A) on the Book of Psalms
(P. B. Version), chiefly grounded on the Fathers. 2 vols..
Fcap. 8vo.   *Oxf.* & *Lond.* Parker. 1859.

*Of the High Church school, and rather strained in places, but
abounding in sweet spiritual thoughts. We have read it with
pleasure and profit, though with some caution.*

460 PLUMER (WILLIAM S., DD., LL.D.) Studies in the Book of
Psalms. Imp. 8vo.   *Edinb.*, A. & C. Black. 1867.

A huge volume, compiled from such works as were accessible to the
author in the United States. Full of instructive comment, but not very
original, or remarkably learned.

461 PRACTICAL ILLUSTRATION (A) of the Book of Psalms ; by the Author
of the Family Commentary on the New Testament. [? Mrs. Thomson.]
2 vols. 8vo. *York*, 1826.

For families. Consisting of remarks which would occur to any motherly person.

462 PRIDHAM (ARTHUR). Notes and Reflections on the Book of
Psalms. Cr. 8vo.   *Lond.*, James Nisbet & Co. 1869.

Spiritual reflections of an excellent kind, but not very striking.

463 REMARKS upon the Psalms as Prophetic of the Messiah. 8vo. *Lond.*,1843.

Mere outlines: of no consequence.

464 ROGERS (J., M.A.) The Book of Psalms in Hebrew, metrically arranged ;
with Selections from the various Readings of Kennicott and De Rossi, and
from the Ancient Versions. 2 vols., 12mo. *Oxf.*, 1833.

For the Hebrew scholar only.

465 ROSENMÜLLER (ERNEST F. C. 1768—1835). Annotations
on the Messianic Psalms. Translated. 12mo.   *Edinb.*,
T. & T. Clark. 1841.

It may be altogether our own fault, but we cannot make any use of
this volume. No doubt these scholastic notes have a value ; but commentaries upon inspired Scripture written in the same style as one might
write upon Ovid or Horace are not to our taste. *Gesenius* praises this
work for its criticisms. We wish there had been a little religion in it, but
perhaps if there had been it would have been the religion of neology.

466 RYLAND (R. H., M.A.) The Psalms restored to Messiah.
Sm. 8vo. 6/. *Lond.*, Nisbet. 1853.

Written with an admirable design. Good, but not very able. The
subject still demands the pen of a master.

467 SHERIFFE (Mrs.) Practical Reflections. 2 vols., 12mo. *Lond.*, 1820.

We hope they benefited the printer ; they will not help the reader much.

468 SPURGEON (CHARLES HADDON). The Treasury of David :
containing an Original Exposition of the Book of Psalms ; a
Collection of Illustrative Extracts from the whole range of
literature ; a Series of Homiletical Hints upon almost every
verse ; and Lists of Writers upon each Psalm.

Vol. I. Pss. I-XXVI.; Vol. II. Pss. XXVII-LVIII.; Vol. III. Pss. LVIII.-LXXXVII.; Vol. IV. Pss. LXXXVIII.-CX.; Vol. V. Pss. CXI.-CXIX.; Vol. VI. Pss. CXX-CL. $24.75, Zondervan.

To be completed in six volumes, if God permit. Reviewers have handled this book with remarkable kindness, and the public have endorsed their judgment by largely purchasing the volumes already issued. It would not become us to say more.

469 STREET (STEPHEN, M.A.) A New Literal Version ; with a Preface and Notes. 2 vols., 8vo. *Lond.*, 1790.

One hardly desires a rigidly literal translation of a poetic book, for the beauty and spirit are lost. The notes are purely critical and are superseded by later works

470 THOLUCK (AUGUSTUS F., D.D., Ph.D.) A Translation and Commentary. Translated from the German by J. Isidor Mombert. 8vo. *Lond.*, Nisbet & Co. 1856.

Tholuck is one of the most spiritual of German interpreters. Though we cannot say that this is equal to some others of his works, yet he is a great writer, and always deserves attention.

471 THRUPP (JOSEPH FRANCIS, M.A.) An Introduction to the Study and Use of the Psalms. 2 vols., 8vo. *Lond.* and *Camb.*, Macmillan & Co. 1860.

Though not the best, it is still a learned and helpful work of its class.

472 TUCKER (WILLIAM HILL, M.A.) The Psalms [P. B. Version], with Notes, showing their Prophetic and Christian Character. Post 8vo. 6/- *Lond.*, 1840.

The writer refers all the Psalms to Christ, and writes many weighty things, but we cannot place him in the front rank among expositors.

473 WAKE (W. R.) A Literal Version of the Psalms into Modern Language, according to the Liturgy translation. 2 vols., Cr. 8vo. *Bath.*, 1793.

Think of a translation of a translation. The author was Wake, but not awake, or he would never have wasted so much good paper.

474 WALFORD (WILLIAM. *Late Classical and Hebrew Tutor at Homerton*). A New Translation, with Notes, Explanatory and Critical. 8vo. *Lond.*, 1837.

Contains some useful notes, good, but not specially remarkable.

475 WEISS (BENJ. *Missionary to the Jews, Algiers*). A New Translation, Exposition, and Chronological Arrangement of the Book of Psalms, with Critical Notes. 8vo. *Edinb.*, W. Oliphant & Co. 1852.

The Psalms are arranged in a new order, and are very hard to find. The author is dogmatic to the last degree. Our estimate of his work is not so high as his own.

476 WILCOCKS (THOMAS, A.M. *Puritan.* 1549—1608). A very godly and learned exposition upon the whole Book of Psalms. [*Works.* Folio.] *See No.* 336.

Short spiritual remarks, followed by many doctrinal inferences, calculated to suggest topics to preachers.

477 **WILSON** (W., D.D.) The Psalms ; with an Exposition, Typical and Prophetical, of the Christian Dispensation. 2 vols. 8vo. *Lond.*, Nisbet. 1860.

We have consulted Wilson with advantage and often quoted from him in the " Treasury of David," He is a clear, gospel Expositor, and has written much that is weighty and precious.

478 WOODFORD (SAMUEL). A Paraphrase. 4to. *Lond.*, 1667.

Poor rhymes ; though the preface says of the author—

"At length the skilful way you found,
With a true ear judg'd the melodious sound,
And with a nimble hand run descant on the Hebrew ground."

It would seem from this that the poem scrambles on all-fours, and we think it does.

479 WRIGHT (ABRAHAM). A Practical Commentary, wherein the Text of every Psalme is Practically expounded, according to the Doctrine of the Catholick Church, in a way not usually trod by Commentators ; and wholly applyed to the Life and Salvation of Christians. Very thin folio. 1661.

Wright selects the more remarkable verses, and comments upon them in a deeply spiritual, quaint, and suggestive manner. His work is extremely rare.

480 ZILLWOOD (J. O.) The Psalms, arranged in Parallelisms, with Notes, chiefly from Bishops Horne and Horsley. 2 vols., 8vo. *Lond.*, 1855.

The student had better get *Horne* and *Horsley* for himself, and he will have no need of this.

CONSIDERABLE PORTIONS OF THE PSALMS.

481 **BAKER** (SIR RICHARD. 1568—1645). Meditations and Disquisitions on the First, and Seven Penitential Psalms, viz., the 6, 32, 38, 51,102, 130, & 143. 4to. *Lond.*, 1640.

Meditations and Disquisitions on the Seven Consolitarie Psalms, viz., the 23, 27, 30, 34, 84, 103, and 116. 4to. *Lond.*, 1640.

O rare Sir Richard Baker ! Knight of the flowing pen. His " Meditations and Disquisitions " are altogether marrow and fatness. We have often tried to quote from him and have found ourselves so embarrassed with riches that we have been inclined to copy the whole book. Why it has not been reprinted, and made to pass through fifty editions, we cannot tell. Poor man, he became a surety and smarted, dying in poverty in the Fleet. Were there any Christians alive in those days?

482 BARKER (FREDERICK, M.A.) Thirty-six Psalms ; with Commentary and Prayer, for use in families. Cr. 8vo. Jackson, 1854.

What platitudes people will write for *the use of families.* Families will best use these commentaries and prayers by lining their cake tins with them.

483 BERTRAM (R. A.) The Imprecatory Psalms. Six Lectures. 12mo. *Lond.*, Elliot Stock. 1867.

Contains some very sensible remarks upon a subject which no doubt bewilders certain of the weaker sort.

484 BOWMAN (HETTY). Studies in the Psalms. 12mo. *Lond.*, The Book. Society, and John Snow & Co. 1869.

Outlines of teaching upon a few Psalms. The authoress begs that these " Studies " may not in any sense be considered as a commentary : we do not so consider them.

485 **BOYS** (JOHN, D.D. *Dean of Canterbury.* 1571—1625). *Workes.* Folio, 1629. An Exposition of the Proper Psalms used in our English Liturgy. (See under *New Testament.*)

One of the richest of writers. From his golden pen flows condensed wisdom. Many of his sentences are worthy to be quoted as gems of the Christian classics.

486 COPE (SIR ANTHONY. *Chamberlain to Queen Catherine Parr*). Meditation on Twenty Select Psalms. Reprinted from the edition of 1547. Small square 8vo. *Lond.*, John Ollivier. 1848.

More curious than valuable. The style is scholastic and pointless.

487 DIDHAM (R. CUNNINGHAM, M.A.) I.—XXXVI.— New Translation : made by means of Arabic Lexicons, Syriac New Testament Words, the Ancient Versions, Bishop Lowth's Parallelisms, and Parallel Places, whereby the Scriptural Messianic Canon that our Lord Christ is the Key to the Psalm is upheld, &c. 8vo. 15/- *Lond.*, Williams & Norgate. 1870.

Principally consists of denunciations of other writers. As the price has descended from 15/- to 1/9 for *new* copies, the verdict of the public is pretty definite.

488 LUTHER (MARTIN). A Commentary on Psalms I.—XI. ; and on Psalm LI., in Vol. 3 ; on Psalms XII.—XXII. and on Psalm II. in Vol. 4, of *Select Works of Luther.* Translated by Rev. H. Cole. [4 vols. 8vo. *Lond.*, 1824.

A Commentary on the Psalms, commonly called the Psalms of Degrees [CXX.—CXXXIV]. 8vo. *Lewes*, 1823. Also a *black letter* 4to., 1577, and other editions of this work.

Luther needs no trumpeter.

489 PITMAN (J. R., M.A.) A Course of Sermons on some of the Chief Subjects in the Book of Psalms ; abridged from eminent divines of the Established Church. 8vo. *Lond.*, Longmans. 1846.

We have seldom obtained much from these sermons. A far better selection might have been made ; at the same time, some of the discourses are admirable.

490 ROLLOCK (ROBERT. 1555—1598). An Exposition upon some select Psalms. 12mo. 1600.

Rollock's works are rare. He wrote in Latin, and his language is made more dull than need be by the translator. All his writings are masterly.

491 STRIGELLIUS (VICTORINUS. 1524—1569). Part of the Harmony of King David's Harp. Translated by R. Robinson. [In four parts.] 4to. 1582 to 1596.

This volume the expositor is not at all likely to see, and there is, therefore, the less need for us to speak of it. *Strigellius* was the friend of *Luther* and *Melancthon*, and a man of sound sense and vast learning.

492　**WILLIAMS** (ISAAC, B.D.)　The Psalms interpreted of
　　　Christ.　[Vol. I., Psalms I.—XXVI.]　Thick 12mo.
　　　Lond., Rivingtons.　1864.

*This writer is of the High Church school, but he is very spiritual
and deep, and we seldom turn to him without profit.*

THE PENITENTIAL PSALMS.

[The Penitential Psalms are seven in number.　Psalms 6, 32, 38, 51,
102, 130, and 143.　For 102 some substitute 25.]

493　**BAKER** (SIR R.)　*See No.* 481.

494　**DONNE** (JOHN.　1573—1631).　Sermons on the Peni-
　　　tential Psalms.　In Vols. II. and III. of his *Works*. [6 vols.,
　　　8vo.,　　　1839.]

A right royal writer, whose every line is a pearl.

495　FISHER (JOHN.　1459—1535).　Fruytful saynges of Dauid.　*Black Letter.*
　　　4to., 1509; 8vo., 1555.　Reprinted in 12mo., 1714.
Dry and tedious: in the stiff antique style.

496　HAYWARD (SIR JOHN, LL.D.　*Died* 1627).　David's Tears.
　　　[On VI., XXXII., and CXXX. only.]　4to., 1623; 12mo.,
　　　1649.
After the Puritanic method : full of point and pith.

497　OXENDEN (CHARLES).　Sermons on the Seven Penitential Psalms, preached
　　　during Lent.　12mo.　1838.

To listen to these sermons must have afforded a suitable Lenten penance to those
who went to church to hear them.　There their use began and ended.

498　**SYMSON** (ARCHIBALD).　A Sacred Septenarie ; or, a
　　　Godly and Fruitfull Exposition on the Seven Psalmes of
　　　Repentance.　4to.　1638.

A marrowy author, full of instruction.

SEPARATE PSALMS.

[The following works are arranged according to the order of the
Psalms, to assist reference.　We have not attempted to include all
writers in this list].

499　Psalm I.—SMITH (SAMUEL.　1583—1665). David's Blessed Man.
　　　Ninth edition, 18mo.　1635.　　　　　Reprinted in Nichol's
　　　Commentaries, with *Pierson* (No. 527) ; and *Gouge* (No. 560).
Very popular in its day, and worthily so.

500 I.—STONHAM (Matthew). A Treatise on the First Psalme. 4to. 1610.

Somewhat dry, scholastic and out of date; but still an interesting and instructive piece of old divinity.

501 II., XLV., CX.—HARPUR (George, B.A.) Christ in the Psalms. A Series of Discourses. Cr. 8vo. *Lond.,* Wertheim & Co. 1862.

Discourses of a high order as to ability, but the historico-prophetic interpretations here given do not commend themselves to us.

502 II.—PITCAIRN (David). Zion's King. Cr. 8vo. *Lond.,* J. H. Jackson. 1851.

This author does not err on the side of conciseness. His book is a meritorious effort, but we have found it somewhat heavy reading.

503 IV., XLII., LI., LXIII.—**HORTON** (Thomas, D.D. *Died* 1673). Choice and Practical Expositions. Folio. 1675.

A marvellous homiletical exposition. Horton's discourses are very full of divisions, but then he always has plenty of solid matter to divide. Ministers will find teeming suggestions here.

504 XV.—CARTWRIGHT (Christopher). Commentary. 4to. 1658.

A learned and weighty work; not readily met with.

505 XV.—DOWNAME (George, D.D.) Lectures. 4to. 1604.

Lectures by one of the race of giant divines.

506 XV.—TURNBULL (Richard). Four Sermons on Psalm XV. 4to. 1606. Forming last part of volume on James and Jude.

By a popular and edifying preacher of the olden times

507 XVI.—DALE (Thomas, M.A. *Canon of St. Paul's.*) The Golden Psalm. 12mo. 1847.

Good, simple discourses ; the headings might suggest a course of sermons.

508 XVI.—FRAME (James). Christ in Gethsemane. Cr. 8vo. 1858.

A sterling, well-intentioned and well-executed comment. The text has to be a little twisted to suit the theory of the interpreter, but we do not suppose that *Mr. Frame* is conscious of it. He is one of the best of modern discoursers upon the Psalms.

509 XVIII.—**BROWN** (John, D.D.) The Sufferings and Glories of the Messiah. 8vo. *Edinb.,* 1853.

Like all Dr. Brown's productions, this is a work of the highest order. Clear, full, and, in the best manner, exegetical.

510 XIX.—**REEVE** (J. W.) Lectures on the Nineteenth
   Psalm. Cr. 8vo.   1863.

*By one of the ablest preachers among the Evangelical Episco-
palians. Scriptural, thoughtful, and original.*

511 XIX.—RICHARDSON (J. WILBERFORCE). Illustrations of the
   Nineteenth Psalm. Cr. 8vo.   *Lond.*, John Snow & Co.
   1870.

Sound in doctrine, but verbose and common-place.

512 XX., verses 1—6.—BOWND (NICHOLAS, D.D.) Medicines for
   the Plague [Twenty-one Sermons]. 4to. 1604.

Racy, quaint, extremely rare.

513 XXII.—FRAME (JAMES). The Song of the Cross. Cr. 8vo.
   Lond., S. W. Partridge & Co. 1872.

This is valuable, as *Mr. Frame's* books generally are.

514 XXII.—STEVENSON (JOHN, D.D., *Hon. Canon of Canterbury*).
   Christ on the Cross : an Exposition of the Twenty-second Psalm.
   Post 8vo.   *Lond.*, Bagsters.

The best of *Dr. Stevenson's* books. Exceedingly precious in its un-
veiling of the Redeemer's sorrows. We have derived personal spiritual
benefit from the perusal of this gracious exposition, and are unable
to judge it critically.

515 XXIII.—STEVENSON (JOHN, D.D., *Hon. Canon of Canterbury*).
   The Lord our Shepherd : An Exposition of the Twenty-third
   Psalm. Post 8vo.   *Lond.*, Bagsters.

Too wire-drawn, but it is golden wire.

516 XXIII.—**BAKER** (SIR R.)   *See No.* 481.

517 XXIII.—DALE (THOMAS, M.A.) The Good Shepherd and the
   Chosen Flock. 12mo. 1847.

Somewhat ordinary evangelical discourses.

518 XXIII., LXII., LXXIII.—LXXVII.—HOOPER (JOHN, *Bishop and Martyr*).
   Certain Comfortable Expositions. [In Parker Society's edition of Hooper's
   Works.]

The cramped style and antiquated matter repel the reader.

519 XXIII.—MILLER (ANDREW). Meditations on Twenty-third and
   Eighty-fourth Psalms. 12mo. *Lond.*, G. Morrish.

Discursive, but devout ; more useful to the heart than the head.

520 XXIII.—PATON (JAMES, B.A.) The Children's Psalm : Twelve
   Meditations and Twelve Spiritual Songs. 12mo. *Lond.*,
   Passmore & Alabaster. 1870.

Worthy of much commendation. It is unfortunate that the title leads
the reader to expect a book for children, whereas the author intended to
edify *the children of God* of an older growth.

521 XXIII.—SEDGWICK (OBADIAH, B.D.) The Shepherd of Israel. 4to. 1658.

Sedgwick was one of the most eminent preachers of the time of the Commonwealth. His commenting is solid and lively.

522 XXIII.—SMITH (SAMUEL). The Chiefe Shepheard; or An Exposition on yᵉ XXIII Psalme. 18mo. 1625.

All the writings of *Samuel Smith* are good, but not so full of memorable sentences and pithy sayings as certain others of their date.

523 XXIII.—STOUGHTON (JOHN, D.D.) The Song of Christ's Flock. 12mo. *Lond.*, 1860.

Devout practical meditations, but we don't see how a flock can sing.

524 XXIII.—THORNTON (J., *of Billericay*). The Shepherd of Israel. 12mo. 1826.

We need no longer wonder how spiders make such long threads with such little material, for here is an equally amazing instance of spinning. Plentiful quotations of Scripture, and venerable anecdotes are here used as substitutes for thought, not as aids to it.

525 XXV.—HALKET (LADY ANNE. 1622—1699.) Meditations. 8vo. *Edinb.*, 1778.

This lady was eminent for medicine as well as theology; she left twenty-one volumes: this and another book of meditations appear to be all that have been reprinted.

526 XXV.—**MOSSOM** (ROBERT, *Bishop of Londonderry. Died* 1679). The Preacher's Tripartite, contains Divine Meditations upon Psalm XXV. Folio. 1657.

Thoroughly devotional, eminently consolatory, and deeply experimental. Mossom is a fruitful writer.

527 XXVII., LXXXIV., LXXXV., LXXXVII.—PIERSON (THOMAS, M.A. 1570—1633). Excellent Encouragements against Afflictions. 4to. 1647. [Reprinted in Nichol's Commentaries, with *Smith*, No. 499 ; and *Gouge*, No. 560].

Pierson was not the richest or most overflowing of the old divines, but yet one who stood in the front rank.

528 XXXII.—BINGHAM (CHARLES H , B.A.) Lectures. Post 8vo. 1836.
Tame sermons. Faultlessly feeble. Good, but no good.

529 XXXII.—**LEIGHTON** (ROBERT, *Archbishop of Glasgow.* 1611—1684).

In some editions of Leighton's collected works will be found choice meditations on this Psalm, and also on Psalms IV. and CXXX. Everything that fell from his pen is worth its weight in diamonds.

530 XXXII.—TAYLOR (THOMAS, D.D.) David's Learning, or Way
    to True Happiness. 4to. 1617.   Also in his *Works.*
    Folio. 1660.

On account of *Taylor's* great knowledge of the Scriptures, he was
commonly called " the illuminated Doctor." *Fuller* calls him " a grave
divine, a painful preacher, and a profitable writer." He is one of the
richest in matter of all the Puritans.

531 XXXII.—REEVE (J. W., M.A.) Lectures.   Cr. 8vo.
    Lond., Nisbet. 1859.

Orthodox, spiritual, and suggestive lectures, by an evangelical clergyman.

532 XXXII.—WILLARD (SAMUEL).   The Truly Blessed Man.
    8vo. *Boston, N.E.*   *Rare.*

One of the first books printed in the United States.   An old-fashioned
exposition.   The price is caused by its rarity rather than its value.

533 XL.—FRAME (JAMES). Christ and his Work. Cr. 8vo.
    Lond., Snow & Co. 1869.

Well done.   Though differing from the author at times, we are grateful
for such real help.

534 XLII.—MACDUFF (J. R., D.D.) The Hart and the Water-
    brooks. Sm. cr. 8vo. *Lond.*, Nisbet. 1860.

See remarks on other books by this copious writer. (*Nos.* 308, 315, &c.)

535 XLII., XLIII.—MARCH (H.) Sabbaths at Home. 8vo.
    1823.

Profitable reading, rendered all the more pleasing by the introduction
of very choice poetry. Not important to the expositor.

536 XLII.—**SIBBES** (RICHARD, D.D.) The Soul's Conflict
    and Victory over itself by Faith. 12mo. 1635, etc.
    Works, Vol. I., Nichol's edition.

*Mainly upon verses 5 and 11. Sibbes never wastes the student's
time; he scatters pearls and diamonds with both hands.*

537 XLV.—BENNETT (THOMAS). Sermons on the Forty-fifth
    Psalm. Sm. 8vo. *Edinb.*, 1781.

Twenty-four sermons after the manner of *Ralph Erskine*, in which
Jesus is all in all. What more need be said in their praise?

538 XLV.—PENNEFATHER (WILLIAM, M.A.) The Bridegroom
    King. A Meditation on the Forty-fifth Psalm. 18mo.
    Lond., J. F. Shaw & Co.

Rather a meditation than an exposition. A fitting book for a sick bed.
The little chapters might lie, like wafers made with honey, upon the
praiseful tongue of the suffering believer. The beloved writer has now
gone to see the King in his beauty, of whom he had those glimpses
here which enabled him to pen this tiny volume.

539   XLV.—TROUGHTON (W.) The Mystery of the Marriage Song. 12mo. 1656.
An old work with nothing new or striking in it.   Remarkably tame and meagre for a work of that exuberant period.   Let it alone.

540   XLV.—PITCAIRN (DAVID).   The Anointed Saviour.   12mo. 1846.
Contains an exposition of part of Psalm XLV., as applied to Messiah's first and second advents.   Good, yet it reads rather wearily to us.

541   LI.—ALEXANDER (THOMAS, M.A.)   The Penitent's Prayer. Cr. 8vo.   Lond., Nisbet.   1861.
Our friend the late *Dr. Alexander* of Chelsea handled this Psalm well.

542   LI.—DE COETLOGON (CHARLES EDWARD, A.M.   *Died* 1820).   The Portraiture of the Christian Penitent.   2 vols., 12mo.   1775.
Very proper.   We see nothing in the book but platitudes decorously expressed.

543   LI.—BIDDULPH (THOMAS T., A.M., 1763—1838).   Lectures on Psalm LI.   8vo., 1830 ; 12mo., 1835.
Lectures far above the average of such lucubrations, making up a very fair exposition.

544   LI.—BULL (JOHN, M.A.)   Sermons on the Fifty-first Psalm. 8vo. 1824.
Another specimen of sermons published by subscription.   The poor curate was no doubt the better for the profits, and nobody was any the worse.   Clipston church was not set on fire by the flaming eloquence of the preacher, nor was the country disturbed by any fanatical excitement produced by his excessive zeal.

545   LI.—HIERON (SAMUEL.   1572—1617).   David's Penitentiall Psalme opened.   4to.   1617.
Hieron was a conforming Puritan.   His works were once exceedingly popular and they are still esteemed.

546   LI.—**HILDERSHAM** (ARTHUR. *Puritan.* 1563—1631). One Hundred and Fifty-two Lectures upon Psalm LI. Folio.   1635 and 1642.
Hildersham was one of the most tried of the Nonconforming ministers, and at the same time one of the most able.   He is copious and discursive, we had almost said long-winded.   Both Willet and Preston speak of him in the highest terms.

547   LI.—**MORGAN** (JAMES, D.D.)   The Penitent.   12mo. *Belfast*, M'Comb ; *Lond.*, Hamilton.   1855.
The excellent doctor first wrote this exposition for his own spiritual benefit, then preached it for the edification of his flock, and lastly published it for the good of us all.   This is a worthy pedigree for a book, and the book itself is worthy of the pedigree.

548   LI.—**PAGE** (SAMUEL, DD. *Died* 1630).   David's Broken Heart.   4to.   1637 and 1646.
Every page is like a bank note for value.   Here are homiletical materials in abundance.

549 LI.—SMITH (Samuel). David's Repentance. 18mo. 16th
     Edition. 1655. (*See Nos.* 499 *and* 522).

It will be seen from the numerous editions that this work was well
received in its author's lifetime.   He tells us that he spent the spare
hours of a long sickness in publishing this short exposition, and thus the
world is all the healthier for his illness.

550 LXVIII., CX.—DIXON (Richard, A.M., F.R.S.)   A New
     Interpretation of the Sixty-eighth Psalm: with an Exposition of
     the Hundred and Tenth Psalm. 4to.   *Oxf.,* 1811.

This author, in a most interesting manner, traces out the analogy
between this Psalm and the Song of Deborah.   Those who like choice
pieces of writing upon the literature of Scripture will be gratified by the
perusal of this exposition.

551 LXXIII.—PARRY (Edward. *Bishop of Killaloe*).   David
     Restored ; or an Antidote against the Prosperity of the Wicked
     and the Afflictions of the Just. 8vo.   1660.

Not super-excellent, nor free from blemishes, but containing much of
sterling value.

552 LXXXII.—HALL (Thomas, B.D.   1610—1665).   The Beauty
     of Magistracy. An Exposition of Psalm LXXXII. 4to.   1660.
     [In Vol. IV. of Swinnock's Works, Nichol's edition.]

This exposition has always nestled in the bosom of *Swinnock's*
works.   We agree with *Dr. Jenkyn's* criticism—"The style is terse
and clear, though grave and theological, and the matter is solid and
judicious."

553 LXXXIV.—HEMINGE (Nicholas.   1513—1600).   The Faith of the
     Church Militant. 8vo.   1581.
     A Danish divine of high repute in his own day.   Some of his works were
turned into English; but the translations, like the originals, are now left in undeserved
oblivion.

554 XC.—SMITH (Samuel). Moses, his Prayer. 18mo.   1656.

See our notes on Nos. 499, 522, and 549.

555 XCIX., CI., CII.—EDERSHEIM (Alfred, D.D.)   The Golden
     Diary of Heart Converse with Jesus.   1873.   Contains Exposi-
     tions of Psalms XCIX., CI., CII.

Sweet and spiritual ; worth purchasing.

556 CIII—STEVENSON (John, D.D.   *Hon. Canon of Canterbury*).
     Gratitude. An Exposition of the Hundred and Third Psalm.
     Post 8vo.   *Lond.,* S. Bagster & Sons.

Somewhat diffuse, but at the same time too good to be criticized.

557 CVII.—HYPERIUS (Andrew Gerard. 1511—1564). A
Special Treatise of God's Providence and Comfort against all
kinds of Crosses and Calamities, to be drawn from the same;
with an Exposition of the One Hundred and Seventh Psalme.
From the Latin. *Black Letter.* 8vo. 1602. *Scarce.*

This author has written in Latin upon many subjects, but his works
are now little known. He was a learned Lutheran.

558 CVII.—ROMAINE (William, M.A. 1714—1795). A Practical
Comment on Psalm CVII. 8vo. Fifth edition. 1767.
Also in *Works, IV.*

Romaine's doctrine and style of writing are well known. He could
not be accused of overlaying the truth with much learning. The
thought is gracious, sound, and practical, but the style is just a little dull.

559 CX.—**REYNOLDS** (Edward, D.D. *Bishop of Norwich.*
1599—1676). Explication of the One Hundred and
Tenth Psalm. 4to., 1632 and 1635; 12mo., 1837.
Also in *Works.*

*Surpassingly clear and elaborate. Reynolds was a man of vast
learning and thoroughly evangelical spirit.*

560 CXVI.—GOUGE (William, D.D. *Puritan.* 1575—1653). The
Saints' Sacrifice. 4to. 1632. *Scarce.*   Reprinted in Nichol's
Commentaries, with *Smith,* No. 499; and *Pierson,* No. 527.

Gouge's method of cutting up his exposition into sections and dis-
cussing everything in propositions, is very tedious to the reader, but we
judge it to be advantageous to the preacher. At any rate *Gouge* has
often given us a hint. He was a man of great learning.

561 CXIX.—**BRIDGES** (Charles, M.A.) Exposition.
Twenty-second edition. Cr. 8vo. *Lond.,* 1857.

*Worth its weight in gold. Albeit that the work is neither learned
nor very original we prize it for its surpassing grace and unction.*

562 CXIX.—COWPER (William. *Bp. of Galloway.* 1566— 1619).
A Holy Alphabet for Sion's Scholars. A Commentary upon
CXIX Psalm. Folio. *Lond.,* 1613; and in *Works.* Folio. 1629.

Dr. M'Crie gives a high character to all *Cowper's* works, and says
that a vein of practical piety runs through them, while the style is
remarkable for ease and fluency. This remark applies emphatically to
the "Holy Alphabet." We have found it very delightful reading.

563 CXIX.—GREENHAM (Richard. *Puritan.* 1531—1591). An
Exposition of the 119 Psalme. *Works.* Folio. *Lond.,* 1612.

We regret that this comment is not published separately, and is
only to be procured by purchasing the rest of *Greenham's* works. The
style, however, is antique and cramped, and *Manton* and *Bridges* are
quite enough.

564 CXIX.—**MANTON** (Thomas, D.D. 1620—1677). One
hundred and ninety Sermons on the One Hundred and
Nineteenth Psalm. Folio, *Lond.*, 1725 ; 3 vols., 8vo.,
Lond., 1842 ; 3 vols (with Life), 1845.

*Fully up to Manton's highest mark, and he is well known to have
been one of the chief of the Puritan brotherhood. The work is long,
but that results only from the abundance of matter.*

565 CXIX.—SANDERSON (R. B., Esq., B.A.) Lord's Day Literature: or,
Illustrations of the Book of Psalms from the Hundred and Nineteenth
Psalm consecutively. 12mo. *Lond.*, 1842.

We cannot call this an exposition, its title far more accurately describes it. The
author takes occasion from the text to plead for those points of doctrine and practice
into which he had been led by the Spirit of God. He was an eminently conscientious
man, a bold believer, and a Baptist.

566 CXX.—CXXXIV.—ARMFIELD (H. T., M.A. *Vice-Principal,
Theol. Coll., Vicar of the Close, and Minor Canon of Sarum*).
The Gradual Psalms : a Treatise on the Fifteen Songs of
Degrees, with Commentary, based on Ancient Hebrew, Chaldee,
and Christian Authorities. 8vo. *Lond.*, J. T. Hayes. 1874.

A wonderfully interesting book from a literary point of view ; perhaps
more singular than profitable ; but in many respects a publication which
we should have been sorry to have missed. The homiletical student
will not be able to make much use of it.

567 CXX.—CXXXIV.—COX (Samuel). The Pilgrim Psalms ;
an Exposition of the Songs of Degrees. 8vo. *Lond.*,
Daldy, Isbister & Co. 1874.

*This will be greatly valued by intelligent readers. A noble series
of sermons would be pretty sure to grow out of its attentive perusal.
Mr. S. Cox is a great expositor.*

568 CXX.—CXXXIV.—LUTHER (Martin). *See No.* 488.

569 CXX.—CXXXIV.—**M'MICHAEL** (N., D.D.) The Pilgrim
Psalms. Cr. 8vo. *Edinb.*, Oliphant. 1860.

A capital work, full of sound doctrine perfumed with devotion.

570 CXX.—CXXXIV.—NISBET (Robert, D.D.) The Songs of
the Temple Pilgrims. *Lond.*, Nisbet. 1863.

Dr. Nisbet regards the " Songs of Degrees as affording so complete
an exhibition of the phases of religious sentiment, as to make these
short poems a transcript of the feelings of the whole Church ; a miniature
Bible for the use of all." He has expounded in this spirit, with well-
chosen language, and produced a very valuable and instructive book.

571 CXXII.—WILLET (Andrew). In *Willet's* Harmonie and Exposition of the
Books of Samuel there is " a brief exposition of the 122 Psalm."

Willet ought to have known better than to twist a psalm to the honour and glory of
James I. As a learned man he says good things, and as a courtier foolish things.

572 CXXX.—**HUTCHESON** (George). Forty-five Sermons
Psalm CXXX. 8vo. *Edinb.,* 1691. *Scarce.*
*We have already advised the purchase of anything and every-
thing by Hutcheson. Be sure not to confound this with Hutchinson.*

573 CXXX.—**LEIGHTON** (Robert). *See No.* 529.

574 CXXX.—**OWEN** (John, D.D.) A Practical Exposition
on the One Hundred and Thirtieth Psalm. *Lond.* 4to.
1669 and 1680. R. Tract Society's edition. 18mo.
*One of the best known and most esteemed of John Owen's works.
It is unnecessary to say that he is the prince of divines. To master
his works is to be a profound theologian. Owen is said to be prolix,
but it would be truer to say that he is condensed. His style is
heavy because he gives notes of what he might have said, and passes
on without fully developing the great thoughts of his capacious mind.
He requires hard study, and none of us ought to grudge it.*

575 CXXX.—SIBBES (Richard, D.D.) The Saints' Comforts.
18mo. 1638. *Works,* Vol. VI. Nichol's Edition.
Notes on five verses only. Published without the author's sanction, it
is incomplete, but very full as far as it goes, and considering its brevity.

576 CXXX.—WINSLOW (Octavius, D.D.) Soul-Depths and Soul-
Heights; an Exposition of Psalm CXXX. Cr. 8vo. *Lond.,*
J. F. Shaw. 1874.
Not very deep nor very high, but pleasant spiritual reading.

BOOKS OF SOLOMON.

577 KEIL and DELITZSCH'S Commentaries. Salomonic Writings.
Ecclesiastes, Song of Solomon. $3.50. Eerdmans.

578 **LANGE'S** Commentaries. Proverbs, Ecclesiastes, and
Song of Solomon. By Dr. Otto Zöckler.
$3.95. Zondervan.
*We cannot say that we admire Zöckler's interpretation of the
Song of Solomon. The volume contains much that we do not like,
but its value is considerable. It is a pity that the value of the
volumes in this series varies so much.*

579 NOYES (G. R., D.D.) A Translation of Proverbs, Ecclesiastes,
and Canticles, with Notes, &c. 12mo. *Boston, U.S.* 1846.
Of *Noyes* upon Ecclesiastes, *Dr. Hamilton* says :—" This interpretation is clear and straightforward, but the American Professor gives to
the book an air of theological tenuity and mere worldly wisdom which
carries neither our conviction nor our sympathy." *Noyes* is a good
literary expositor, but his theological views render him a very poverty-
stricken commentator from a spiritual point of view.

PROVERBS.

580 ALLEN (ROBERT. *Puritan*). Concordances of the Proverbs and Ecclesiastes. 4to. 1612.

An ordinary concordance will answer the purpose far better; but the wonderfully wise, half-crazy *Cruden* had not compiled his invaluable work in *Allen's* days.

581 **ARNOT** (WILLIAM, D.D. *Died* 1875). Laws from Heaven for Life on Earth. 2 vols., cr. 8vo. 1858. Also 1 vol., cr. 8vo. *Edinb.*, Nelson. 1869.

We wish Dr. Arnot had gone steadily through the whole book, for his mind was of an order peculiarly adapted for such a task. Those passages which he dilates upon are set in a clear and beautiful light. For a happy blending of illustrative faculty, practical sound sense, and spirituality, Dr. Arnot was almost unrivalled.

582 **BRIDGES** (CHARLES, M.A.) An Exposition. 2 vols., 12mo. *Lond.*, Seeleys. 1850.

The best work on the Proverbs. The Scriptural method of exposition so well carried out by Bridges renders all his writings very suggestive to ministers. While explaining the passage in hand, he sets other portions of the word in new lights.

583 BROOKS (J. W., M.A.) A New Arrangement of the Proverbs of Solomon. 12mo. *Lond.*, Seeleys. 1860.

We do not see the use of the arrangement; but those who want the Proverbs classified have the work done for them here.

584 CASE (R. J.) A Commentary. 12mo. *Lond.*, 1822.

The Proverbs themselves are plainer than this author's exposition of them.

585 DAY (WILLIAM. *Formerly Missionary to the South Seas*). A Poetical Commentary. 8vo: 14/- *Lond.*, Simpkin, Marshall & Co. 1862.

The author says, he has "a taste for building rhymes," and he has here gratified it. That is all we can say for his book.

586 DELITZSCH (FRANZ, D.D.) Biblical Commentary. Translated from the German, by M. G. Easton, D.D. 2 volumes $7.00. Eerdmans.

587 DOD (JOHN. *Puritan. Died* 1645). A Plaine and Familiar Exposition of Proverbs, Chapters IX. to XVII. 4to. *Lond.*, 1608-9. [The comment on Chapters XIII. and XIV. appears to have been the work of *Robert Cleaver*. In our copy, containing Chapters XXVIII.—XXX., the names of both *Dod* and *Cleaver* are given, and the last chapter was "penned by a Godly and learned man, now with God."]

Both *Dod* and *Cleaver* were popular as preachers, and their joint works were widely circulated. This book can rarely be met with entire.

588 FRENCH (W., D.D.) and (SKINNER, G., M.A.) A New Translation, with Explanatory Notes. 8vo. *Lond.*, 1831.

These translators endeavour to produce faithful renderings of the text, giving to each word the same sense in all places. They are calm, dispassionate, judicious, and able.

589 HODGSON (BERNARD, LL.D.) The Proverbs of Solomon, with Notes. 4to. *Oxf.*, 1788.

Darling says:—" A good translation; the notes are chiefly philological." We set no store by this mass of letter-press, and we question whether any one else does.

590 HOLDEN (GEORGE, M.A.) An attempt towards an improved Translation, with Notes, &c. 8vo. *Liverpool*, 1819.

Horne says of this work:—"It is one of the most valuable helps to the critical understanding of this book." It is certainly one of the best of *Holden's* productions. We may be wrong, but we could not conscientiously subscribe to *Horne's* opinion.

591 JACOX (FRANCIS). Scripture Proverbs, illustrated, annotated, and applied. Thick cr. 8vo. *Lond.*, Hodder & Stoughton. 1874.

This work illustrates many of the proverbs scattered throughout the Scriptures, and some of those collected by Solomon. *Mr. Jacox* seems to have read everything good and bad, and hence he pours forth a medley of fact and fiction more entertaining than edifying. He reminds us of the elder Disraeli and his "Curiosities of Literature."

592 JERMIN (MICHAEL, D.D. *Died* 1659). Paraphrastical Meditations upon the Book of Proverbs. Folio. 1638.

Very antique, and full of Latin quotations. *Jermin* does not err in excessive spirituality, but the reverse. Those who can put up with his style will be repaid by his quaint learning.

593 **LANGE.** (*See No.* 578.)

594 LAWSON (GEORGE, D.D. 1749—1820). Exposition of the Book of Proverbs. 2 vols., 12mo. *Edinb.* 1821.

A thoroughly sound and useful commentary. *Lawson* wrote popularly and vigorously.

595 MILLER (JOHN. *Princeton, N. J.*) A Commentary, with a New Translation, and with some of the Original Expositions Re-examined. Demy 8vo. Dickinson & Higham. 1875.

This author's interpretations are new, and in our judgment very far removed from accuracy. Certainly the old interpretations are better in many ways. His theory that the Proverbs are spiritual and not secular will not hold water. He needs reading with very great discrimination: if read at all. "Too great innovation" is the author's own suspicion of his work, and we quite agree with him, only we go beyond mere *suspicion*.

596 MUFFET (PETER). A Commentary on the whole Book of Proverbs. 8vo. 1596. [Reprinted, with Cotton's Commentaries on Ecclesiastes and Song of Solomon, in one of the volumes of Nichol's series. Cr. 4to. *Lond.*, Nisbet. 1868.]

Homely, but not very striking. *Mr. Nichol's* choice of commentators for reprinting was not a wise one.

597 NEWMAN (WILLIAM., D.D. *Formerly President of Stepney Theol. Institution*). An improved version. 18mo. *Lond.*, 1839.

Merely the corrected text. A very small affair.

598 NICHOLLS (BENJAMIN ELLIOTT, M.A.) The Book of Proverbs, explained and illustrated from Holy Scripture. 12mo. *Lond.*, Rivingtons. 1858.

Contains very sensible suggestions for the interpretation of proverbs, and gives instances of explanations by geography, natural history, &c. It is a somewhat helpful work.

599 NOYES. (*See No. 579.*)

600 STUART (MOSES). A Commentary on the Book of Proverbs. 8vo. *New York*, 1852.

We have not met with any English reprint of this useful volume. *Dr. Stuart* purposely adapted his work to beginners in Hebrew study. He has set himself to prepare a commentary of explanation only, believing that a hortatory and practical comment every minister ought to be able to make for himself. *Stuart's* introductory matter is highly instructive, though no reader should blindly accept it all.

601 **TAYLOR** (FRANCIS, B.D.) Observations upon the three first chapters of Proverbs. 4to. *Lond.*, 1645.
An Exposition [as above] upon The 4, 5, 6, 7, 8, 9 Chapters, &c. 4to. 1657.
Two volumes (in one) of rich, old-fashioned Puritan divinity.

602 THOMAS (DAVID, D.D.) The Practical Philosopher. Thick 8vo. *Lond.*, Dickinson. 1873.

Dr. Thomas of the " Homilist " is a well-known writer, and a man capable of great things. This work does not equal his " Genius of the Gospel." It contains a large amount of practical comment, written in a rather grandiose style. We can hardly fancy men of business reading this book from day to day as the author proposes.

603 **WARDLAW** (RALPH, D.D.) Lectures. 3 vols., cr. 8vo. *Edinb.*, Fullarton. 1861.

Wardlaw is diffuse, and his views upon " wisdom " are peculiar; but he always repays the reader, and neither Bridges nor Arnot have rendered him obsolete, for he works a different vein, and expounds in a manner peculiar to himself.

604 WILCOCKS (THOMAS, *Puritan.* 1549—1608). A Short yet Sound Commentarie. [*Works. See No.* 336].

Wilcocks briefly sums up the teaching of the verses, and so aids in suggesting topics; in other respects he is rather wearying.

ECCLESIASTES.

605 ANNOTATIONS on the Book of Ecclesiastes. [12mo.] *Lond.* Printed by *J. Streater.* 1669.
By no means remarkable, except for extreme rarity.

606 BEZA (THEODORE). Ecclesiastes. Solomon's Sermon to the People, with an Exposition. Small 8vo. *Camb.*, [1594].
Sure to be weighty and instructive. It is exceedingly rare.

607 **BRIDGES** (CHARLES, M.A.) Exposition of Ecclesiastes. Sq. 8vo. *Lond.*, Seeley & Co. 1860.
After the manner of other works by this devout author, who is always worth consulting, though he gives us nothing very new.

608 BROUGHTON (HUGH. 1549—1612). A Comment upon Ecclesiastes, framed for the Instruction of Prince Henry. 4to. 1605.

Broughton was a far-famed and rather pretentious Hebraist whom *Dr. Gill* quoted as an authority. His work is nearly obsolete, but its loss is not a severe one.

609 **BUCHANAN** (ROBERT, D.D.) Ecclesiastes; its Meaning and its Lessons, explained and illustrated. Sq. 8vo. *Lond., Glasg.,* & *Edinb.,* Blackie & Sons. 1859.

Dr. Buchanan has endeavoured in every instance to give the true meaning of the text. His explanations were composed for the pulpit and delivered there. The work is most important, but strikes us as lacking in liveliness of style.

610 CHOHELETH, or "The Royal Preacher, a Poem." First published in the year 1768. 4to. Reprinted, 8vo., 1830.

This is the work of which *Mr. Wesley* wrote :—"Monday, Feb. 8, 1768. I met with a surprising poem, intituled Choheleth, or the Preacher: it is a paraphrase in tolerable verse on the Book of Ecclesiastes. I really think the author of it (a Turkey merchant) understands both the difficult expressions and the connection of the whole, better than any other, either ancient or modern, writer whom I have seen." We defer to *Mr. Wesley's* opinion, but it would not have occurred to us to commend so warmly.

611 COLEMAN (JOHN NOBLE, M.A.) Ecclesiastes. A New Translation, with Notes. Imp. 8vo. *Lond.,* Nisbet. 1867.

A scholarly translation with important observations.

612 COTTON (JOHN. 1585—1652). A briefe exposition, with practical observations. Small 8vo. *Lond.,* 1654. [Reprinted in Nichol's series of Commentaries. See *Muffet, No.* 596.]

By a great linguist and sound divine. Ecclesiastes is not a book to be expounded verse by verse ; but *Cotton* does it as well as anyone.

613 COX (SAMUEL). The Quest of the Chief Good : Expository Lectures. Sq. 8vo. *Lond.,* Isbister. 1868.

We should find it hard to subscribe to *Mr. Cox's* views of Ecclesiastes, for, to begin with, we cannot admit that its author was not Solomon, but some unnamed Rabbi : nevertheless, " The Quest of the Chief Good" is full of valuable matter, and abundantly repays perusal.

614 DALE (THOMAS PELHAM, M.A.) Ecclesiastes. With a running Commentary and Paraphrase. 8vo. *Lond.,* Rivingtons. 1873.

This author makes all that he can out of the errors of the Septuagint, which he seems to value almost as much as the correct text itself. The new translation is a sort of stilted paraphrase, which in a remarkable manner darkens the meaning of the wise man's words. *Mr. Dale* says he is a man of one book, and we are glad to hear it: for we should be sorry for another book to suffer at his hands.

615 DESVOEUX (A. V.) A Philosophical and Critical Essay on Ecclesiastes. 4to. *Lond.,* 1760.

A curious and elaborate production. Neither in criticism, nor in theology, is the author always sound, and his notes are a very ill-arranged mass of singular learning.

616 GINSBURG (CHRISTIAN D.) Coheleth, or Ecclesiastes ; translated, with a Commentary. 8vo. *Lond.,* Longmans. 1857.

The author does not believe that Solomon wrote the book, and his view of its design is not the usual, nor, as we think, the right one. His outline of the literature of the book is very complete.

617 GRANGER (Thomas). A Familiar Exposition, wherein the
      World's Vanity and the true Felicitie are plainly deciphered.
      4to. *Lond.*, 1621.
Very antique, containing many obsolete and coarse phrases; but
pithy and quaint.

618 GREENAWAY (Stephen). New Translation. 8vo. *Leicester*, 1781.
Confused, eccentric, and happily very rare.

619 **HAMILTON** James, D.D. (1814–1867). Royal Preacher:
      Lectures on Ecclesiastes. Cr. 8vo.   Also 12mo.,
      1851; 16mo., 1854. *Lond.*, Nisbet.
*We have had a great treat in reading this prose poem. It is a
charming production.*

620 **HENGSTENBERG** (E. W., D.D.) Commentary on
      Ecclesiastes. To which are appended : Treatises on the
      Song of Solomon ; on the Book of Job ; on the Prophet
      Isaiah, &c. 8vo.   *Edinb.*, T. & T. Clark. 1860.
*Scholarly of course, and also more vivacious than is usual with
Hengstenberg.*

621 HODGSON (Bernard, LL.D) New Translation. 4to. *Oxf.*, 1791.
Notes neither long, numerous, nor valuable.

622 HOLDEN (George, M.A.) An Attempt to illustrate the Book
      of Ecclesiastes. 8vo. *Lond.*, 1822.
Bridges says that *Holden* " stands foremost for accuracy of critical
exegesis," and *Ginsburg* considers his Commentary to be the best in our
language. We may therefore be wrong in setting so little store by it as
we do, but we are not convinced.

623 JERMIN (Michael, D.D.) Ecclesiastes. Folio. 1639.
The school to which *Jermin* belonged delighted to display their
learning, of which they had no small share ; they excelled in wise
sayings, but not in unction. The fruit is ripe, but lacks flavour.

624 **KEIL & DELITZSCH.** (See *Books of Solomon*. No. 577.)

625 **LANGE.** (See *Books of Solomon*. No. 578.)

626 LLOYD (J., M.A.) An Analysis of Ecclesiastes : with reference
      to the Hebrew Grammar of Gesenius, and with Notes ; to which
      is added the Book of Ecclesiastes, in Hebrew and English, in
      parallel columns. 4to.   *Lond.*, Bagsters. 1874.
This will be esteemed by men who have some knowledge of the
Hebrew. The repeated references to Gesenius would render the book
tedious to the ordinary reader, but they make it all the more valuable
to one who aspires to be a Hebraist.

627 [LUTHER]. An Exposition of Salomon's Booke, called Eccle-
      siastes, or the Preacher. 8vo. Printed by J. Day. *Lond.*, 1573.
Even the British Museum authorities have been unable to find this
octavo for us, though it is mentioned in their catalogue.

628 **MACDONALD** (James M., D.D. *Princeton, N. J.*)
Ecclesiastes. Thick 12mo. *New York.* 1856.
Thoroughly exegetical, with excellent " scopes of argument" following each division : to be purchased if it can be met with.

629 MORGAN (A. A.) Ecclesiastes metrically Paraphrased, with
Illustrations. 4to. *Lond.,* Bosworth. 1856.
This is an *article de luxe*, and is rather for the drawing-room than for
the study. A graphic pencil, first-class typography, and a carefully
written metrical translation make up an elegant work of art.

630 MYLNE (G. W.) Ecclesiastes ; or, Lessons for the Christian's
Daily Walk. 16mo. *Lond.,* 1859.
The author in this little publication does not comment upon the
whole Book ; but the passages he touches are ably explained.

631 NISBET (Alexander. *Died about* 1658). An Exposition, with
Practical Observations. 4to. *Edinb.,* 1694.
One of those solid works which learned Scotch divines of the seven
teenth century have left us in considerable numbers. In our judgment
it is as heavy as it is weighty.

632 NOYES. (*See No.* 579).

633 PEMBLE (William, M.A 1591—1623). Salomon's Recantation and Repentance ; or, the Book of Ecclesiastes briefly and
fully explained. Thin 4to. *Lond.,* 1628.
Anthony à Wood calls *Pemble* " a famous preacher, a skilful linguist,
a good orator, and an ornament to society." Moreover, he was a learned
Calvinistic divine. This " Recantation " is a minor production. The
style is scholastic, with arrangements of the subjects such as render it
hard to read. We confess we are disappointed with it.

634 PRESTON (Theodore, M.A.) A translation of the Commentary
of Mendelssohn from the Rabbinic Hebrew; also a newly-
arranged English Version. 8vo. *Lond.,* 1845.
A book more prized by linguists than by preachers. We might with
propriety have named this *Mendelssohn's* Commentary, for so it is.

635 PROBY (W. H. B., M.A.) Ecclesiastes for English Readers. Thin 8vo.
Lond., Rivingtons. 1874.
About 45 pages, and these are quite enough. What has come to a man's brain
when he prophecies that Antichrist will take away the daily sacrifice, that is, "forbid
the eucharistic bread and wine," and then adds: "To this awful time there is probably
a mystical reference in the words of our present book (XII. 6), 'While the silver cord
is not loosed, or the golden bowl broken, or the pitcher broken at the fountain, or the
wheel broken at the cistern.' For *silver* and *gold* signify respectively, in the symbolic
language of Scripture, *love* and *truth*: thus the loosening of the silver cord will mean
the love of many waxing cold, and the breaking of the golden bowl will mean the
failure of truth from the earth ; and we understand, then, that in the last awful time
there will be no longer any speaking of the truth in love. And as the 'wells of salvation' in Isaiah XII. 3, are the sacraments and other means of grace, so the breaking
of the pitcher and the wheel may signify the cessation of those ministries by which
the sacraments and other means of grace are dispensed."

636   REYNOLDS (Edward, D.D. *Bishop of Norwich.* 1599—1676).
       Annotations. *Works.* Vol. IV. 8vo. *Lond.,* 1826. Reprinted,
       by Dr. Washburn. 8vo. *Lond.,* 1811.
   See Westminster Assembly's Annotations (*No.* 2), for which *Reynolds*
wrote this : he is always good.

637   SERRANUS, or, DE SERRES (John. 1540—1598). A Godlie and
       Learned Commentary upon Ecclesiastes, newly turned into English, by
       John Stockwood, Schoolmaster of Tunbridge. 8vo. *Lond.,* 1585.
   Serranus was a Protestant pastor at Nismes, of such moderate opinions, and such
objectionable modes of stating them, that he was about equally abhorred by Romanists
and Protestants. He is said to have been very inaccurate in his learning.

638   **STUART** (Moses). A Commentary on Ecclesiastes.
       12mo.   *New York.,* 1851.
   *Full and minute, with most instructive introductions. It is
unnecessary to say that Moses Stuart is a great authority, though
not all we could wish as to spirituality.*

639   TYLER (Thomas, M.A.) Ecclesiastes ; a Contribution to its Interpretation.
       8vo.   *Lond.,* Williams & Norgate. 1875.
   This writer is no doubt a profound thinker, but we do not set much store by the
result of his thinkings. He maintains that the writer of Ecclesiastes was a Jew who
had travelled abroad, and heard the Stoic philosophers and their opponents at
Athens. He seems to think that his point is proved, but it is the merest surmise
possible. The work is not at all to our taste.

640   **WARDLAW** (Ralph, D.D.) Lectures on Ecclesiastes.
       2 vols., 8vo. 1821. 2 vols., 12mo. 1838. Oliphant & Co.'s
       edition, in 1 vol.,   1871.
   *Wardlaw is always good, though not very brilliant. He may be
relied upon, when not critical, and he generally excites thought.*

641   WEISS (Benjamin). New Translation and Exposition, with
       Critical Notes. 12mo.   *Lond.,* Nisbet & Co. 1856.
   It is pleasing to find a converted Jew engaged upon this Book. *Mr.
Weiss* says many good things, but frequently his interpretations and
remarks are more singular than wise.

642   YCARD (Fr. *Dean of Achonry*). Paraphrase. 8vo. *Lond.,* 1701.
   The dean supposes the Royal Preacher to have been interrupted by an impudent
sensualist, and so he gets rid of the difficulty of certain passages by putting them into
the scoffer's mouth. The theory is not to be tolerated for a moment.

643   **YOUNG** (Loyal, D.D.) Commentary, with introductory
       Notices by McGill and Jacobus. 8vo. *Philadelphia,* 1865.
   *This American comment is highly spoken of by eminent judges,
and appears to have been carefully executed. It is able and solid,
and at the same time enlivened with originality of thought, vivacity
of expression, and practical pungency.*

644   SMITH (John, M.D., M.R.C.P.L.) King Solomon's Portraiture
       of Old Age, wherein is contained A Sacred Anatomy both of
       Soul and Body, with an account of all these Mystical and

Ænigmatical Symptomes, expressed in the six former verses of the 12th Chap. of Ecclesiastes, made plain and easie to a mean Capacitie. 8vo. *Lond.*, 1666.

A curious book by a Physician, who brings his anatomical knowledge to bear upon the twelfth chapter of Ecclesiastes, and tries to show that Solomon understood the circulation of the blood, &c. *Matthew Poole* introduced the substance of this treatise into his *Synopsis*, and in that huge compilation he speaks eulogistically of the author, with whom he resided. We mention it because of its singularity.

SONG OF SOLOMON.

645 AINSWORTH. (See under *Pentateuch*, No. 72).

646 AVRILLON (JOHN BAPTIST ELIAS. 1652—1729). The Year of Affections; or, Sentiments on the love of God, drawn from the Canticles, for every day of the year. Fcap. 8vo. *Lond.* and *Oxf.*, Parker & Co. 1847.

One of the series of Romish authors, issued by *Dr. Pusey*. It is a deeply spiritual work, after the manner of the mystics. It might have been written by *Madame Guyon*. Despite its occasional Popery and sacramentarianism, it contains much choice devotional matter.

647 **BEZA** (THEODORE). Sermons upon the three first chapters of Canticles, translated out of the French, by John Harmar. 4to. *Oxf.*, 1587.

These thirty-one sermons are a well of instruction, very precious and refreshing. The unabbreviated title indicates a controversial use of the Song, and we were therefore prepared to lament the invasion of the dove's nest of the Canticles by the eagle of debate; but we were agreeably disappointed, for we found much less of argument, and much more of the Well-Beloved, than we looked for.

648 BEVERLEY (T.) An Exposition of the Divinely prophetick Song of Songs, which is Solomon's; beginning with the reign of David, and ending in the glorious Kingdom of our Lord Jesus Christ. 4to. 1687.

This maundering author finds in Canticles the history of the church from David to our Lord, and rhymes no end of rubbish thereon. Truly there is no end to the foolishness of expositors. We suppose there must be a public for which they cater, and a very foolish public it must be.

649 BRIGHTMAN (THOMAS). A Commentary on the Canticles, wherein the Text is Analised, the Native Signification of the Words Declared, the Allegories Explained, and the Order of Times whereunto they relate Observed. 4to. *Lond.*, 1644. [See under *Daniel* and *Revelation*.]

Brightman was a writer of high renown among the prophetic students of the seventeenth century. With singular strength of the visionary faculties he sees in the Canticles "the whole condition of the church from the time of David, till time shall be no more." Expounding on this theory needs an acrobatic imagination.

650 **BURROWES** (George. *Prof. Lafayette Coll. U.S.)*
      Commentary. Cr. 8vo. *Philadelphia,* 1853.

*Mr. Moody Stuart says :—" The excellent work of Dr. Burrowes
is specially fitted to remove the prejudices of men of taste against the
Song of Solomon, as the medium of spiritual communion between
the soul and Christ. We welcome it as a valuable contribution to
us from our transatlantic brethren."*

651 BUSH (Joseph, M.A.) The Canticles of the Song of Solomon.
      A Metrical Paraphrase, with Explanatory Notes and Practical
      Comments. Post 8vo. *Lond.,* Hatchards. 1867.

A good compilation, with a helpful translation. For popular use.

652 CLAPHAM (Enoch). Salomon; his Songs expounded. 4to. *Lond.,* 1603.
      Clapham was a voluminous author of very remarkable attainments. He wrote also
on the first fourteen chapters of Genesis. This work is rare as angels' visits.

653 **COLLINGES** (John, D.D. 1623—1690). The Inter-
      courses of Divine Love betwixt Christ and his Church,
      metaphorically expressed by Solomon in Canticles I. and
      II. 2 vols., 4to. *Lond.,* 1676.

*Nine hundred and nine quarto pages upon one chapter is more
than enough. The materials are gathered from many sources
and make up a mass of wealth. On the second chapter there are
five hundred and thirty pages. It would try the constitutions of
many modern divines to read what these Puritans found it a
pleasure to write. When shall we see their like?*

654 COTTON (John, B.D. 1585—1652). A Brief Exposition, describing the
      estate of the Church in all ages thereof, both Jewish and Christian, and
      modestly pointing at the gloriousness of the restored estate thereof. 8vo.
      Lond., 1642. [Reprinted in Nichol's Series. See *Muffet, No.* 596.]
      Cotton explains the sacred love-song historically, and misses much of its sweetness
by so doing. We should never care to read his exposition while *Durham,* and *Gill,*
and *Moody Stuart* are to be had.

655 DAVIDSON (William, Esq.) A Brief outline of an Examina-
      tion of the Song of Solomon. 8vo. *Lond.,* 1817.

A precious work by one whose heart is warm with the good matter.
He sees in the Song the history of the Church of Christ.

656 DOVE (John, D.D.) The Conversion of Solomon, a Direction to holiness of
      Life ; handled by way of Commentarie upon the whole Booke of Canticles.
      Profitable for young men which are not yet mortified, for old men which are
      decrepit and have one foote in the grave, and for all sorts of men which have
      an intent to renounce the vanities of this world, and to follow Jesus Christ.
      4to. *Lond.,* 1613.
      A quaint old work. The student will do better with the moderns. Moreover, this
Dove is rare, and seldom lights on poor men's shelves.

657 **DURHAM** (James. 1622—1658). Clavis Cantici ; or,
      an Exposition of the Song of Solomon. 4to. *Lond.,*
      1668 and 1723. Also 12mo., *Aberdeen.* 1840.

Durham is always good, and he is at his best upon the Canticles.

He gives us the essence of the good matter. For practical use this work is perhaps more valuable than any other Key to the Song.

658 FENNER (DUDLEY). The Song of Solomon, in Verse, with an Exposition. *Middleburgh.* 8vo. 1587. 4to.

Moody Stuart says:—" This is a faithful and excellent translation, accompanied by an admirable exposition. There is no poetry in it, but the renderings are often good, and the comment valuable." We have not met with it.

659 FLEMING (ROBERT. *Died* 1716). The Mirrour of Divine Love unvail'd, in a Poetical Paraphrase of the Song of Solomon. Sm. 8vo. 1691.

The *poetry* is after the same manner as that of *Quarles*, and though not without merit, it is too antiquated to be admired in the present day. This is the *Fleming* who interpreted the Apocalyptic vials, and was fortunate enough to hit upon the date of the French revolution and other events connected with the decline of the Papal power. His prophetic work has been reprinted, but not this limping poetry.

660 FRANCIS (ANN. *Died* 1800). A Poetical Translation ; with Notes, Historical, Critical, and Explanatory. 4to. *Lond.*, 1781.

Framed on a fanciful theory. Verses flowing and feeble. Insignificant.

661 FRY (JOHN, A.B.) New Translation, with Notes, and an attempt to interpret the sacred allegories. 8vo. *Lond.*, 1811.

Fry's work may be called the supplement and complement of *Dr. Good's.* He divides the Songs into idyls, and gives notes in the same manner as *Good;* but he also plunges into the spiritual meaning of the blessed Song, and so far is to be preferred.

662 GIFFORD (MR.) A Dissertation on the Song of Solomon. 8vo. *Lond.*, 1751.

Worthless rhymes. This man dares to say that the Song is a pastoral, composed by Solomon for the amusement of his lighter hours, before God had given him the divine wisdom for which he was afterwards so eminent.

663 **GILL** (JOHN, D.D.) An Exposition of the Book of Solomon's Song. Folio. *Lond.*, 1728. Not contained in the author's Exposition of the Old and New Testament. An 8vo. edition was published by Collingridge, *Lond.*, 1854.

The best thing Gill ever did. He could not exhaust his theme, but he went as far as he could towards so doing. He is occasionally fanciful, but his work is precious. Those who despise it have never read it, or are incapable of elevated spiritual feelings.

664 GINSBURG (CHRISTIAN D.) A Translation, with a Commentary, Historical and Critical. 8vo. *Lond.*, Longmans. 1857.

Written upon an untenable theory, viz., that the Song is intended "to record an example of virtue in a young woman, who encountered and conquered the greatest temptations, and was eventually rewarded." This grovelling interpretation needed the aid of great liberties with the text, and a few interpolations, and the author has not hesitated to use them. However learned the book may be, this vicious theory neutralizes all.

665 GOOD (JOHN MASON, M.D., F.R.S.) Song of Songs ; or, Sacred Idyls translated ; with Notes, Critical and Explanatory. 8vo. *Lond*, 1803.

By a man of great learning. It is not at all spiritual, or even expository, in the theological sense, but treats the Canticles as an Oriental drama, explaining its scenery and metaphors from a literary point of view.

666   GREEN (WILLIAM, M.A.) Song of Solomon. In "The Poetical Parts of
        the Old Testament translated, with Notes." 4to. 1781.

Critical only. *Orme* says, "the translations are in general very accurate and elegant
specimens of biblical interpretation."

667   GUILD (WILLIAM, D.D. 1586—1657). Love's Intercourse
        between the Lamb and his Bride. 8vo. *Lond.*, 1658.

A rare old work : but we prefer *Durham.* The author was one of
the better sort of the Scotch Episcopalians.

668   GYFFARD (GEORGE). Fifteen Sermons upon the Song of
        Solomon. 8vo. 1598 to 1612.

We have several times met with this writer's name coupled with that
of *Brightman* as in his day regarded as a very learned writer, but we
cannot procure his work. Possibly some reader of this Catalogue may
yet present us with it. We beg to assure him of the gratitude which we
already feel, in the form of "a lively sense of favours to come."

669   HARMER (THOMAS. 1715—1788). Outlines of a New Com-
        mentary on Solomon's Song, drawn by the help of instructions
        from the East. 8vo. *Lond.*, 1768.

"This book is not well arranged, but is otherwise one of the most
ingenious, modest, and interesting of all the treatises on the outward
sense of the Song."—*Moody Stuart.*

670   **HENGSTENBERG.** (See under *Ecclesiastes*, No. 620.)

671   HODGSON (BERNARD, LL.D.) Solomon's Song translated from
        the Hebrew. 4to. *Oxf.*, 1786.

Moody Stuart says that this is "a good translation," and therefore
we suppose it is so, but we do not admire it. It does not even refer to
the mystical sense, and it mars the poetry of the Song. *Dr. Hodgson*
renders ch. vi. ver. 9:—" My pigeon, my undefiled is but one." This is
an alteration, but certainly not an emendation. The name of the bride's
mother he discovers to have been Talmadni. Wonderful !

672   HOMES (NATHANIEL. *Died* 1678). A Commentary on the
        Canticles. *Works.* Folio. 1652.

This goes to the very marrow of spiritual teaching, and uses every
word and syllable in a deeply experimental manner with great unction
and power. *Homes,* however, spiritualizes too much, and is both too
luscious in expression and too prolix for these degenerate days.

673   HOUGHTON (WM.) Translation. 8vo.   *Lond.*, Trübner. 1865.
Useless. The Song is viewed as a secular poem on chaste love.

674   IBN EZRA (ABRAHAM). Commentary on the Canticles, after the first
        recension. Edited from two MSS., with a Translation, by H. J. Matthews,
        B.A. 12mo. *Lond.*, Trübner & Co. 1874.
The original Hebrew of the Song, with a Jewish comment, which conveys but little
instruction. In this small book the student will have a specimen of Jewish exposition.

675   **IRONS** (JOSEPH, *of Camberwell.* 1786—1852). Nymphas.
        A Paraphrastic Exposition. 16mo. *Lond.*, 1844.
Outside of his own circle we fear that this work by the late

Joseph Irons is little known. It is a paraphrase in blank verse, rendered in a very spiritual manner. We confess that we look upon the little book with admiring eyes, though we know that the critics will sneer both at us and it.

676 **KEIL & DELITZSCH.** (See *Books of Solomon, No. 577.*)

677 KRUMMACHER (F. W., D.D.) Solomon and the Shulamite. Sermons on the Book of Canticles. 16mo. *Lond.,*1838.
Touches only upon a few portions. Short and sweet.

678 **LANGE.** (See *Books of Solomon, No. 578.*)

679 LITTLEDALE (R. F.) A Commentary. From Ancient and Mediæval Sources. 12mo. *Lond.,*J.Masters. 1869. S. 4/6.
Littledale is a close follower of *John Mason Neale*, and here reproduces the beauties and the deformities of mediæval spiritualizing. Great judgment will be needed to extract the good and true from the mass of semi-popish comment here heaped together. If discretion be used, jewels of silver and jewels of gold may be extracted.

680 MACPHERSON (PETER, A.M.) The Song of Songs shown to be constructed on Architectural Principles. Post 8vo. *Edinb.*, 1856.
"His supposition that this song consists of verses written round an archway, is so entirely gratuitous, that it is only misguiding and deceptive."—*A. Moody Stuart.*

681 **METRICAL MEDITATIONS** on the Canticles. [Anon.] 16mo. *Lond.,* Wertheim. 1856.
Exceedingly well rendered: noteworthy both from a literary and religious point of view. The author seizes the meaning of the Song, and repeats it in well-chosen words.

682 MILLER (ANDREW). Meditations. 12mo. *Lond.,* Morrish.
First published in the Plymouthite magazine, "Things New and Old." Devotional, and glowing with the light of fellowship with Jesus.

683 **MOORE** (DANIEL, M.A.) Christ and his Church. A Course of Lent Lectures on the Song of Solomon. Sm. cr. 8vo. *Lond.,* H. S. King & Co. 1875.
These lectures treat upon the first chapter only, but they do so in an admirable manner. Moore has evangelized Littledale.

684 [NEALE (JOHN MASON, D.D.)] Sermons on the Canticles, preached in a Religious House. By a Priest of the Church of England. 12mo. *Lond.,* Masters. 1857.
By that highest of high churchmen, *Dr. Neale.* These sermons smell of Popery, yet the savour of our Lord's good ointment cannot be hid. Our Protestantism is not of so questionable a character that we are afraid to do justice to Papists and Anglicans, and therefore we do not hesitate to say that many a devout thought has come to us while reading these "sermons by a Priest of the Church of England."

685   NEWTON (ADELAIDE L.)   The Song of Solomon compared with
        other parts of Scripture.   Cr. 8vo.   *Lond.*, Nisbet.   1871.
        [The earlier editions were published anonymously.]
Miss Newton's book is very dear to spiritual minds ; it is full of that
quiet power which comes from the Spirit of God through deep experience
and precious fellowship with the Well-Beloved.

686   NOYES.   (*See No.* 579.)
This author sees in the Canticles nothing but a collection of amatory
songs, written without express moral or religious design.   Blind !

687   PERCY (THOMAS, D.D.   *Bishop of Dromore.*   1729—1811).   New Transla-
        tion : with a Commentary and Annotations. [Anon.] 8vo. *Lond.*, 1764.
 His theory of the sacred Song is dead, and not worthy of a monument in our pages.
We trust that not a *relic* will remain.   *Percy* did very well with his ballads, but he had
better have let the Song of Songs alone.

688   POWER   (PHILIP BENNET, M.A.)   Failure   and   Discipline :
        Thoughts on Canticles V.   16mo.   *Lond.*, Wertheim.
Upon the fifth chapter only.   *Mr. Power* always writes attractively.
His book is "linked sweetness," but not "long drawn out."

689   REFLECTIONS ON CANTICLES ; or, the Song of Solomon,
        with Illustrations from Modern Travellers and Naturalists.
        [Anon.] 12mo. *Lond.*, S. W. Partridge & Co.   1870.
Has much sweetness, and a fair measure of freshness.

690   ROBOTHAM (JOHN).   Exposition. 4to. *Lond.*, 1652.
Very solid ; but not to be compared with *Durham, No.* 657.   It is
just a little dull and commonplace.

691   ROMAINE (WILLIAM, M.A.)   Discourses upon Solomon's Song.
        8vo.   *Lond.*, 1789.
Twelve excellent sermons from verses taken out of the Song.   They
do not summarize the book, nor form a commentary, but are simply a
selection of spiritual discourses by one of the most eminent Calvinistic
divines of the last century.

692   **SIBBES** (RICHARD, D.D.   1577—1635).   Bowels Opened ;
        or, a Discovery of the Neere and Deere Love, Union and
        Communion betwixt Christ and the Church.   Sermons
        on Canticles IV., V., and VI.   4to.   1639, etc.
        [*Works II.* Nichol's edition.]
*Sibbes never writes ill.   His repute is such that we need only
mention him.   His title is most unfortunate, but in all else his
" discovery " is worthy of our commendation.*

693   SKINNER (JOHN.   *Bishop of Aberdeen.*   1721—1806).   Essay towards a literal
        or true radical Exposition.   *Works II.* 2 vols., 8vo. *Aberdeen*, 1809.
    Not very important.   The Bishop closes his exposition with the following prayer
for those who do not believe in the mystical sense :—" God forgive the fools and open
their eyes."   Pretty strong for a Bishop !

694 **STUART** (A. Moody, M.A.) Exposition, with Critical Notes. 8vo. *Lond.*, Nisbet 1860.

Although this admirable author expounds the Song upon a theory which we do not quite endorse, we do not know where to find a book of equal value in all respects. He has poetry in his soul, and, beyond that, a heart like that of Rutherford, fired with love to the Altogether Lovely One. We thank him for this noble volume.

695 THE BRIDE OF CHRIST; or, Explanatory Notes on the Song of Solomon. [Anon.] 18mo. *Lond.*, Seeleys. 1861.

A little book for general use; not for students.

696 THE THREEFOLD MYSTERY : Hints on the Song of Songs, viewed as a Prophecy of the Double United Church of Jew and Gentile. By the author of "The Gathered Lily." 12mo. *Lond.*, Partridge & Co. 1869.

It seems to us to be a wild fancy that all ecclesiastical history is condensed into the Canticles ; hence we do not value this book.

697 **THRUPP** (John Francis). New Translation, with Commentary. Cr. 8vo. *Lond.*, Macmillan. 1862.

We are highly pleased with this work. It defends the usual Christian interpretation by the conclusions of sober criticism, and shows that the spiritual sense is confirmed by the investigations of modern scholarship. In the introduction the author deals heavy blows at the sceptical school, and at those who, like Ginsburg, content themselves with imputing a merely moral meaning to the blessed Canticle of love.

698 WEISS (Benjamin). The Song of Songs unveiled : a New Translation and Exposition. Cr. 8vo. W. Oliphant & Co. 1859.

This author believes that the Song sets forth the history of Israel and her relation to the Covenant Angel from Horeb to Calvary. Beyond a few Eastern illustrations, nothing of value is contributed to existing materials. The work is thoroughly evangelical.

699 WILCOCKS (Thomas). Exposition. *Works.* Folio. 1624.

Short, and somewhat in the manner of a paraphrase. This venerable author gives a doctrinal summary of each verse, and from this we have frequently been directed to a subject of discourse.

700 WILLIAMS (Thomas). A New Translation, with a Commentary and Notes. 8vo. *Lond.*, 1801. Second edition, 1828.

This volume is little known, but its value is above the average of Canticles literature. We have read many of the remarks with pleasure, but most of them are to be found in the standard commentaries.

701 WOODFORD (Samuel, D.D.) Paraphrase in Verse. 8vo. 1679.

Better than many poetical paraphrases, but still below the mark of true poetry.

702 WRIGHT (M.) The Beauty of the Word in the Song of Solomon. Cr. 8vo. *Lond.*, Nisbet & Co. 1872.

A purely spiritual commentary, casting no light upon the text, but drawing much from it. More devotional than expository. The figures of the allegory are pressed as far as they should be, perhaps further.

WORKS ON PROPHECY.

[Volumes upon this subject are so extremely numerous and so varied in their opinions that we confine ourselves to the few which follow. The reader is also referred to works upon the Apocalypse.]

703 **DAVISON** (JOHN, B.D. 1777—1834). Discourses on Prophecy ; its Structure, Use, and Inspiration. [*Warburtonian Lectures.*] 8vo. *Oxf.*, 1845.

Elliott calls this "Davison's noble Work on Prophecy." This is one of the Warburtonian lectures, and we would here note that those lectures are all upon prophecy, and are many of them by first-class men, and therefore worthy of study. Of course they greatly vary in value according to the ability of the lecturers.

704 FABER (GEORGE STANLEY, B.D. 1773—1854). Calendar of Prophecy, or a Dissertation on the Prophecies which treat of the Seven Times, and especially of the latter Three Times and a Half. 3 vols., 8vo. *Lond.*, 1828.   12mo. editions,

Faber is one of the great rabbis of prophecy. He was a man of almost boundless learning and industry. His characteristics are said to have been "strong masculine sense, extensive classical erudition, and *a hearty love of hypothesis.*" This last quality, no doubt, led him to expound prophecy, and also disqualified him for doing it well.

705 **FAIRBAIRN** (PATRICK, D.D.) Prophecy: its Distinctive Nature, Special Functions, and Proper Interpretation. 8vo.   *Edinb.*, T. & T. Clark. 1856.

A standard work by one who is at home with the subject.

706 FLEMING (ROBERT. 1630—1694). The Fulfilling of the Scripture. Fifth edition. Folio. *Lond.*, 1726,   2 vols., 8vo., 1801,   2 vols., 12mo., 1845,

This we mention because it is generally placed under this head, but it is not an exposition of prophecy at all. It is an elaborate treatise upon the fact that the Scriptures are fulfilled, and the word of the Lord is true. As such it deserves the high encomiums so freely showered upon it by the eminent divines of *Fleming's* own time, and it abundantly justifies the issue of so many editions.

707 **HENGSTENBERG** (E. W.) The Messianic Prophecies of Isaiah and the other Prophets.

These remarks are contained in Hengstenberg's Christology, which is a standard work on the subject. (See No. 67.)

708 **KEITH** (ALEXANDER, D.D.) Evidence of the Truth of the Christian Religion, derived from the literal Fulfilment of Prophecy ; as illustrated by the History of the Jews, and by the Discoveries of recent Travellers. Thirty-sixth edition. Thick 8vo. 1848.

Horne says, "The multiplied editions which have been required

within a very few years sufficiently attest the high estimation in which Mr. Keith's work is deservedly held;" and we may add that the improvements and additions have increased its value, and that fresh editions have shown that it is still appreciated.

709 **NEWTON** (THOMAS, D.D., *Bp. of Bristol.* 1704—1782). Dissertations on the Prophecies which have been fulfilled, and are fulfilling. Numerous editions. 2 and 3 vols., 8vo. Also, 1 vol., 8vo. *Lond.*, W. Tegg.

A standard work of a laborious and learned author; rather laborious reading. The Bishop must not be trusted upon the New Testament prophecy. Theologically his standing is very dubious.

THE PROPHETS.

710 **KITTO** (JOHN, D.D.) "Isaiah and the Prophets." In *Daily Bible Illustrations.* (See No. 41).
Should be consulted wherever the readings touch upon a passage.

711 LOWTH (BISHOP) and others. A Literal Translation of the Prophets from Isaiah to Malachi, with Notes by Lowth, Blayney, Newcome, &c. 5 vols. 8vo. *Lond.*, 1836.
Concerning each of the five volumes we refer the reader to our notices under the separate books.

712 LOWTH (WILLIAM, B.D., 1661—1732, *Father of Bp. Lowth*). Commentary on the Prophets. 4 vols. 4to. *Lond.*, 1714.
This is *Lowth's* part of *Patrick* (*No.* 50). He was more spiritual than those with whom he became associated, which is not saying much.

713 NOYES (GEORGE R., D.D.). A New Translation of the Hebrew Prophets. 3 vols., 12mo. *New York*, 1849.
We are bound to commend this author's learning, taste, and candour, even though we differ widely from him. The reader must not look for savour or spiritual quickening, but use the work as a literary help only.

714 WILLIAMS (ROWLAND, D.D.) The Hebrew Prophets during the Assyrian and Babylonian Empires. Translated afresh from the Original, with Illustrations. 2 vols., 8vo. *Lond.*, Williams & Norgate. 1866—71.
The author does not admit that there are references to the Messiah in the Prophets. Whatever he may have written, this fatal error deprives it of value. A man writing in that fashion should have been a rabbi in the synagogue, and not a minister among professed Christians.

ISAIAH.

715 **ALEXANDER** (JOSEPH ADDISON). Prophecies of Isaiah, earlier and later. 2 volumes in one. $8.95. Zondervan.
Dr. Hodge says of the author: "I regard Dr. Joseph Addison

Alexander as incomparably the greatest man I ever knew—as incomparably the greatest man our Church has ever produced." He wastes no space, but gives the essence of exposition.

716 **ALEXANDER** (JOSEPH ADDISON). Isaiah Translated and Explained. An Abridgment of the preceding. 2 vols. 12mo. *New York*, 1858.

This abridgment of the larger work is by no means a small affair. For all ordinary purposes it is voluminous enough. We cannot too strongly recommend it.

717 **BARNES** (ALBERT). Notes on Isaiah. Enlarged Type Edition, edited by Robert Frew, 2 volumes. $7.00 Baker.

A good popular exposition, though not the most learned.

718 BIRKS (T. R., M.A.) Commentary on Isaiah, and a revised Translation. 8vo. *Lond.*, Rivingtons. 1871.

Written for the *Speaker's Commentary*, and, though not inserted therein, it strikes us as being far superior to that work. It is a great treasure to the student of this much neglected prophet.

719 CALVIN (JOHN). Commentarie on Isaiah. Translated by C. Cotton. Folio. *Lond.*, 1609.

The translation of the Calvin Translation Society will be better.

720 CHEYNE (T. K., M.A.) The Book of Isaiah chronologically arranged. An Amended Version. Cr. 8vo. *Lond.*, Macmillan & Co. 1870.

We do not as a rule believe in these re-arrangements; the book of Isaiah is best as we have it. The tone of the interpretation in this instance is not such as we can delight in; what the evangelical teacher has a right to expect is totally absent. The work is of the Broad School; the notes are, however, learned and somewhat suggestive.

721 ,, ,, Notes and Criticisms on the Hebrew Text of Isaiah. Cr. 8vo. *Lond.*, Macmillan & Co.

The *Westminster Review* speaks of it as "a piece of scholarly work, very carefully and considerately done." It may be so.

722 **COWLES** (HENRY, D.D.) Isaiah, with Notes. 12mo. *New York*, D. Appleton & Co. 1869.

Cowles writes more popularly than Alexander, and, though he is not so profound an authority, we have read him with pleasure.

723 DAY (WILLIAM). An Exposition of the Book of Isaiah. Folio. 1654.

Day does not throw much light upon the text: he says he wrote for his children, and certainly he is childish enough.

724 DELITZSCH (FRANZ.) Biblical Commentary on Isaiah. 2 vols. $7.00. Eerdmans.

"The author has long been honourably distinguished among the scholars of Germany. He occupies, indeed, a position always peculiar to himself; for, whilst his attainments in Hebrew philology and Talmudical lore are of the highest order, he unites with these a genuine appreciation of evangelical truth and godliness." So says the *Literary Churchman*. For our own part, we are not enraptured with *Delitzsch*.

725 EWALD (H.) The Prophet Isaiah. Chapters I.—XXXIII. From the German. By Octavius Glover. Cr. 8vo. *Lond.*, Bell & Sons. 1869.
Decidedly sceptical; but yet it may be useful as leading the reader to appreciate the poetic beauty of the book. Question if the good to be gained equals the risk incurred. Our verdict is to the contrary.

726 FRASER (ALEXANDER). Paraphrase with Notes. 8vo. *Edinb.*, 1800.
Of very small value.

727 GALLOWAY (WILLIAM BROWN, M.A.) Isaiah's Testimony for Jesus. A Series of Discourses. 8vo. *Lond.*, G. Bell & Sons. 1864.
A congregation which would listen to such lectures as these must be a very select one indeed. The writer goes most thoroughly and learnedly into his subject.

728 HENDERSON (EBENEZER, D.D.) Isaiah, translated from the Hebrew; with a Commentary. 8vo. 1840. Second and best edition. 1857. *Scarce*
The author has given no doctrinal or practical observations, as he conceived that others had furnished these in abundance; he has confined himself to eliciting the real meaning of the words, and has thereby rendered great service to all expositors who have wit enough to make use of his critical assistance. To the less instructed reader, *Dr. Henderson's* work will appear to be dull and savourless; but to those who only need to have the language translated, and are able to supply reflections for themselves, it will be of much service.

729 GOVETT (R. JUNIOR, M.A.) Isaiah Unfulfilled. Exposition, with new Version and Critical Notes. 8vo. *Lond.*, 1841.
We have not met with this publication.

730 JENOUR (ALFRED, M.A.). The Book of Isaiah, translated, with Notes and Practical Remarks. 2 vols., 8vo. *Lond.*, 1830.
This appears to us to be a faithful translation; the commentary and practical reflections are instructive and gracious.

731 KEITH (ALEXANDER, A.M.). Isaiah as it is; or, Judah and Jerusalem the subjects of Isaiah's prophesying. Cr. 8vo. *Edinb.*, 1850.
The student will consult with benefit this valuable contribution to the explanation of a most important, but neglected book.

732 KELLY (WILLIAM). Lectures on Isaiah. *Lond.*, G. Morrish. 1871.
This eminent divine of the *Brethren* school sometimes expounds ably, but with a twist towards the peculiar dogmas of his party.

733 LOWTH (ROBERT, D.D., F.R.S., *Bp. of London.* 1710—1787). Isaiah, Translation with Notes. 8vo. Numerous editions, a modern one, 8vo. *Lond.*, W. Tegg. *See No.* 711.
Smith's Dictionary remarks that *Bp. Lowth's* incessant correction of the Hebrew text is constantly to be mistrusted. This seriously diminishes *Lowth's* value, but this is a grand work notwithstanding.

734 LYTH (JOHN, D.D.) Homiletical Treasury. 12mo.   *Lond.*, Elliot
      Stock. 1868.

This should have been to the preacher a book of the utmost value, for it consists
wholly of outlines and hints for sermons, but these are frequently poor and commonplace.   The design is superlatively practical, and had the execution been better we
should have rejoiced in it.

735 MACCULLOCH (ROBERT, D.D.) Lectures on Isaiah. 4 vols.
      8vo. *Lond.* 1791—1805.

In these days we need condensation.   This author would have been
far more valued if he had compressed his matter into one volume.   He
is good, but verbose.   Some authors toil not, but they spin ; *Macculloch*
both toils and spins.

736 MACLACHLAN (MRS., *of Maclachlan*). Notes on the unfulfilled Prophecies
      of Isaiah. [Anon.] 8vo.   *Lond.*, Nisbet. 1868.

This authoress treats Isaiah as a Jewish book only, and refers all the prophecies to
that nation.   We do not agree with her fundamental principle.

737 MANCHESTER (GEORGE MONTAGUE, DUKE OF). Short Notes on Isaiah,
      chap. V.—XII. 8vo. 1852.

We confess that we cannot enjoy the very singular style of the Duke's prelections,
but there are some who set great store by them.   We wonder why.

738 **NOYES** (G. R.) *See No.* 713.

739 STOCK (JOSEPH, M.A., *Bishop of Killalla*). Isaiah in Hebrew and English.
      With Notes. 4to. 1803.

The notes are few, but are said by the *British Critic* to be "uncommonly valuable
for their depth and acuteness."   We should not have thought so.   *Stock* alters the
renderings of *Lowth*, but seldom improves them.   We judge him to be over estimated.

740 SMITH (R. PAYNE, D.D., *Dean of Canterbury*). The Authen-
      ticity and Messianic Interpretation of the Prophecies of Isaiah
      Vindicated, in Sermons before the University of Oxford. 8vo.
      Oxf. and *Lond.*, J. H. & J. Parker. 1862.

A work which would be invaluable in a discussion with Jews.   It
meets their objections, and also those advanced by neologians, and by
the writers of *Essays and Reviews.*

741 VERNEY (LADY). Practical Thoughts on the First Forty
      Chapters of Isaiah. 8vo. *Lond.*, Nisbet. 1858.

Some sensible spiritual hints will be found in these remarks.   As an
exposition it is one of the least.

742 WHISH (J. C., M.A.) A Paraphrase of the Book of Isaiah, with
      Notes. 12mo.   *Lond.*, Seeley & Co. 1862.

Somewhat helpful.   The paraphrasing is not prolix, and it does, as
a rule, aid the reader in getting at the literal sense.   With the spiritual
teaching *Mr. Whish* has not intermeddled.

743 WHITE (SAMUEL, M.A.) Commentary on Isaiah, wherein the
      literal sense is briefly explained. 4to. *Lond.*, 1709.

This author keeps to the literal sense and is very severe upon
spiritualizers, of whose vagaries he gives specimens.   In aiming at one
excellence he misses others, and fails to see Christ where he certainly
is, thus rendering his remarks less valuable to the Christian mind.

PARTS OF ISAIAH.

[There are many works upon separate chapters of this book, but it does not fall in with our plan to go so much into detail as to enumerate them all. We thought it would be useful to our readers if we mentioned a few.]

744 MACDUFF (J. R., D.D.) " Comfort ye, Comfort ye :" God's words of comfort addressed to his Church in the last twenty-seven chapters of Isaiah. Cr. 8vo. *Lond.*, Nisbet. 1872.

Dr. Macduff translates into popular language the teachings of great expositors, and does it to perfection. For an hour's pleasant and holy reading commend us to *Dr. Macduff.*

745 **CALVERT** (THOMAS). Mel Cœli, Medulla Evangelii; or, The Prophet Isaiah's Crucifix. An Exposition of the Fifty-third Chapter of Isaiah. 4to. 1867.

Precious and practical. Just what the title would lead us to expect—marrow and fatness ; honey from the Rock, Christ Jesus.

746 **DURHAM** (JAMES). Christ Crucified ; or, the Marrow of the Gospel, holden forth in Seventy-two Sermons on Isaiah liii. Editions, folio, 4to., and 8vo.

This is marrow indeed. We need say no more: Durham is a prince among spiritual expositors.

747 MACDONOGH (T. M.) Messiah as revealed in Is. liii. Founded upon Manton (748). 12mo. *Lond.*, 1858.

This is a serving up of the next work in the form of lectures. We do not admire abridgments, and especially those which make alterations and additions ; still it is likely that many have read *Macdonogh's Manton* who might never have fallen in with *Manton's Manton.*

748 **MANTON** (THOMAS, D.D.) A Practical Exposition on the whole Fifty-third Chapter of Isaiah. 8vo. *Lond.*, 1703. Also in *Works*, Vol. III. Nichol's Puritan Series.

Manton needs no praise from us. Whatever he does is done in a style worthy of a chief among theologians. He is, however, seldom too brief, and his own bulk hinders his being read. Preachers of long sermons should take a hint from this.

749 MARGOLIOUTH (MOSES, B.A.) Six Lectures on Isaiah liii., &c. 8vo. *Lond.*, Hatchards. 1846.

Well worth a careful reading.

750 STEWART (JAMES HALDANE, M.A.) Lectures upon Isaiah LV. 12mo. *Lond.*, Hatchards. 1846.

Nine sweet evangelical discourses, in a lively, impressive style.

JEREMIAH AND LAMENTATIONS.

[We would call special attention to the volume of the *Speaker's Commentary* upon this Book. It is by *Dr. Payne Smith*, Dean of Canterbury, and deserves much praise.]

751 BLAYNEY (BENJAMIN, D.D. *Died* 1801). Jeremiah and Lamentations. New Translation, with Notes. 8vo. *Lond.*, 1836. (*See No.* 711.)

Blayney belonged to a past school of clever men, too apt to suggest new readings, and more able to appreciate literary beauties than spiritual teachings. He was a zealous follower of *Lowth*, but he lacked the fine taste and poetic genius of his master.

752 BROUGHTON (HUGH). The Lamentations of Jeremy translated. With Explications. 4vo. 1608.
Incomprehensible. One of *Broughton's* wilder pieces. It may as well die.

753 **HULL** (JOHN, D.D.) Exposition upon part of Lamentations. 4to. *Lond.*, 1618.
Full of quaintnesses. Marrowy throughout.

754 KEIL (K. F. 1754—1818). Commentary on Jeremiah and Lamentations. 2 vols. $7.00. Eerdmans.
We have already indicated the direction in which *Keil* is serviceable. For exact interpretation he is esteemed, but he is too cold and formal ever to be a favourite.

755 **LANGE'S COMMENTARY.** Jeremiah and Lamentations. By Dr. C. W. Nägelsbach. 1 vol. $3.95. Zondervan.
" *Whoever becomes possessed of this great work will have, in a comprehensive form, the results of all ancient and modern exegesis, with an apparatus criticus of surprising copiousness.*"—*British Quarterly Review.*

756 LOWTH (WILLIAM, M.A.) A Commentary on Jeremiah and Lamentations. 4to. *Lond.*, 1718. (*See Nos.* 50 and 712).
This forms a part of what is known as *Bp. Patrick's Commentary.* *Orme* says that *Lowth* is " one of the most judicious commentators on the prophets, *and he never prophesies himself.*" We wish we could say this of all writers on prophetic subjects.

757 SMITH (THORNLEY). The Prophet of Sorrow; or, Life and Times of Jeremiah. Cr. 8vo. *Edinb.*, Oliphant. 1875.
Not a commentary; but as it casts light on the character and times of the prophet it deserves a place here.

758 SWIFT (DANIEL). Zion's sufferings: an Exposition of Lamentations V. 12mo. *Lond.*, 1654.
Strong, rough, coarse. Excessively rare.

759 UDALL (John) A Commentarie upon the Lamentations of
Jeremy. [Anon.] 4to. *Lond.*, 1599.

In this extremely rare work the author has laboured after brevity, and
has given the abridgment of many discourses ; hence, to those who can
procure it, it is all the more useful.

EZEKIEL.

760 ALLEINE (William). The nine last chapters of Ezekiel unfolded. 8vo. 1679.

Very rare ; will interest interpreters of prophecy.

761 **COWLES** (Henry, D.D.) Ezekiel and Daniel ; with
Notes, Critical, Explanatory, and Practical. Thick cr. 8vo.
New York, D. Appleton & Co. 1867.

*In his own way this author is one of the most instructive of
American writers; he is clear and definite, and leaves his meaning
impressed upon the mind. His scholarship is respectable.*

762 **FAIRBAIRN** (Patrick, D.D.) Ezekiel. Exposition; with
New Translation. 8vo. *Edinb.*, T. & T. Clark. 1851.

*This exposition has passed through three editions, and has gained
for its author a high place among elucidators of difficult parts of
Scripture. Dr. Fairbairn has a cool judgment and a warm heart;
he has cast much light upon Ezekiel's wheels, and has evidently felt
the touch of the live coal, which is better still.*

763 **GREENHILL** (William, M.A. 1591–1677). Exposition
of Ezekiel. 5 vols. 4to. 1645—1667. Reprinted in a
thick imp. 8vo. volume, 1827, and now issued in Nichol's
Commentaries. *Lond.*, Nisbet. 1863.

*We always get something out of Greenhill whenever we refer to
him. He had not, of course, the critical skill of the present day,
but his spiritual insight was keen. He rather commented on a
passage than expounded it.*

764 GUTHRIE (Thomas, D.D.) The Gospel in Ezekiel.
$2.95. Zondervan.

Very little of Ezekiel, and a great many of those flowers of eloquence
which rendered *Dr. Guthrie* so famous. We can hardly regard it as
an exposition. It only dwells upon the latter part of the 36th chapter.

765 **HENDERSON** (Ebenezer, D.D.) Ezekiel. With Commentary. 8vo. *Lond.*, Hamilton. 1855.

Valuable condensed notes.

766　HENGSTENBERG (E. W., D.D.) The Prophecies of Ezekiel
　　　elucidated. Demy 8vo.　　　　　*Edinb.*, T. & T. Clark. 1869.
　　We have frequently characterised this author's writings. They are
clear, cold, and dry, like a fine moonlight night in the middle of winter.
A man needs a peculiar mind to *enjoy Hengstenberg;* but all educated
students can *profit* by him.

767　KEIL (K. F.) Ezekiel 2 volumes $7.00. Eerdmans.

768　**LANGE.** Commentaries on Ezekiel and Daniel. $4.95.
　　　Zondervan.

769　NEWCOME (WILLIAM, D.D., *Abp. of Armagh.* 1729—1800).
　　　Improved version, metrical arrangement, and explanation. 4to.
　　　Dublin, 1728. 8vo. *Lond.*, 1836, &c. (*See Lowth and others,
　　　No.* 711).
　　Dr. Fairbairn says :—" The notes are of a very brief description,
chiefly explanatory of the meanings given in the translation ; and both
the translation and the notes proceed to a large extent on the vicious
principle, very prevalent at the time, of getting rid of difficulties in the
sense by proposed emendations of the text." Yet *Newcome* showed
both learning and diligence in this improved version.

DANIEL.

770　AMNER (R.) Essay towards interpretation. 8vo. *Lond.*, 1776.
　　Written on the absurd hypothesis that the prophecies were all fulfilled before the
death of Antiochus Epiphanes.

771　AUBERLEN (CARL AUGUST, Ph.D.) The Prophecies of Daniel
　　　and the Revelation, by C. A. A. Translated by Adolphe Saphir.
　　　8vo. *Edinb.*, T. & T. Clark. 1856.
　　Not a textual commentary, but a treatise upon the mysterious prophecies. *Auberlen's* spirit is reverential and his views are evangelical,
or we should not have found *Mr. Saphir* translating it. He acknowledges his indebtedness to *Roos*, No. 799. We must leave the interpretations to be judged by those who are learned in such subjects.

772　**BARNES** (ALBERT). Notes. Enlarged Type Edition,
　　　edited by Robert Frew, 2 volumes $7.00. Baker.
　　*Dr. Wardlaw said of this work:—"I have examined the 'Notes'
of the Rev. Albert Barnes on a considerable variety of testing
passages ; and, so far as my examination has gone, I feel confident
in pronouncing them to be characterized, in no ordinary degree, by
discriminative judgment, sound theology, unostentatious learning,
practical wisdom, and evangelical piety."*

773　BIRKS (T. R., M.A.) Exposition of the first two Visions of
　　　Daniel. Fcap. 8vo.　　　　*Lond.*, Seeleys. 1845.

774 BIRKS (T. R., M.A.) The Two Later Visions of Daniel historically explained. Fcap. 8vo. *Lond.*, Seeley. 1846.

We must leave judgment upon this work and the preceding one to those skilled in prophetic interpretation.

775 BRIGHTMAN (THOMAS. *Puritan.* 1557—1607). A most comfortable Exposition of the last and most difficult part of the Prophecie of Daniel, from the 26th verse of the 11th Chapter to the end of the 12th Chapter, wherein the restoring of the Jewes and their calling to the faith of Christ after the utter overthrow of their three last enemies is set forth in live'y colours. 4to. *Lond.*, 1644.

This exposition and the author's commentary on Canticles are appended to his work on Revelation, and do not appear to have been published separately. In his title-page *Brightman* is called a *bright* and worthy man, and in the preface we are told that " he shined every way and was a *Brightman* indeed." His work is rather a curiosity than a treasure.

776 BROUGHTON (HUGH. 1549—1612). Daniel's Chaldee Visions. *Works.* Folio. *Lond.*, 1662.

This author was pedantic and eccentric, but yet a man of real learning. His works have almost disappeared. In his own day some considered him a sage and others a quack. He was a little of both.

777 **CALVIN** (JOHN). Commentaries upon Daniel. Reprint of C. T. S. edition, 2 volumes $7.00. Eerdmans. *Also in Calvin's complete works.*

778 COLEMAN (THOMAS). Decision, exemplified in Daniel. 8vo. *Lond.*, 1858.

This is by the author of " Memorials of Independent Churches." It is intended for children and is suitable for them.

779 **COWLES** (HENRY, D.D.) *See under Ezekiel, No. 761.*

780 DANIEL : Statesman and Prophet. [Anon]. 8vo. *Lond.*, Religious Tract Society. [N.D.]

A valuable popular addition to the literature of the book of Daniel. Objections to its authenticity and inspiration are met, and the assaults of infidels are made to bring out the evidences of Divine authority with all the greater clearness. We are delighted with the volume, which is beautifully got up. Every student and minister should have a copy.

781 DARBY (JOHN NELSON). Studies. *Lond.*, W. H. Broom.

The name of the writer sufficiently indicates the character of the book.

782 DESPREZ (PHILIP S., B.D.) Daniel ; or, the Apocalypse of the Old Testament. 8vo. *Lond.*, Williams & Norgate. 1865.

This work is of the *Essays and Reviews* school. The author cannot see the Messiah in Daniel. It is worse than useless.

783 **ELLIOTT** (E. B.) *See under Revelation.*

784 FRERE (JAMES HATLEY, Esq.) A Combined View of the Prophecies of Daniel, Ezra, and St. John. 8vo. *Lond.*, 1826.

This has been esteemed by many in its day, but we do not recommend its purchase.

785 **GAUSSEN** (S. R. LOUIS). Daniel, explained for Young Persons. 2 vols. 8vo. *Lond.*, J. & C. Mozley. 1874.

This is a work for children only. We hope it will not set our Sunday School teachers explaining to their little ones the image and its toes, the he-goat, and all the other marvels. If they do attempt it we wish them as well through their task as Professor Gaussen.

786 **HARRISON** (BENJAMIN, M.A., *Archdeacon of Maidstone*). Prophetic Outlines of the Christian Church and the Antichristian Power, as traced in the Visions of Daniel and St. John. [*Warburtonian Lectures.*] 8vo. 1849.

We like the manner of this book. The author has been content throughout to trace the true outline of interpretation without entering on a detailed examination of counter theories; and he has done this in the spirit of Bishop Ridley, who said upon a kindred subject, "Sir, in these matters I am so fearful, that I dare not speak further than the very text doth, as it were, lead me by the hand."

787 HENGSTENBERG (E. W.) Dissertations on the Genuineness of Daniel and the Integrity of Zachariah. 8vo. *Edinb.*, T. & T. Clark. 1848.

Much valuable matter is brought out by the discussion ; but few of us have time to go into it, or any need to do so ; for we are fully persuaded of the integrity of all the prophets, and of their books too.

788 HUIT (EPHRAIM. *Puritan*). The whole Prophecie of Daniel Explained. 4to. *Lond.,* 1643.

Huit's short doctrinal summaries of the verses will bring useful subjects before the preacher's mind ; otherwise *Huit* is not very remarkable.

789 IRVING (EDWARD, M.A. 1792—1834). Babylon and Infidelity foredoomed of God ; A Discourse on Daniel and the Apocalypse. 2 vols., 12mo. *Glasg*, 1826 ; also one vol. 8vo.

More of rolling sound than anything else.

790 **KEIL** (K. F.) Commentary on the Book of Daniel. $3.50. Eerdmans.

" We have just had occasion to make ourselves acquainted with Keil's book on Daniel, and we can speak of it in very high terms. It is marked by great erudition, rare accuracy, and much spiritual thoughtfulness."—Evangelical Magazine.

791 KELLY (WILLAM). Notes. 12mo. *Lond.*, Morrish. 1870.

It needs minds of a peculiar organization to enjoy Plymouth writings. They abound in peculiar phraseology, which only the initiated can understand. We are sorry to see such a mind as Mr. Kelly's so narrowed to party bounds.

792 KNOX (J.) Reflections on Daniel. Small 8vo. 1849.

This book is unknown to us.

793 MANCHESTER (GEORGE MONTAGUE, DUKE OF). The Times of Daniel, Chronological and Prophetical. 8vo. *Lond.*, 1845.

This work has received the most enthusiastic praise fiom German writers, who dwell with pleasure upon his being "erudite and illustrious." The duke's writing is certainly *sui generis*. He is by no means a favourite author with us.

794 MILES (CHARLES POPHAM, B.A.) Lectures, with Notes. [Chap. I—VII]. 2 vols. 12mo. *Lond.*, Nisbet. 1840-41.

Commendable sermons and good notes.

795 MORE (Henry, D.D., F.R.S. 1614—1687). A Plain and Continued
Exposition of the several Prophecies of Daniel. 4to. *Lond.*, 1681.

If a man had no more than *More* on Daniel he would certainly long for more, and need a work more spiritual and more suggestive.

796 NEWTON (Sir Isaac, F.R.S. 1642—1727). Observations on
Daniel and the Apocalypse. 4to. *Lond.*, 1733; 8vo., 1831.

The author's name will always keep this book in repute. The spiritual student will not glean much from it. Sir Isaac's fame does not rest on his expositions. The following extract we cannot forbear inserting in this place :—" The folly of interpreters has been, to foretell times and things by this prophecy [the Apocalypse], as if God designed to make them prophets. By this rashness they have not only exposed themselves, but brought the prophecy also into contempt. The design of God was much otherwise. He gave this and the prophecies of the Old Testament, not to gratify men's curiosities by enabling them to foreknow things, but that after they were fulfilled they might be interpreted by the event; and his own providence, not the interpreter's wisdom, be then manifested thereby to the world."

797 PARKER (Thomas. *Puritan. Died* 1677). Daniel expounded. 4to. *Lond.*, 1646.

This learned book is enough to perplex and distract any ordinary mortal, but probably *Dr. Cumming* and brethren of his school would revel in it. We had sooner read a table of logarithms.

798 **PUSEY** (Edward Bouverie, D.D. *Regius Professor of Hebrew*). Daniel the Prophet. Nine Lectures. 8vo. *Lond.*, J. Parker & Co. 1869.

To Dr. Pusey's work on Daniel all subsequent writers must be deeply indebted, however much they may differ from him in other departments of theological study.

799 **ROOS** (Magnus Frederick. 1727—1803). Exposition of such of the Prophecies of Daniel as receive their accomplishment under the New Testament. Translated by E. Henderson. 8vo. *Edinb.*, 1811.

Dr. Henderson gently chides those who are not sufficiently intent upon prophetical interpretation. There would be fewer of such delinquents if expositors were more reasonable. Roos, however, is dull to a dreadful degree: we should say that nobody ever read him through, except his translator. He is very devout, and this is the saving point about his book. We cannot tell whether the views of Roos are correct or not, for we cannot keep awake while reading him. As far as we have gone we have seen some reason to question.

800 **RULE** (William Harris, D.D.). Historical Exposition of Daniel. Cr. 8vo. *Lond.*, Seeley & Co. 1869.

A notably interesting exposition, bringing historical facts and memorials to bear upon the prophecy. It is not merely readable, but attractive.

801   STRONG (Leonard). Lectures. 12mo.   *Lond.*, Yapp. 1871.
Notes of instructive lectures.

802   STUART (Moses).   A Commentary on the Book of Daniel.
8vo.   *Boston, U. S.*   1850.
Stuart gives quite an independent interpretation, and fails to see the
Pope and his *Cardinals* in Daniel, for which we like him all the better.
We do not accept his conclusions, but he is always worthy of respect.

803   TREGELLES (S. Prideaux, LL.D.)   Remarks on the Prophetic
Visions of Daniel.   Cr. 8vo.   *Lond.*, Bagsters.   1852.
Tregelles is deservedly regarded as a great authority upon prophetical
subjects.

804   WELLS (Edward, D.D.)   Daniel explained.   4to.   *Lond.*, 1716.
This is a different work to that mentioned in No. 61.   It is of no great value.

805   WILLET (Andrew).   Hexapla in Danielem.   Folio.   1610.
Dr. Williams says that this is a work of much information, as it contains the "opinions of many authors on each point of difficulty." He adds
that in none of his expositions does *Willet* "discover more skill and
judgment than in the present work."

806   WILSON (Joseph, A.M.)   Horæ Propheticæ ; or Dissertation on
the Book of Daniel.   8vo.   *Oundle*, 1824.
We consider this to be of more than average worth.

807   WINTLE (Thomas, B.D.   1737—1814).   Daniel, an Improved Version,
with Notes.   4to.   *Oxf.*, 1792 ; 8vo., *Lond.*, 1836.   (*See No.* 711.)
Learned notes, mainly philological, with a translation on the plan of *Lowth.*

808   WODROW (Robert).   Destiny of Israel, as unfolded in the Eighth and
succeeding Chapters of Daniel.   12mo.   Blackie & Son.   1844.
This devout author follows the system of *Sir Isaac Newton* and *Bishop Newton.*
His calculations as to the year 1843 were disproved by history.

809   WOOD (William, A.M.)   Lectures on the first Seven Chapters of Daniel.
12mo.   *Lond.*, Cleaver.   1847.
Plain sermons of no great expository value.

MINOR PROPHETS.

810   BARLEE (Edward).   Explanatory Version of the Minor Prophets.   12mo.   *Lond.*, Pickering.   1839.
One of the best paraphrases we have ever met with.

811   COWLES (Henry, D.D.)   The Minor Prophets, with Notes.
Cr. 8vo.   *New York*, D. Appleton & Co.   1867.
" This work is designed for both pastor and people.   It embodies
the results of much research, and elucidates the text of sacred Scripture
with admirable force and simplicity."—*New York Christian Intelligencer.*

812 DANÆUS, or DANEAU (LAMBERT. *Eminent French Protestant Divine.* 1530—1596). A fruitfull Commentarie upon the Twelve Small Prophets. Translated by John Stockwood, Minister at Tunbridge. 4to. *Lond.,* 1594. A translation of a work famous in its day, but of small service now.

813 HENDERSON (EBENEZER, D.D.) The Twelve Minor Prophets. Large 8vo. *Lond.,* Hamilton & Co. 1845. *Scarce.* A learned critical work, not spiritually or doctrinally suggestive, but simply explanatory of the text. This author denounces the theory of a double sense in prophecy; we, none the less, believe it to be a fact.

814 **HUTCHESON** (GEORGE). Briefe Exposition of the 12 Small Prophets. 3 vols., sm. 8vo. *Lond.,* 1655; 1 vol., folio, 1657. *Get it. Hutcheson is always rich. He resembles Dickson.*

815 **KEIL** (K. F.) Commentary on the Minor Prophets. 2 vols., $7.00. Eerdmans. " *Dr. Keil is at his best in this Commentary; and to all who have ventured on this obscure region we can promise an intelligent guide and a serviceable light in this work. We ourselves, under his guidance, have resumed the study of these beautiful and instructive Scriptures with renewed vigour and growing delight."— Nonconformist.*

816 KELLY (WILLIAM). Lectures. Cr. 8vo. *Lond.,* Broom. 1871. *Mr. Kelly* finds in the Minor Prophets a great many things which we cannot see a trace of—for instance, he here discovers that we shall lose India. It is a pity that a man of such excellence should allow a very superior mind to be so warped.

817 **LANGE.** Commentary on the Minor Prophets. Edited by Dr. Schaff. $3.95. Zondervan. *The commentaries on the different prophets are by various authors; hence their value differs. As a whole the volume is excellent, but not so good as Keil.*

818 NEWCOME (WILLIAM, D.D. *Abp. of Armagh.* 1729—1800). Improved Version, Metrical Arrangement, and Explanation. With all the Principal Notes of *Horsley* on Hosea, and *Blayney* on Zechariah. 8vo. *Lond.,* 1836. (*See No.* 711.) A celebrated critical work of a past age, but not expository. *Newcome* was too fond of new readings to be safely followed.

819 **PUSEY** (E. B., D.D.) The Minor Prophets. With a Commentary. Enlarged Type Edition complete in 2 volumes (uniform with Barnes Notes) $7.00. Baker.

All authorities speak of this work with great respect and so would we; but it is evident that Dr. Pusey is far too much swayed by patristic and mediæval commentators.

820 RANDALL (JAMES, M.A.) Sermons on the Books of Joel,.
     Jonah, Nahum, Micah, and Habakkuk. 8vo. *Lond.*, 1843.
Superior sermons ; but what are they among so many prophets ?

821 STOKES (DAVID, D.D.) Paraphrase. 8vo. *Lond.*, 1659.
Of no importance.

HOSEA.

822 **BURROUGHES** (JEREMIAH. *Puritan.* 1599—1646).
     Exposition of the Prophesie of Hosea. 4 vols. 4to.
     Lond., 1643—1651. [The original work does not include
     Chapter XIV., upon which there is an Exposition by
     Sibbes, and another by *Bp. Reynolds.* The reprint, by
     James Sherman, contains the Exposition completed by
     Hall and *Reynolds.* Nichol's Series of Commentaries.
     1 vol., imp. 8vo.   Nisbet, 1863.
*Masterly. A vast treasure-house of experimental exposition.
With the exception of Adams, we prefer it to any other of the
expositions reprinted under the editorship of Mr. Sherman.*

823 HORSLEY (SAMUEL, *Bishop of St. Asaph*). Hosea. Translated
     from the Hebrew ; with Notes. 4to. *Lond.*, 1804.
     And in Vol. 2 of Biblical Criticism.
Horsley occasionally succeeds in elucidating obscurities, but frequently
his treatment of the text reminds one of the old army surgeons who cut
and hacked their patients without mercy. This translation is still valued,
but is to be followed with discretion.

824 **DOWNAME** (JOHN, B.D. *Died* 1644). Lectures upon
     the Four First Chapters of Hosea. 4to. *Lond.*, 1608.
*An exposition of the richest kind. Get it by all means, if you
can.*

825 DRAKE (WILLIAM, M.A.) Notes, critical and explanatory, on the Prophecies
     of Jonah and Hosea. 8vo. *Camb.*, Macmillan & Co. 1853.
For Hebraists only.

826 NEALE (JAMES, M.A.) Hosea. Translation, Commentary, and
     Notes. Royal 8vo. *Lond.*, 1850.
We do not think many ministers will value it for homiletical purposes.

827 POCOCK (EDWARD, D.D. 1604—1691). Commentary on Hosea.
     In Vol. 2 of his *Works* ; 2 vols. folio. *Lond.*, 1740.
Orme says *Pocock* was " one of the finest Oriental scholars, and certainly the first Arabic scholar of his age." His book is a treasury filled
with the products of laborious research.

828 WOLFENDALE (J.) Homiletical Commentary on Hosea. [In progress: being Part 5 of the Preacher's Commentary.] *+* *Lond.*, R. D. Dickinson. [1875.]

On an excellent plan, and moderately well executed. With *Burroughes* and others to quarry from, and so good a method to work by, *Mr. Wolfendale* ought to have produced a better book; but even as it is he deserves a measure of commendation.

829 **SMITH** (SAMUEL). An Exposition upon the Sixth Chapter of the Prophesie of Hosea. 4to. *Lond.*, 1616.

In Smith's usual quiet, rich, expository manner.

830 MARGOLIOUTH (MOSES, B.A.) Genuine Repentance, and its Effects. Exposition of Hosea XIV. 8vo. *Lond.*, 1854. Respectable discourses.

831 **REYNOLDS** (EDWARD, D.D., *Bp. of Norwich.* 1599— 1676). An Explication of the Fourteenth Chapter of Hosea, in Seven Sermons. 4to. 1649. Reprinted by the Religious Tract Society. 18mo. See also under *Burroughes*, No. 822.

Reynolds was one of the greatest theological writers in an age of great divines. He worthily takes place with Burroughes.

832 **SIBBES** (RICHARD, D.D.) The Returning Backslider, or a Commentary upon Hosea XIV. 4to. 1639, etc. Also in Vol II. of his *Works*, Nichol's edition.

Manton says of Sibbes, that he had a peculiar gift in unfolding the great mysteries of the Gospel in a sweet and mellifluous manner, and therefore he was by his hearers usually termed the Sweet Dropper, *"sweet and heavenly distillations usually dropping from him with such a native elegance as is not easily to be imitated." This commentary on Hosea is a fair specimen of his style.*

JOEL.

833 CHANDLER (SAMUEL, D.D.) A Paraphrase and Critical Commentary on Joel. 4to. *Lond.*, 1735.

Chandler makes very few remarks of a spiritual kind, but explains the letter of the word with considerable skill. In writing upon Joel he does not appear to the same advantage as in his "Life of David." He does not effect much in clearing up the "things hard to be understood" in the prophet, and he is of the old broad school.

834 HUGHES (JOSEPH, B.A.) The Prophecy of Joel. The Hebrew Text metrically arranged, with a New Translation and Critical Notes. Fcap. 8vo. *Lond.*, Bagsters.

A purely literary treatise, useful to Hebraists only.

835   POCOCK (Edward, D.D.) A Commentary on Joel. *Works*, vol. I.
      Folio. *Oxf.*, 1691. [The same volume contains his commen-
      taries on Micah and Malachi.]
Full of antique learning. Holds a high place among the older
comments, but will never again be popular.

836   ROWLEY (Adam Clarke, M.A.) Joel. Metrical Translation.
      Sq. 8vo. *Lond.*, Hamilton. 1867.
The translation has been carefully executed. The notes are illustrative and literary only; they do not profess to open up the moral and
spiritual teaching of the prophet. Could *Adam Clarke* rise from the
dead, he would rejoice to find his grandson following in his footsteps.

837 **TOPSELL** (Edward).   Times Lamentations; or, An
      Exposition on the Prophet Joel. 4to. *Lond.*, 1599.
Among the old English commentaries Topsell is the writer on
Joel. He has the usual force, homeliness, piety, and fulness of the
Puritan period.

838   UDALL (John).   The true remedie against Famine and Warres.
      Fiue Sermons vpon the first Chapter of the prophesie of Joel.
      Lond. 12mo. 1586.
We gave so high a price for this small *black letter* volume that we
should like to make it profitable to our brethren, and therefore we commend to the more starchy of them the following extract, which will also
serve to show how the old preachers lashed with vigour the fashions of
the times. *Udall* says: "For the feeding of our monstrous humour of
vanity, how many thousands of quarters of the finest wheat, which God
ordained for the food of man, are yearly converted into *that most devilish*
device of starch. A sin so abominable that it doth cry so loudly in the
Lord's ears for vengeance, as his justice must needs proceed against us
for it, without speedy repentance."

AMOS.

839   BENEFIELD (Sebastian, D.D. 1559—1630). A Commentary
      upon the first Chapter of the Prophecie of Amos. Delivered
      in twenty-one Sermons. 4to. *Lond.*, 1629. Upon the second
      chapter, in twenty-one Sermons, 1620. Upon the third chapter,
      in seventeen Sermons, 1629.

Dr. Benefield was Lady Margaret Professor in Oxford, a Puritan and
thorough Calvinist. His volume was, in its time, the standard Commentary on Amos. It is somewhat prolix and plentifully sprinkled with
Latin; it only discusses three chapters in 953 pages.

840   HALL (Thomas, B.D., *Puritan*, *Born* 1610). An Exposition ;
      by way of Supplement, on the fourth, fifth, sixth, seventh, eighth,
      and ninth Chapters of Amos. 4to. *Lond.*, 1661.

Hall took up Amos where *Benefield* left off. He says he studied brevity, and perhaps he succeeded, for he does not quite fill 600 pages with six chapters.   The two quartos make up a complete work, of an antique type, not suitable to modern tastes, ncr up to the mark of present criticism, but still instructive.   What Puritan s not?

841   RYAN (VINCENT WILLIAM, M.A.) Lectures on Amos.   12mo.
        Lond., Seeleys.   1850.

A commendable series of Lectures; the more valuable because so few moderns have ventured to touch the subject.

OBADIAH.

842   **MARBURY** (EDWARD, A.M. *Died about* 1655). Obadiah.
        4to. *Lond.*, 1649.   Reprinted, with his Commentary
        upon Habakkuk, in Nichol's Series. Cr. 4to.   *Lond.*,
        Nisbet. 1865.

Far more lively than Rainolds. His spirituality of mind prevents his learning becoming dull. He says in the preface, " all my desire is to do all the good I can," and he writes in that spirit.

843   PILKINGTON (JAMES, B.D., *Bp. of Durham.* 1520—1575).
        In the "Works of Bishop Pilkington," reprinted by the *Parker
        Society*, there are Commentaries on Haggai, Obadiah, and
        Nehemiah.

Full of the minor as well as the major controversies of the Reformation period, and therefore the less interesting to us.   In its own day it was *the* master-work on the two prophets, Haggai and Obadiah.

844   RAINOLDS (JOHN, D.D. 1549—1607). The Prophecie of
        Obadiah opened and applyed. 4to. 1613.   Reprinted, with his work on Haggai, and *King* on Jonah, in one
        volume of Nichol's Series. Cr. 4to.   *Lond.*, Nisbet. 1864.

Full of classical stories and learned allusions; but more useful when first written than now.   The author was one of the most learned men the world ever produced, but he is not likely to be a favourite with modern readers.

JONAH.

[This unloveable Prophet has found more Commentators than any other; partly we suppose because the angles of his character excite greater interest, but mainly because we have some knowledge of his life, and therefore are able to realise his personality.   He has received quite as much attention as he deserves in proportion to other Prophets.]

845   **ABBOTT** (GEORGE, *Abp. of Canterbury.* 1562—1633).
        An Exposition upon the Prophet Jonah. 4to. 1613.

Abbott was a renowned Calvinistic divine, and one of the trans-
lators of the present version of the Bible. No set of works on
Jonah would be complete without this learned, laborious, and com-
prehensive exposition. It is, of course, very antique in style; but,
like " old wine," it is none the worse for its age.

846 BENJOIN (GEORGE). Jonah. Translation, with Notes. 4to. *Camb.*, 1796.
Plenty of paper. *Horne* says this work "is literally good for nothing."

847 **CALVIN** (JOHN). Lectures upon the Prophet Jonas.
Translated by N. Baxter. 4to. *Lond.*, 1578.

This of course is fuller than the Commentary, and, as the work
of a revered master, is beyond our criticism.

848 CUNNINGHAM (J. W., A.M.) Six Lectures on the Book of
Jonah. Fcap. boards. *Lond.*, Hatchards. 1833.
Good simple Lectures.

849 DESPREZ (P. S., D.D.) The Book of Jonah. Illustrated by
Discoveries at Nineveh. 12mo. 1857.

To make *Layard* illustrate Jonah was a good idea, and it has been
well carried out by this author.

850 DRAKE (WILLIAM, M.A.) Notes on Jonah and Hosea. 8vo.
Camb., Macmillan & Co. 1853.
Entirely critical. Only useful to Hebrew scholars.

851 EDWARDS (HENRY). Exposition of the Book of Jonah. 12mo.
Long Sutton, Swain. 1837.
Fourteen plain, earnest, practical sermons.

852 EPHRAEM SYRUS. (*Died about* 379). A Metrical Homily on the Mission
of Jonah. Translated from the original Syriac, by Henry Burgess, LL.D.
Cr. 8vo. *Lond.*, Sampson Low & Co. 1853.
A literary curiosity—nothing more.

853 **EXELL** (JOSEPH S.) Practical Readings on the Book of
Jonah. Cr. 8vo. *Lond.*, Elliot Stock. 1874.

Mr. Exell, in a very unpretending but able way, brings to light
the practical lessons of Jonah. Paxton Hood calls these readings
" admirable," and we concur in the verdict.

854 **FAIRBAIRN** (PATRICK, D.D.) Jonah: Life, Character.
and Mission. 12mo. *Edinb.*, Johnstone. 1849.

The life and times of the prophet are set in a clear light; and the
nature and design of his mission fully explained. The work is well
done, and is by far the ablest English treatise on this prophet.

855 **FULLER** (THOMAS, D.D.) Notes upon Jonah. [In
"A Collection of Sermons." Sm. 8vo. *Lond.*, 1656.]
Mr. Tegg has reprinted Fuller's Comment on Ruth, and
Notes upon Jonah, in one small 8vo. vol. 1868.

Full of wisdom, and fuller of wit; in fact, too full of the soul
of the latter, for they are far too short.

856 GAUSSEN (S. R. LOUIS, *Theol. Prof., Geneva*). Jonah, the Prophet. Lessons on his Life. 18mo. *Lond.*, Religious Tract Society. [N. D.]
Addresses to a Sunday School at Geneva.

857 HARDING (THOMAS). Expository Lectures. 12mo. *Lond.*, 1856.
What intelligent man in this kingdom could learn anything from these lectures? The worthy man writes only such self-evident truisms as must have occurred to anybody and everybody who has read his Bible.

858 HOOPER (JOHN. *Bishop and Martyr*). An oversyghte and deliberacion uppon the holy prophet Jonas : made and uttered before the Kinges Majesty and his most honorable Councell, by Jhon Hoper, in Lent last past. Comprehended in seuen Sermons. 16mo. *Lond.*, 1550. Reprinted by the Parker Society. 8vo. *Camb.*, 1843.
It would not repay the student to buy Hooper's works for this short piece. The language is antique, and the thought not of the newest.

859 JONES (THOMAS, *of Creaton*). Jonah's Portrait. 12mo. 1827.
"Jonah's Portrait" was very popular fifty years ago, and deservedly so, for *Mr. Jones* sketches it with considerable power. We should fancy that Jonah's portrait, as he sat under his withered gourd, was not a thing of beauty, or a joy for ever.

860 KING (JOHN, *Bp. of London*. 1559—1621). Lectures upon Jonas. 4to. *Oxf.*, 1600, etc. Reprinted in Nichol's Series of Commentaries. (*See Rainolds*, No. 844).
Quaint and rich, with a little occasional quiet mirth. It was *the* book of its time. Some will think it out of date, others will, like *Grosart*, prize the work of "the Bishop with the royal name."

861 MACPHERSON (A.) Lectures. 18mo. *Edinb.*, 1849.
Far superior to the general run of lectures.

862 **MARTIN** (HUGH). The Prophet Jonah. Cr. 8vo. *Lond.*, W. Isbister & Co. 1866.
A first-class exposition of Jonah. No one who has it will need any other. It is not a small treatise, as most of the Jonah books are; but it contains 460 pages, all rich with good matter. It is out of print, and ought to be republished. What are publishers at to let such a book slip out of the market?

863 MUIR (A. S.) Lessons from Jonah. Cr. 8vo. *Lond.*, 1857.
A lively, popular, and earnest book, in a specially florid style. The author talks a great deal about "the Son of Amittai ;" why not say Jonah? We are tempted to pull the finery to pieces; but we stay our hand, for there is really something good in these "lessons."

864 **PEDDIE** (JAMES, D.D. 1759—1845). A Practical Exposition of the Book of Jonah. 12mo. *Edinb.*, 1842.
"*The pungent remarks peculiar to the Ralph Erskine school make the Jonah of Dr. Peddie a favourite wherever it is known.*"

865 PRESTON (MATTHEW MORRIS, M.A.) Lectures. 8vo. *Lond.*, 1840.
Ordinary sermons. Better ones can be bought for a penny.

866   QUARLES (FRANCIS). A Feast for Wormes. A Poem on the
      History of Jonah. 4to. *Lond.*, 1620.
Quaint and rather bombastic verse, but full of meaning.

867   **RALEIGH** (ALEXANDER, D.D.)   The Story of Jonah.
      Cr. 8vo.   *Edinb.*, A. & C. Black.   1875.
*Dr. Raleigh calls your attention to every touch of the strange
picture which hangs before us in the life of Jonah. Although we
do not always endorse the Doctor's remarks, we can but marvel at
the beauty and power of his descriptions and reflections.*

868   TWEEDIE (W. K.)   Man by Nature and Grace ; or, Lessons
      from Jonah. 12mo. *Edinb.*, Johnstone & Hunter. 1850.
A good practical work, expounding the book of Jonah for Christian
edification.

869   SIMPSON (JAMES). Discourses from Jonah I. 8vo. *Edinb.*, 1816.
Very little in the sermons, but their titles are singularly happy, and in themselves
enough to afford subjects of discourse to preachers.

MICAH.

[Since there is so very little upon this book the student should refer
to works on the Minor Prophets as a whole.   There are some excessively rare authors and also works in Latin ; but these do not fall
within our range.]

870   POCOCK (EDWARD, D.D.)   *See No.* 835.

HABAKKUK.

871   **MARBURY** (EDWARD, A.M.) Commentarie. 4to. *Lond.*,
      1650.   For Reprint, *See No.* 842.
*Here Marbury holds the field alone among old English authors,
and he does so worthily.   There is about him a vigorous, earnest
freshness which makes his pages glow.*

HAGGAI.

872   GRYNÆUS (JOHN JAMES, D.D. 1540—1617). Haggeus, the Prophet ;
      a most plentiful Commentary, gathered out of the Publique Lectures of
      Dr. J. J. Grynæus. 12mo. *Lond.*, 1586.
Grynæus was a voluminous author, and commented on most of the books of
Scripture, but only this work has been turned into English, and it is now seldom
met with.

873 **MOORE** (T. V., D.D., *of Richmond, Va., U.S.*) Haggai, Zechariah, and Malachi. A New Translation, with Notes. 8vo. *New York*, 1856; *Lond.*, 1858.
A capital book. Most useful to ministers.

874 PILKINGTON (*Bishop*). See under *Obadiah*, No. 843.

875 RAINOLDS (JOHN, D.D.) Haggai; Interpreted and Applyed. 4to. 1613 and 1649. For Reprint, *See No.* 844.
Rainolds was the tutor of *Hooker*, and had a main hand in our authorised version of the Bible. *Bishop Hall* says, "the memory, the reading of that man were near a miracle." We ought to be enraptured with a Commentary from such a divine, but we confess that we are not.

ZECHARIAH.

876 BLAYNEY (BENJAMIN, D.D.) Zechariah. A New Translation, with Notes. 4to. *Oxf.*, 1797.
This learned author writes after the manner of *Lowth*, but has neither *Lowth's* taste nor poetic vein. His notes will not suggest sermons, but will be philologically useful if cautiously read.

877 HENGSTENBERG (E. W.)
In his "Christology" (for which *See No.* 67) *Hengstenberg* has given a thorough and elaborate exposition of the greater part of Zechariah and Malachi. He is too grammatical and dry to be generally interesting.

878 KIMCHI (DAVID. *A celebrated Spanish Rabbi. Died about* 1240). Commentary on Zechariah. Translated from the Hebrew by Rev. A. M'Caul, A.M. 8vo. *Lond.*, 1837.
This enables the English reader to see how the Jews themselves understood the Prophets, and this is worth knowing.

879 **MOORE** (T. V.) *See* under *Haggai*, No. 873.

880 PARK (I. R., M.D.) An Amicable Controversy with a Jewish Rabbi on the Messiah's coming; with an entirely new Exposition of Zechariah. 8vo. *Lond.*, 1832.
The words "entirely new exposition" put us on our guard, and did not entice us to read. The caution was needful. This author explains the prophecy spiritually, and asserts that "the spiritual is the most literal interpretation." We more than doubt it.

881 PEMBLE (WILLIAM, M.A. *Puritan.* 1591—1623). A Short and Sweet Exposition upon the First Nine Chapters of Zechariah. In his *Works.* Folio. *Oxf.*, 1659, and *Lond.*, 1635.
Richard Capel says: "Amongst the hardest bookes of Scripture the Prophets may have place, and amongst the Prophets, *Zechary* is a deepe, wherein an elephant may swimme, and therefore I cannot but commend the wisdom of that man of God (the author of this booke), who bestowed his learning and his paines to open the mysteries of this Prophecie. Death

ended his dayes ere he could quite finish his worke, and great weakness hindered an intended supplement." *Pemble* was a learned Calvinistic divine, and his writings are highly esteemed, but not very captivating.

882 STONARD (JOHN, D.D. 1769—1849). Commentary on Zechariah, with a Corrected Translation, and Critical Notes. 8vo. *Lond.*, 1824.
An earnest attempt to expound this prophecy; we do not think the author has succeeded, but he has written some good things.

883 **WARDLAW** (RALPH, D.D.) Lectures on Zechariah. [Posthumous Works, Vol. III.] Cr. 8vo. *Edinb.*, A. Fullerton & Co. 1862.
Written in the Doctor's old age; but we prefer it, in some respects, to other volumes of his lectures. We always consult it.

MALACHI.

884 MOORE (T. V., D.D.) *See* under *Haggai*, No. 873.

885 POCOCK (EDWARD, D.D.) *See* under *Joel*, No. 835.

886 SCLATER (WILLIAM, D.D.) Brief and Plain Commentary upon Malachy. 4to. *Lond.*, 1650.
Not equal to the general standard of Puritan comments. The editor of the work rightly says, "the method is, for the chapters themselves, analytical; for the practical observations, synthetical." We are quaintly told that he would start the hare with any man; that is to say, he would suggest thought and leave others to pursue its track.

887 STOCK (RICHARD, M.A. 1568—1626). A Commentary upon Malachy. Whereunto is added an Exercitation upon the same Prophecy by Samuel Torshell. Folio. *Lond.*, 1641. [Reprinted, together with *Bernard* and *Fuller* on Ruth. Cr. 4to. *Lond.*, Nisbet. 1865.] *See No.* 262.
Contains a *stock* of knowledge, and more than a sufficient stock of quotations from the fathers. *Torshell* printed the book fifteen years after *Stock's* death, and finding it to be written for a popular audience only, he added an examination of the original and a few notes in a more learned style, to make a complete commentary. The two authors have thus composed *the* work upon Malachi.

888 WATSON (THOMAS. *Puritan*). Notes on Malachy III. 8vo. 1682.
This would be a great find if we could only come at it, for *Watson* is one of the clearest and liveliest of Puritan authors. We fear we shall never see this commentary, for we have tried to obtain it, and tried in vain.

May God bless this effort to assist his ministers in the study of the Old Testament.

COMMENTARIES ON THE NEW TESTAMENT.

[See also under *Whole Bible* Nos. 1—65. In many cases the New Testament may be had separately.]

889 **ALFORD** (HENRY, D.D., *Dean of Canterbury*). The Greek Testament ; with a Critically Revised Text, &c. 4 vols., 8vo. *Lond.*, 1856—61. (*See* page 17 of this work). Rivingtons, and G. Bell & Sons.

890 „ „ The New Testament for English Readers. 4 parts. 8vo. Rivingtons, and G. Bell and Sons. 1872. (*See* page 18).

891 „ „ The New Testament Authorized Version Revised. Long Primer, Cr. 8vo., Brevier, Fcap. 8vo., Nonp. Sm. 8vo., Rivingtons, and Isbister & Co.

892 „ „ How to Study the New Testament. Part 1, Gospels and Acts ; Part 2, Epistles (first section) ; Part 3, Epistles (second section) and Revelation. Sm. 8vo. *Lond.*, W. Isbister & Co. 1868.

All critics speak of Alford with respect, though they consider that something better than his Greek Testament is still needed. He is, for the present at any rate, indispensable to the student of the original. With some faults, he has surpassing excellencies. We specially commend 892 to the careful reading of young ministers.

893 ASH (EDWARD, M.D.) Notes and Comments on the New Testament. 3 vols. Sm. 8vo. *Lond.*, 1849—50.
Remarks such as any plain, thoughtful reader would make offhand.

894 **BARNES** (ALBERT). Notes on the New Testament. Enlarged Type Edition, edited by Robert Frew, 11 volumes $35.00. Baker.

Everybody has this work, and therefore can judge for himself, or we would both commend and criticize. (See page 13).

895 BAXTER (RICHARD. 1615—1691). Paraphrase on the New Testament, with Notes. 4to., 1685. 8vo., 1810.
The notes are in *Baxter's* intensely practical and personal style, and show the hortatory use of Scripture ; but they are not very explanatory.

896 **BENGEL** (JOHN ALBERT. 1687—1752). Gnomon of the New Testament, translated into English. With Original Notes. 5 vols., Demy 8vo.

Edinb., T. & T. Clark. (*See also No.* 909.)
See our remarks upon pages 15 and 16.

897 **BEZA** (THEODORE). Newe Testament, Translated out of Greeke, by Theod. Beza. Sm. fol. *Lond.*, 1596.

The compact marginal notes are still most useful. The possessor of this old black letter Testament may think himself happy.

898 **BIBLICAL MUSEUM (The).** By James Comper Gray. Revised edition reissued as Gray and Adams Bible Commentary. 6 volumes $24.75. Zondervan.

Most helpful in suggesting divisions, and furnishing anecdotes. Multum in parvo. Our opinion of it is very high. It is not critical, but popular. The author has used abbreviations in order to crowd in as much matter as possible. (See No. 5.)

899 **BLOOMFIELD** (S. T., D.D.) The Greek Testament, with English Notes ; chiefly original. 2 vols., 8vo. *Lond.*, 1841.

900   „   „   Additional Annotations on the New Testament. 8vo. *Lond.*, 1850.

We frequently get more from Bloomfield than from Alford, though he is not so fashionable. His notes are full of teaching.

901   „   „   Recensio Synoptica Annotationis Sacræ ; being a Critical Digest of the most important Annotations on the New Testament. 8 vols., 8vo. *Lond.*, 1826.
            [A considerable part of this work was included in recent editions of the editor's Greek New Testament.]

"It would be impossible to convey to our readers an adequate idea of the mass of information which the learned author has brought to bear upon the numerous passages which he has undertaken to illustrate, and we can safely say, that the enquirer will find very few of which Mr. Bloomfield has not given a complete and satisfactory exposition."—Quarterly Theological Review.

902 BOWYER (WILLIAM, F.S.A. 1699—1777). Critical Conjectures and Observations on the New Testament. From various authors. 4to. *Lond.*, 1812.

According to *Orme*, the best that can be said for these conjectures is, that they are ingenious ; but who wants conjectures at all ?

903 **BOYS** (JOHN, D.D., *Dean of Canterbury*. 1571—1625). Exposition of the Dominicall Epistles and Gospels used in our English Liturgie throughout the whole yeere. Folio. *Lond.*, 1638.

Racy, rich, and running over. We marvel that it has not been reprinted. English churchmen ought not to leave such a book in its present scarcity, for it is specially adapted for their use. Boys is all essence. What a difference between the John Boys of 1638 and the Thomas Boys of 1827 ! Note well the name.

904   BOYS (THOMAS, M.A.)   The New Testament, with a plain exposition for
      the use of families.   4to.   *Lond.*, 1827.

Ordinary readers might be benefited by the practical observations and evangelical
applications and exhortations; but students do not require this *Boys'* exposition.

905   BURKITT   (WILLIAM.   1650—1703).   Expository Notes.
      Numerous editions, folio, 4to., and 8vo.   Mr. Tegg publishes
      it in 2 vols., 8vo.   (*See* page 20).

We liked *Burkitt* better when we were younger.   He is, however, a
homely and spiritual writer, and his work is good reading for the many.

906   **CHALMERS** (THOMAS, D.D., LL.D.) Sabbath Scripture
      Readings.   Posthumous Works, vol. IV.   (*See No.* 11).

*The readings are not upon every portion of Scripture, neither
can they be viewed as a full exposition of any part thereof.   They
are precious fragments of immortal thought.*

907   CHRYSOSTOM.   Homilies on Matthew, 3 vols.,   John,
      2 vols.,   Acts, 2 vols.,   Romans, 1 vol. ; 1 and 2
      Corinthians, 3 vols.,   Commentaries on Galatians and
      Homilies on Ephesians, 1 vol. ; Philippians, Colossians, and
      Thessalonians, 1 vol. ; Timothy, Titus, and Philemon, 1 vol.,
      8vo.   *Library of the Fathers.*   *Lond.*, J. Parker & Co.

Enough of solid truth and brilliant utterance will be found here to
justify this father's title of " Golden Mouth "; but still all is not gold
which fell from his lips, and to modern readers *Chrysostom* is not so
instructive as he was to his own age.

908   CHURTON (EDWARD, M.A.), and JONES (WILLIAM BASIL, M.A.)
      The New Testament.   With a Plain Explanatory Comment.
      2 vols., Cr. 8vo.   *Lond.*, Murray.   1869.
Meant for private or family reading; with brief notes and well-
executed engravings.   An elegant work.

909   **CRITICAL   ENGLISH   TESTAMENT,** (The).   An
      Adaptation of Bengel's Gnomon, with Notes, showing
      the Results of Modern Criticism and Exegesis.   3 vols.,
      Cr. 8vo.   *Lond.*, Isbister.   1869.

" *The editors of this valuable work have put before the English
reader the results of the labours of more than twenty eminent commentators.   He who uses the book will find that he is reading
Bengel's suggestive 'Gnomon,' modifying it by the critical investigations of Tischendorf and Alford, and comparing it with the
exegetical works of De Wette, Meyer, Olshausen, and others, and
adding to it also profound remarks and glowing sayings from
Trench and Stier.*"—*Evangelical Magazine.*

*We have heard this opinion questioned; but with all discounts
the book is a good one.*

910 CUMMING (John, D.D.) Sabbath Evening Readings. Issued
  as follows :—The Four Gospels, in 4 vols.,   Acts,
  Romans,   Corinthians,   Galatians, Ephesians, and
  Philippians,   James, Peter, and Jude,   Revelation,
  Lond., Arthur Hall, Virtue & Co. 1853, &c.

Dr. Cumming is always evangelical, and his style is very attractive.
These works are rather for popular reading than for students ; but they
are good as a whole, and their spirit is excellent. The doctor has
written too fast, and borrowed too much ; but he interests and edifies.

911 DALLAS (Alexander, A.M.) The Cottager's Guide to the New Testament.
  6 vols. 12mo. *Lond.*, Nisbet. 1839—45.

Six volumes for cottagers ! How could they ever buy them ? If bought, how could
they refrain from sleeping while trying to read them ? The "Guide" could be of no
possible use to a sensible man, except as an opiate.

912 DALTON (W., A.M.) Commentary. Edited by Rev. W. Dalton, A.M.
  2 vols. 8vo. *Lond.*, Seeleys. 1848.

Not of use to preachers. Prepared for family reading, and mainly taken from
Henry and *Scott.* There are quite enough of these compilations.

913 DAVIDSON (David). Critical Notes. 2 vols., 18mo. *Edinb.*, 1834.

Two small thick volumes : really a *pocket* commentary. Although the notes are
good, the student had better spend his money on larger and better books.

914 DODDRIDGE (Philip, D.D. 1702—1751). Family Expositor ;
  With Critical Notes. Many editions. 6 vols., 4to. ; 5 vols.
  8vo. ; 4 vols. 8vo. ; and 1 vol., imp. 8vo.,   *Lond.*, Tegg.

"The late *Dr. Barrington*, Bishop of Durham, in addressing his
clergy on the choice of books, characterises this masterly work in the
following terms :—' I know no expositor who unites so many advantages
as *Doddridge* ; whether you regard the fidelity of his version, the fulness
and perspicuity of his composition, the utility of his general and historical
information, the impartiality of his doctrinal comments, or, lastly, the
piety and pastoral earnestness of his moral and religious applications.'"
Later interpreters have somewhat diminished the value of this work.

915 ERASMUS (Desiderius. 1467—1536). Paraphrase. *Black
  Letter.* 2 vols. Folio. *Lond.*, 1548 and 1551.

This paraphrase was appointed by public authority to be placed in all
churches in England, and the clergy were also ordered to read it. The
volumes are very rare, and expensive because of their rarity.

916 GELL (Robert, D.D. *Died* 1665). Gell's Remains ; or, Select Scriptures
  explained. 1 or 2 vols. Folio. *Lond.*, 1676.

A queer collection of remarks, criticisms, and fancies, in a huge volume. *Baxter*
called *Gell* "one of the sect-makers." He was, no doubt, a singular man, an
Arminian, and one who had great respect for "the Learned Societie of Astrologers."

917 GILPIN (William, A.M. 1724—1804). Exposition of the New Testament.
  4to. 1790. Fourth edition. 2 vols. 8vo. 1811.

Half paraphrase, half very free translation. Notes meagre. Useful to buttermen.

918 GIRDLESTONE (Charles, M.A.) New Testament. Lectures
  for Families. 2 vols. 8vo. *Lond.*, 1835.

Profitable household reading.

919　GUYSE (JOHN, D.D. 1680—1671). The Practical Expositor. 3 vols., 4to., 1739—52 ; 6 vols., 8vo., 1775, &c.

The day of paraphrases is past. *Dr. Guyse* was ponderous in style, and we question if at this date he is ever read. *Doddridge's Expositor* is far better.

920　HAMMOND (HENRY, D.D.) Paraphrase and Annotations. Folio. *Lond.*, 1675. *Works*, vol. III. Also in 4 vols., 8vo. *Oxf.*, 1845.

Though *Hammond* gives a great deal of dry criticism, and is Arminian, churchy, and peculiar, we greatly value his addition to our stores of biblical information. Use the sieve and reject the chaff.

921　HEYLYN (JOHN, D.D.) Theological Lectures at Wesminster Abbey ; with an Interpretation of the New Testament. 2 vols., 4to. *Lond.*, 1749—61.

Five volumes with absolutely nothing in them beyond a spinning out of the text.

922　KNATCHBULL (SIR NORTON, *Bart. Died* 1684). Annotations upon some Difficult Texts. 8vo. *Camb.*, 1693.

Much valued in its day ; but far outdone by more recent critics.

923　**LANGE** (J. P., D.D.) Commentary. 24 volumes complete on Old and New Testament. $97.80. Zondervan. Also sold as separate volumes.

See under separate books.

924　**LEIGH** (SIR EDWARD). *See No.* 44.

925　LINDSAY (JOHN). New Testament; with Notes. [Selected from Grotius, Hammond, &c.] 2 vols. folio. *Lond.*, 1736.

A condensation of other writers—very well done.

926　McCLELLAN (JOHN BROWN, M.A.) New Testament. A New Translation, Analyses, Copious References, and Illustrations from Original Authorities, Harmony of the Gospels, Notes, and Dissertations. In 2 vols., 8vo. Vol. I. The Gospels, with the Harmony. 30/- *Lond.*, Macmillan & Co. 1875.

This work is what it professes to be, and we need say no more. It is, however, a very expensive luxury at the publishing price.

927　**MAYER** (JOHN, D.D.) New Testament. 2 vols., Folio. 1631.　(*See pages* 10 *and* 11.)

928　MEYER (Dr. H. A. W. *Oberconsistorialrath, Hannover*). Commentary on the New Testament. Messrs. T. & T. Clark are issuing a Translation of *Meyer's* Commentary. They have issued Romans, 2 vols.; Galatians, 1 vol.; John's Gospel, 1 vol.

A very learned Commentary, of which *Bp. Ellicott* speaks in the highest terms. *Meyer* must be placed in the first class of scholars, though somewhat lower down in the class than his admirers have held. Apart from scholarship we do not commend him. *Alford* was certainly no very rigid adherent of orthodoxy, yet he says of *Meyer* that he is not to be trusted where there is any room for the introduction of rationalistic opinions. Whatever credit may be due to him for accurate interpretation, this is a terribly serious drawback. It is well to be warned.

929　NEWCOME (WILLIAM, D.D., *Abp. of Armagh.* 1729—1800). Attempt towards revising our English Translation and Illustrating the Sense by Notes. 2 vols., royal 8vo. *Dubl.*, 1796.

Newcome was a critical scholar whose works enjoyed a high repute. Unhappily, the Unitarians brought out an "Improved Version," professedly based upon *Newcome's* and this led the public to question *Newcome's* orthodoxy, but there was little reason for doing so. Few of our readers will care for this cold literal interpretation.

930 PENN (GRANVILLE, F.S.A.) The Book of the New Covenant; being a Critical Revision of the English Version. 8vo. *Lond.*, 1836.

931   ,,   ,,   Annotations on the Book of the New Covenant. 8vo. 1837.

932   ,,   ,,   Supplemental Annotations. *Lond.*, 1838.
These books are too learned for much to be learned from them ; perhaps if they had been more learned still they would have been useful.

933 PLATTS (JOHN). Self-Interpreting Testament. 4 vols., 8vo. *Lond.*, 1827.
A sort of Biblical Commentary. A concordance will answer the purpose.

934 QUESNELL (PASQUIER. 1634—1719). New Testament. 4 vols., 8vo. *Lond.*, 1719—1725. [The Gospels have been reprinted. 3 vols., 12mo. *Glasg.*, 1830.
A sweet and simple French writer who says many good things of a. very harmless character.

935 SUMNER (JOHN BIRD, *Archbishop of Canterbury*). Practical Exposition of the Gospels, Acts, Epistles of Paul, James, Peter, John, and Jude. 9 vols., 8vo. 1833 to 1851.
Sumner's Expositions are very mild and can generally be bought very cheap. The public are pretty good judges, and the price indicates the value. The qualities which procure an archbishopric are not such as qualify a man to be an eminent expositor.

936 TOWNSEND (GEORGE, M.A.) New Testament. Arranged in Chronological Order. Notes. 2 vols., 8vo. *Lond.*, 1838.
This harmony has always been in repute ; but we confess we like the New Testament best as we find it.

937 TROLLOPE (WILLIAM, M.A.) Analecta Theologica. 2 vols., 8vo. *Lond.*, 1830—35.
A condensation of the opinions of eminent expositors, very well executed, and useful except so far as superseded by more modern works.

938 WALL (WILLIAM, D.D. 1645—1727-8). Brief Notes. 8vo. *Lond.*, 1730.
Explains some difficulties, but is far surpassed by other annotators.

939 **WESLEY** (JOHN). *See No. 62.*

940 WHEDON (D. D., D.D. *Meth. Epis. Ch., America*). Popular Commentary. To be completed in 5 vols., cr. 8vo.   Hodder & Stoughton.
Dr. Whedon lacks common sense, and is no expositor. He is furiously anti-calvinistic, and as weak as he is furious.

941 WHITBY (DANIEL, D.D. 1638—1726). *See No. 50.*
This is a part of *Patrick, Lowth*, &c.

942 WILSON (WILLIAM, B.D. 1762—1800). Explanation of the New Testament by the early opinions of Jews and Christians concerning Christ. 8vo. *Camb.*, 1838.
Follows a deeply interesting line of investigation. It is not a commentary, but is too good to be omitted.

943 WORSLEY (JOHN). Translation, with Notes. 8vo. *Lond.*, 1770.
Translation second rate, criticism none, notes very short.

THE FOUR GOSPELS.

944 ADAM (THOMAS. 1701—1784. *Of Wintringham*). Exposition of the Gospels. 2 vols., 8vo. *Lond.*, 1837.

Short and sweet; but *Adam* is not the first man as an expositor.

945 AQUINAS (THOMAS. 1224—1274). Catena Aurea. Commentary, collected out of the Fathers. 6 vols., 8vo. *Lond.* and *Oxf.*, Parker. 1870.

The Fathers are over-estimated, by a sort of traditionary repute, for we question if they are much read. This collection of extracts we always look into with curiosity, and sometimes we find a pearl.

946 **BONAR** (HORATIUS, D.D.) Light and Truth. (*See No. 6.*)

947 BOUCHIER (BARTON, A.M.) Manna in the House. Vol. I., Matthew and Mark; Vol. II., Luke; Vol. III., John. Thick 12mo. *Lond.*, J. F. Shaw. 1853—4.

Mr. Bouchier writes sweetly, and his books aid the devotions of many families. Ministers may read them with profit; but they are not exactly intended for them.

948 **BROWN** (JOHN, D.D., *of Edinburgh*). Discourses and Sayings of our Lord. Three large 8vo. vols. *Edinb.*, Oliphant & Co. 1852.

Of the noblest order of exposition. Procure it.

949 BURGON (J. W., D.D.) Plain Commentary for devotional reading. 5 vols., fcap. 8vo. *Lond.*, Parker. 1870.

Ryle says: "This is an excellent, suggestive, and devout work; but I cannot agree with the author when he touches upon such subjects as the Church, the sacraments, and the ministry."

950 CAMPBELL (GEORGE, D.D., F.R.S. *Edinb.* 1719—1796). The Gospels translated, with Notes. 4 vols., 8vo. *Aberd.*, 1814.

Clear and cold. *Orme* says it is "one of the best specimens of a translation of the Scriptures in any language." The preliminary dissertations are valuable; the notes are purely critical.

951 CHOICE NOTES on Matthew, drawn from Old and New Sources. [Also on Mark, Luke, and John.] Cr. 8vo. *Lond.*, Macmillan & Co. 1868—69.

These are taken from the grander treasuries of *Prebendary Ford* (*No.* 955). We have mentioned them because those who could not afford to buy *Ford's* books might be able to get these.

952 CLARKE (SAMUEL, D.D. 1673—1729). Paraphrase, with Notes. 2 vols., 8vo. *Lond.*, 1741; *Oxf.*, 1816.

We do not care for paraphrases. *Clarke* was a learned man, but an unsafe guide.

953 DENTON (W., M.A.) The Gospels for the Sundays and other Holy Days of the Christian year. 3 vols., 8vo. *Lond.*, G. Bell & Co. 1860—63.

Curates will find this just the thing they need for sermonizing.

954 [ELSLEY.] Annotations on the Gospels and Acts. 3 vols.,
       8vo. *Lond.*, 1827.
Wholly critical and philological.

955 **FORD** (JAMES, M.A.)   The Gospels, illustrated from
       Ancient and Modern Authors.   4 vols., 8vo.   Matthew,
           Mark,   Luke,   John,   *Lond.*, Masters.
       1856—72.
*Those who wish to see what the Fathers said upon the Gospels,
and to read the choicest sayings of the early Anglican bishops, cannot do better than consult Ford, who has made a very rich collection. Some of the extracts do not materially illustrate the text, but
they are all worth reading.*

956 FORSTER (JOHN, M.A.) The Gospel Narrative, with a Con-
       tinuous Exposition. Imp. 8vo. *Lond.*, J. W. Parker. 1845.
A paraphrase upon a good system, carefully executed, and instructive.
Thoroughly Anglican.

957 GILBY (WILLIAM S., M.A.) Spirit of the Gospel. 8vo. *Lond.*, 1818.
Interesting remarks on certain texts. All can be found in other writers.

958 HALL (CHARLES H.) Notes, for the use of Bible Classes.
       2 vols., 8vo. *New York* and *Lond.*, 1857.
This book is as full of reverence to Bishops and other Episcopal
arrangements as if it had been "appointed to be read in Churches."
American Episcopalians can evidently be very thorough.   Notes poor.

959 **JACOBUS** (MELANCTHON W., *Pennsylvania*).   Notes.
       3 vols., cr. 8vo.   *Edinb.*, W. Oliphant. 1868—69.
*Jacobus is sound and plain, and is therefore a safe guide to
Sunday-School teachers and others who need to see the results of
learning without the display of it.*

960 **JUKES** (ANDREW).   Characteristic Differences of the
       Gospels considered, as revealing various relations of the
       Lord Jesus. Cr. 8vo.   *Lond.*, Nisbet. 1853.
*Remarks prompting thought ; containing in a small compass a
mass of instruction.*

961 **LANGE** (J. P.) *See No.* 923.
The Gospels are among the best of the series.

962 LYTTLETON (LORD GEORGE). Gospels and Acts, with Notes. Sm. 8vo.
       Lond., Rivingtons. 1856.
Such remarks as most teachers could make for themselves.

963 NORRIS (JOHN, *Canon of Bristol*). Key to the Gospel Narra-
       tive. Sm. 8vo.   *Lond.*, Rivingtons. 1871.
" *Canon Norris* writes primarily to help 'younger students' in studying
the Gospels. But the unpretending volume is one which all students
may peruse with advantage. It is an admirable manual for those who
take Bible Classes through the Gospels."—So says the *London Quarterly.*

964 OLSHAUSEN (HERMANN, D.D.) Commentary on the Gospels and Acts. 4 vols., demy 8vo. Cheap edition, 4 vols., cr. 8vo. *Edinb.*, T. & T. Clark. 1848—1860.

Olshausen is mentioned by *Alford* as so rich in original material, that he has often cited him in his "New Testament for English Readers." He is one of the most devout of the Germans, and a great scholar; but we are not enamoured of him.

965 OXENDEN (ASHTON, *Bishop*). Short Lectures on the Sunday Gospels. 2 vols., 12mo. *Lond.*, Hatchards. 1869, &c.

Why *Oxenden's* books sell we do not know. We would not care to have them for a gift. "Milk for babes" watered beyond measure.

966 PEARCE (ZACHARY, D.D., *Bishop of Rochester*. 1690—1774). Commentary. Gospels, Acts, and 1 Corinthians. 2 vols., royal 4to. *Lond.*, 1777.

A huge mass of learning, said by great divines to be invaluable. To most men these volumes will simply be a heap of lumber.

967 RIDDLE (J. E., M.A.) Commentary. Royal 8vo. 1843.

Choice extracts selected by the author of the well-known Latin Dictionary. Ministers should make such collections for themselves rather than purchase them.

968 RIPLEY (HENRY J. *Prof. Newton Theol. Instit. U.S.*) The Gospels, with Notes. 2 vols., post 8vo. *Boston, U.S.*, 1837.

Adapted for Sunday-School use. Simple, brief, and practical.

969 **RYLE** (J. C., B.A.) Expository Thoughts on the Gospels, 4 volumes. $18.95. Zondervan. Also sold as separate volumes, $4.95 each.

We prize these volumes. They are diffuse, but not more so than family reading requires. Mr. Ryle has evidently studied all previous writers upon the Gospels, and has given forth an individual utterance of considerable value.

970 STABBACK (THOMAS, A.B.) Gospels and Acts, with Annotations. 2 vols., 8vo. *Falmouth*, 1809.

Very useful in its day, but quite out of date.

971 **STIER** (RUDOLPH, D.D.) The Words of the Lord Jesus. 8 vols. in 4. 8vo. T. & T. Clark. 1869.

972 „ „ The Words of the Risen Saviour, and Commentary on the Epistle of St. James. 8vo. *Edinb.*, Clark. 1859.

No one can be expected to receive all that Stier has to say, but he must be dull indeed who cannot learn much from him. Read with care he is a great instructor.

973 **STOCK** (EUGENE). Lessons on the Life of our Lord. For the Use of Sunday School Teachers. 8vo. *Lond.*, Ch. of England S. S. Institute. 1875.

For real use a thoroughly commendable book. Teachers and preachers have here more matter given them on the lesson than they are likely to use. Admirable!

974 TOWNSON (THOMAS, *Archdeacon of Richmond*. 1715—1792).
    Discourses on the Gospels. 2 vols., 8vo. 1810.
Bishop Lowth welcomed this as "a capital performance." It is only
so from *Lowth's* point of view.

975 TRAPP (JOSEPH, D.D. 1679—1747). Notes. 8vo. 1748.
This *Trapp*, grandson of the famous commentator, is the author of a wretched
pamphlet upon "the nature, folly, sin, and danger of being righteous overmuch." He
opposed *Whitfield* and *Wesley* with more violence than sense. His work is utterly
worthless, and we only mention it to warn the reader against confounding it with the
productions of the real old *Trapp*.

976 **TRENCH** (R. CHENEVIX, D.D., *Abp. of Dublin*). Studies
    on the Gospels. 8vo.   *Lond.*, Macmillan & Co. 1874.
*Masterly studies on important topics. Students will do well to
read also Trench's " Sermon on the Mount." We do not always
agree with this author, but we always learn from him.*

977 WARREN (ISRAEL, D.D.) Sunday-School Commentary. 8vo.   1872.
An American work imported by Hodder and Stoughton. Notes slender.

978 WATSON (RICHARD). Exposition of Matthew and Mark.
    Demy 8vo.,   12mo.,   *Lond.*, 66, Paternoster Row.
Arminian views crop up at every opportunity. The notes are meant
to elucidate difficulties in the text, and frequently do so.

979 **WESTCOTT** (BROOKE FOSS, M.A.) Introduction to the
    Study of the Gospels. Cr. 8vo.   *Lond.*, Macmillan
    & Co. 1860.
*Worthy of high commendation. The author knows the German
writers, but is not defiled by their scepticism. He is a man of deep
thought, but displays no pride of intellect. A man had need be a
thorough student to value this Introduction : it is not an introduction to the Gospels, or to the reading of them, but to their study.*

980 WIESELER (KARL). Chronological Synopsis of the Gospels. 8vo.
    Lond., Bell & Daldy. 1864.
This important work formed the basis both of the *Synopsis Evangelica* of *Tischendorf*, and of the *Historical Lectures on the Life of our Lord* by *Bishop Ellicott*. It is
much to be regretted that so many novel interpretations and baseless hypotheses
should have marred the book ; but, notwithstanding all drawbacks, it must be a
masterly work to have received the heartiest commendation of the greatest scholars of
the day. Only the more advanced student will care for this Synopsis.

981 WILLIAMS (ISAAC, B.D.) Devotional Commentary. 8 vols.,
    cr. 8vo.   viz: Thoughts on the Study of the Gospels.
    Harmony of the Evangelists. The Nativity. Second Year of
    the Ministry. Third Year of the Ministry. The Holy Week.
    The Passion. The Resurrection. *Lond.*, Rivingtons. 1873.
Anglican popery for quartz, and sparkling grains of precious gospel
largely interspersed as gold. We cannot imagine any spiritual man
reading these works without benefit, if he knows how to discriminate.

HARMONIES OF THE GOSPELS.

[As these are somewhat aside from our plan, we mention but few. That they are very numerous may be gathered from the following list given in *Smith's Dictionary*.—Osiander, 1537; Jansen, 1549; Stephanus, 1553; Calvin, 1553; Cluver, 1628; Calov, 1680; Chemnitz, 1593 (continued by *Leyser* and *Gerhard*, 1704); Calixt, 1624; Cartwright, 1627; Lightfoot, 1654; Cradock, 1668; Lancy, 1689; Le Clerc, 1699; Tomard, 1707; Burmann, 1712; Whiston, 1702; Rus, 1727–8—30; Bengel, 1736; Hauber, 1737; Büsching, 1766; Doddridge, 1739—40; Pilkington, 1747; Macknight, 1756; Berthing, 1767; Griesbach, 1776, 97, 1809, 22; Newcome, 1778; Priestly, 1777, in Greek, and 1780, in English; Michaelis, 1788, in his Introduction; White, 1799; Planck, 1809; Keller, 1802; Mutschelle, 1806; De Wette and Lücke, 1818; Hess, 1822; Sebastiani, 1806; Matthaei, 1826; Kaiser, 1828; Roediger, 1829; Clausen, 1829; Greswell, 1830; Chapman, 1836; Carpenter, 1838; Reichel, 1840; Gehringer, 1842; Robinson, 1845, in Greek, 1846, in English; Stroud, 1853; Anger, 1851; Tischendorf, 1851.]

982 **CALVIN** (JOHN). A Harmony of Matthew, Mark, and Luke. Translated by Rev. W. Pringle. 3 vols. $10.50. Eerdmans.

There are older translations of this noble work, but they are less suitable to modern taste than Mr. Pringle's. Calvin only harmonized three of the evangelists, but he did his work in his usual superb manner.

983 **CLARKE** (GEORGE W.) Harmony, with Notes, etc. Cr. 8vo. *New York*, 1870.

This American author is greatly indebted to other works. He has produced a very handy book for teachers of youth.

984 DODDRIDGE (PHILIP, D.D.) *See No.* 914.

985 DUNN (SAMUEL). Gospels Harmonized, with Notes: forming a complete Commentary on the Evangelists. Chiefly by Adam Clarke. Thick 8vo. *Lond.*, 1838.

Samuel Dunn has taken *Adam Clarke* as his basis, and then built thereon with stones from *Lightfoot, Macknight, Doddridge, Greswell*, and others. It is, of course, a Wesleyan harmony, and the reader is not long before he discovers that fact; but the names of those concerned are a sufficient guarantee that it is by no means a despicable production.

986 GREENLEAF (SIMON, LL.D., *Dane Professor of Law in Harvard University*). Examination of the Testimony of the Evangelists by the Rules of Evidence administered in Courts of Justice. With an account of the Trial of Jesus. Thick 8vo. *Lond.*, 1847.

The author is an American lawyer, very learned in his profession.
He has issued a treatise upon the laws of evidence, which is a standard
work among his brethren.   It was a happy thought on his part to apply
the laws of evidence to the narratives of the evangelists.   To thoughtful
men of all sorts, but to lawyers especially, this book is commended.

987 **GRESWELL** (EDWARD, B.D.)   Dissertations upon the
     Principles and Arrangement of an Harmony of the
     Gospels.   4 vols., 8vo.   *Oxf.*, 1837.

*" The learned writer has greatly distinguished himself as the
most laborious of modern harmonists.   His work is the most copious
that has appeared, at least since the days of Chemnitz's folios."*
So says Dr. S. Davidson.   To us it seems to be prolix and tedious.

988 LIGHTFOOT (JOHN, D.D.   1602—1675).   Harmony, Chro-
     nicle, and Order of the New Testament.   Folio.   1654.

Lightfoot was a member of the Assembly of Divines, profoundly
skilled in scriptural and Talmudical lore.   He never completed this
harmony, for his plan was too comprehensive to be finished in a lifetime.

989 MACKNIGHT (JAMES. D.D. 1721—1800).   Harmony of the Gospels,
     with Paraphrase and Notes. Fifth edition. 2 vols., 8vo. *Lond.*, 1819.

This author has enjoyed considerable repute and is still prized by many, but we
can never bring our soul to like him, he always seems to us to be so graceless.

990 MIMPRISS (ROBERT).   The Treasury Harmony of the Four
     Evangelists.   Thick demy 4to., 16/-   Also cr. 8vo., two vols.
     in one,   *Lond.*, Partridge & Co.
     Condensed and compressed.   Wonderfully useful.

991 NEWCOME (WILLIAM, *Archbishop of Armagh*).   English Harmony, with
     Notes. 8vo. *Lond.*, S. Bagster. 1827.

Merely the text arranged and a few rather ordinary notes.   We do not see what a
man can get out of it.   But, hush !   It is by an archbishop !

992 **ROBINSON** (EDWARD, D.D., *Prof. Bib. Lit., New York*).
     Harmony on the Authorized Version.   Following the
     Harmony in Greek, by Dr. E. Robinson.   With Notes.
     8vo.   *Lond.*, Religious Tract Society.

*Robinson's Harmony is a work which has met with great accept-
ance, and the Tract Society did well to bring out this work for
those unacquainted with Greek.   The Notes are mainly those of
Robinson ; but Wieseler, Greswell, and others have also been laid
under contribution by the Editor, who has executed his work well.*

993 **STROUD** (WILLIAM, M.D.)   Greek Harmony, with Synop-
     sis and Diatessaron.   4to.   *Lond.*, Bagsters. 1853.

One of the best of the Harmonies.

994 WILLIAMS (ISAAC).   *See No.* 981.

Merely the text arranged, without note or comment.

LIVES OF OUR LORD JESUS CHRIST.

[Here also we can only mention a few leading works.]

See under *Gospels*, especially Nos. 971, 972, 973, and 981.

995 **ANDREWS** (SAMUEL). The Life of our Lord upon the
Earth, in its Historical, Chronological, and Geographical
Relations. $5.95. Zondervan.
*A good book for a student to read through before taking up
larger works. It is a standard work.*

996 BEECHER (HENRY WARD).   Life of Jesus, the Christ.   Earlier
scenes.   Thick 8vo.   *Lond.*, Nelson.   1872.
Here the great genius of *Beecher* glows and burns ; but we are disappointed with his book as a biography of our Lord.

997 BENNETT (JAMES, D.D.)   Lectures on the History of Jesus
Christ.   Second edition.   2 vols., 8vo.   *Lond.*, 1828.
Lively popular lectures, full of matter, well expressed, and possessing
sterling excellence.

998 ELLICOTT (C. J., D.D., *Bp. of Gloucester and Bristol*).   Historical Lectures.   8vo.   *Lond.*, Longmans.   1869.
This great author stands in the highest place of honour ; but having
no sympathy with what he calls "the popular theology," he should be
read with considerable caution.

999 **FARRAR** (F. W., D.D., F.R.S.)   Life of Christ.   2 vols.,
demy 8vo.   *Lond.*, Cassell, Petter & Galpin.   1874.
*THE work upon the subject. Fresh and full. The price is very
high, and yet the sale has been enormous.*

1000 FLEETWOOD (JOHN, D.D.) Life of our Lord Jesus Christ. Also the Lives
of the Apostles and Evangelists. Imp. 8vo. *Lond.*, Mackenzie.
This has had a great run, and is to be found in farm houses and cottages. Why
we cannot tell, except that the sellers of parts and numbers are fine hands at pushing
the trade, and plates and pictures have caught the simple purchasers.

1001 **KITTO** (JOHN, D.D.)   "Life and Death of our Lord."
Daily Bible Illustrations.   (See No. 41.)
Abounds in instructive matter.

1002 **LANGE** (J. P., D.D.)   Life of our Lord Jesus Christ.
With Additional Notes, by Rev. Marcus Dods, D.D.
4 vols., demy 8vo.   *Edinb.*, T. & T. Clark.   1864.
*We constantly read Lange, and though frequently differing from
him, we are more and more grateful for so much thoughtful teaching.*

1003   NEANDER (J. A. W.) The Life of Jesus Christ in its Historical
       Development. Translated by Professors McClintock and
       Blumenthal. Sm. 8vo.   *Lond.,* Bohn. 1853.

Good as an answer to *Strauss,* but unsatisfactory from the standpoint
of evangelical theology.

1004   PRESSENSÉ (EDMOND DE, D.D.) Jesus Christ: his Times,
       Life, and Work. Cr. 8vo.   *Lond.,* Hodder & Stoughton.
       1875. The above work "abridged by the author, and adapted
       for general readers." Cr. 8vo.

There have been many discussions upon the orthodoxy of this work,
but it is a noble production, and is written in an adoring spirit. The
accomplished author has made a valuable contribution to the cause of
truth. Yet we are inclined to agree with the writer who said, "to
write a life of Christ is to paint the sun with charcoal." The life of a
Christian is the best picture of the life of Christ.

1005   YOUNG (JOHN, LL.D.) The Christ of History. Enlarged
       edition. Cr. 8vo.   *Lond.,* Daldy, Isbister & Co. 1869.

"A work of great excellence, eloquence, and logical compactness."
British Quarterly Review.

MIRACLES OF OUR LORD.

[Here, also, we cannot attempt a complete list.]

1006   COLLYER (WILLIAM BENGO, D.D., F.A.S.) Lectures on Scripture
       Miracles. 8vo. *Lond.,* 1812.
       While reading we seem to hear the rustling of a silk gown. The lectures are by
       no means to be despised, but they are far too fine for our taste.

1007   CUMMING (JOHN, D.D.) Lectures on our Lord's Miracles,
       as earnests of the age to come. 12mo. *Lond.,* 1851.

Below the Doctor's usual mark, which is none too high.

1008   HOWSON (J. S., D.D., *Dean of Chester*). Meditations on the
       Miracles. Fcap. 8vo.   *Lond.,* R. Tract Society. [1871.]

Short, simple, but deeply spiritual and suggestive.

1009   KNIGHT (JAMES, A.M.) Discourses on the principal Miracles. 8vo.
       Lond., 1831.
       Mediocre discourses much appreciated by the clergy who borrow their sermons.

1010   MACDONALD (GEORGE, LL.D.) The Miracles of our Lord.
       Cr. 8vo.   *Lond.,* W. Isbister & Co. 1870.

Contains many fresh, childlike, and, we had almost said, dreamy
thoughts. It suggests side-walks of meditation.

1011   MAGUIRE (ROBERT, M.A.) The Miracles of Christ. Sq. 12mo.
       Lond., Weeks & Co. 1863.

We have been agreeably disappointed in this book. The bad paper
offends the eye, but the page bears many living, stirring thoughts. If
the author preaches in this fashion we do not wonder at his popularity.

1012 STEINMEYER (F. L., D.D., *Prof. Theol., Berlin*). The Miracles of our Lord in relation to Modern Criticism. Translated from the German by L. A. Wheatley. 8vo. *Edinb.*, T. & T. Clark. 1875.

No doubt a very scholarly book, and useful to those whose heads have been muddled by other Germans, but we are weary of Teutonic answers to Teutonic scepticisms. We suppose it was needful to hunt down the rationalists, for farmers hunt down rats, but the game does not pay for the trouble.

1013 **TRENCH** (R. C., D.D., *Abp. of Dublin*). Notes on the Miracles of our Lord. 8vo.

Brimming with instruction. Not always to our taste in doctrine; but on the whole a work of highest merit.

PARABLES OF OUR LORD.

[A Selection from a long list, for which *see No.* 1024].

1014 ANDERSON (CHARLES, M.A.) New Readings of Old Parables. Cr. 8vo. *Lond.*, 1876.

We paid four precious shillings for this book, and find seventy pages of rubbish and fifty more of advertisements. Our readers will, we hope, profit by our experience.

1015 **ARNOT** (WILLIAM, D.D. *Died* 1875). The Parables of our Lord. Cr. 8vo. *Lond.*, T. Nelson. 1865.

We do not consider this to be up to our lamented friend's usual high mark of excellence, but it is of great value.

1016 BOURDILLON (FRANCIS, M.A.) The Parables explained and applied. Cr. 8vo. *Lond.*, Religious Tract Society. [N.D.]

Sufficiently common and commonplace. Platitudes sleepily worded.

1017 COLLYER (WILLIAM BENGO, D.D.) Lectures on Scripture Parables. 8vo. *Lond.*, 1815. (*See No.* 1006).

1018 CUMMING (JOHN, D.D.) Foreshadows; or, Lectures on our Lord's Parables. Cr. 8vo. *Lond.*, 1852. (*See No.* 1007).

The Doctor evidently prints his sermons without much revision. They are pleasing, popular, and (of course) rather prophetic.

1019 GRESWELL (E., B.D.) Exposition of the Parables, &c. 5 vols. in 6, 8vo. *Oxf.*, 1834.

A vast heap of learning and language. The work, though padded out, stilted in style, and often fanciful, is a mine for other writers.

1020 GUTHRIE (THOMAS, D.D.) The Parables read in the Light of the Present Day. Cr. 8vo. *Lond.*, Strahan. 1874.

Twelve Parables treated in *Dr. Guthrie's* lively, sparkling manner. Flowers in abundance.

1021 KEACH (BENJ.) Exposition. Folio. *Lond.*, 1701. also 4 vols., 8vo. and 1 vol., imp. 8vo. 1856.

Although our honoured predecessor makes metaphors run on as many legs as a centipede, he has been useful to thousands. His work is old-fashioned, but it is not to be sneered at.

1022   KNIGHT (JAMES, A.M.) Discourses on the Principal Parables.   8vo.
       Lond., 1829.   (*See No.* 1009).

1023   LISCO (FREDERICK GUSTAV).   Parables Explained.   Fcap.
       8vo.   *Edinb.*, T. & T. Clark.   1840.
       Largely composed of citations from *Luther* and *Calvin*.   The remarks
       will assist in elucidating the design of the parables.

1024   **TRENCH** (R. C., D.D.) Notes on the Parables.
       $3.75. Revell; Popular edition. $2.95. Baker.
       *We do not like Trench's theology in many places, but he is a
       capital writer.   The student will find a very complete list of exposi-
       tions on the Parables in the appendix at the close of Trench's work.*

1025   UPJOHN (W.) Discourses on the Parables.   3 vols., sm. 8vo.   1824.
       Earnestly Calvinistic sermons, full of old-fashioned Gospel.   Not very original.

MATTHEW.

[See also works on the Four Gospels.]

1026   ABBOTT (LYMAN, *U.S.A.*) New Testament. Vol. I. Matthew
       and Mark.   Sq. 8vo.,   *Lond.*, Hodder.   1875.
       Intended for workers, and likely to be useful to them.

1027   ADAMSON (H. T., B.D.) Matthew expounded.   Thick 8vo.   *Lond.*,
       Sampson Low.   1871.
       This book reads to us like utter nonsense.   We question if anyone except the
       author will ever be able to make head or tail of it, and he had better be quick about
       it, or he will forget what he meant.

1028   **ALEXANDER** (JOSEPH ADDISON, D.D.)   Matthew
       Explained.   Post 8vo.   *Lond.*, Nisbet.   1870.
       *Dr. Alexander's last work.   He died before it was quite finished.
       It is complete to Chapter XVI.   Its value is great.*

1029   BEAUSOBRE (ISAAC DE, 1659—1738), and L'ENFANT
       (JAQUES, 1661—1728).   A New Version, with a Commentary.
       8vo.   *Camb.*, 1790 ; *Lond.*, 1823, &c.
       The brief notes are purely literal or illustrative, and are remarkably
       pertinent.   The mass of the volume is taken up with an introduction
       to the New Testament.

1030   BENHAM (W.)   Matthew, with Notes.   Cr. 8vo.   *Lond.*,
       National Society.   [1861].
       With this in his hand a teacher would be much aided in conducting
       his class.   It is written by a teacher for teachers.   The remarks are not
       very profound, nor always such as we should endorse, but they are well
       fitted for their purpose.

1031 BLACKWOOD (CHRISTOPHER). An Exposition upon the Ten First Chapters of Matthew. 4to. 1649.

This learned divine became a Baptist through studying the arguments against believers' baptism. This proves his candour. His comment is somewhat out of date, but it is still good.

1032 CLARKE (GEORGE W.) Notes. Cr. 8vo. *New York*, 1870.

Good notes for teachers. Well compiled. A fit companion to No. 983.

1033 **DICKSON** (DAVID). A Brief Exposition of Matthew. 8vo. 1651.

A perfect gem. The work is, to men of our school, more suggestive of sermons than almost any other we have met with.

1034 GODWIN (JOHN H.) New Translation, with Brief Notes. Cr. 8vo. *Lond.*, Bagsters. 1863.

Dr. Godwin is a painstaking elucidator of the word, and his plan is an excellent one. Students in college will value him.

1035 GOODWIN (HARVEY, D.D., *Bp. of Carlisle*). Commentary. Cr. 8vo. *Lond.*, G. Bell & Sons. 1857.

An important work, which may be consulted with advantage.

1036 KELLY (WILLIAM). Lectures on the Gospel of Matthew. $3.00. Loizeaux.

We cannot accept the forced and fanciful interpretations here given.

1037 MARLORATUS [MARLORAT] (AUGUSTINE. 1560—1562). Exposition. Translated by Thomas Tymme. Folio. *Lond.*, 1570.

Marlorate was an eminent French reformer, preacher, and martyr. His commentaries contain the cream of the older writers, and are in much esteem, but are very rare. He wrote on the whole New Testament, but we have in English only the Gospels and Jude.

1038 **MORISON** (JAMES, D.D.) Matthew's Memoirs of Jesus Christ. 8vo. *Lond.*, Hamilton. 1870.

We differ greatly in doctrinal views from Dr. Morison, but we set a great price upon his Matthew and Mark, which deserve the utmost praise.

1039 OVERTON (CHARLES). Expository Preacher. Course of Lectures on Matthew. 2 vols., 8vo. *Lond.*, Nisbet. 1850. *Scarce.*

Solid, sound, soporific sermons ; intended for lay helpers to read, with the prayers appended. They will not make the hearers lie awake at nights, or cause them palpitations of heart through excess of original and striking thought.

1040 PARKER (JOSEPH, D.D.) Homiletic Analysis. Matthew. 8vo. *Lond.*, 1870.

Dr. Parker is an able though somewhat——. But stop, he is a near neighbour of ours.

1041 PENROSE (JOHN). Lectures on Matthew. 12mo. *Lond.*, 1832.

The author says of his work, "no novelty of any kind, no originality either of thought or research will be found in it." Why, then, did he print it ?

1042 **THOMAS** (DAVID, D.D.) Genius of the Gospel. Homiletical Commentary. 8vo. *Lond.*, Dickinson. 1873.
We hardly know a more suggestive book.

1043 WARD (RICHARD). Theologicall Questions, Dogmaticall Observations, and Evangelicall Essays vpon the Gospel according to Matthew. Wherein about two thousand six hundred and fifty profitable Questions are discussed ; and five hundred and eighty points of Doctrine noted, &c., &c. Folio. *Lond.*, 1640.

A huge mass of comment, in which are thousands of good things mostly set forth by way of question and answer. Few could ever read it through ; but to a wise minister it would be a mine of wealth.

MARK.

1044 **ALEXANDER** (JOSEPH ADDISON, D.D.) Mark Explained. Post 8vo.   *Lond.*, Nisbet. 1866.
Alexander expounds Mark as an independent record, and does not constantly tell us to "see Matthew and Luke." Hence the book is complete in itself, and the author's learning and care have made it invaluable.

1045 B. (G.) Practical Commentary on Mark, in Simple and Familiar Language. 12mo.   *Lond.*, Nisbet. 1863.

The different paragraphs are treated under most suggestive headings, which are the most useful parts of the book. Infant baptism is far too prominent ; but the little work is likely to be very helpful.

1046 GODWIN (JOHN H.) Mark. A New Translation, with Notes and Doctrinal Lessons. Cr. 8vo.   *Lond.*, Hodder & Stoughton. 1869.

We like the brief doctrinal lessons, which are rather a new feature. They will serve admirably well as sermon-hints. The notes and translation are really good.

1047 GOODWIN (HARVEY, D.D., *Bp. of Carlisle*). Commentary. Cr. 8vo.   *Lond.*, G. Bell & Sons. 1860.

Contains much very helpful comment. Produced in connection with the Cambridge Working Men's College.

1048 **MORISON** (JAMES, D.D.) A Commentary. Large 8vo.   *Lond.*, Hamilton, Adams & Co. 1873.
A deeply learned work ; we know of none more thorough. Differing as we do from this author's theology, we nevertheless set a high price upon this production.

1049 PETTER (GEORGE). Commentary on Mark. 2 vols., folio. *Lond.*, 1661.
Mr. J. C. Ryle says of this work : " For laborious investigation of the meaning of every word, for patient discussion of every question bearing

on the text, for fulness of matter, for real thoughtfulness, and for continued practical application, there is no work on St. Mark which, in my
opinion, bears comparison with *Petter's*. Like Goliath's sword, there is
nothing like it." We have found far less fresh thought in it than we
expected, and think it rather tedious reading.

LUKE.

[See also on the Gospels. *Oosterzee* in *Lange* is excellent.]

1050 **FOOTE** (JAMES, M.A.) Lectures on Luke. 2 vols. 8vo.
Third edition. *Edinb.*, Ogle & Murray, and Oliver &
Boyd; *Lond.*, Hamilton, Adams & Co. 1858.
*We frequently consult this work, and never without finding in it
things new and old. To preachers who will not steal the lectures,
but use them suggestively, they will be extremely serviceable.*

1051 **GODET** (F., *Professor of Theology, Neuchatel*). Commentary on Luke. Translated by E. W. Shelders, B.A., and
M. D. Cusin. 2 vols., 8vo. *Edinb.*, Clark. 1875.
*Dr. Meyer says: "To an immense erudition, to a living piety,
Godet unites a profound feeling of reality; there is here a vivifying
breath, an ardent love for the Saviour, which helps the disciple to
comprehend the work, the acts, the words of his Divine Master."*

1052 GOODWIN (HARVEY, D.D.) Commentary on Luke. Cr. 8vo.
Lond., G. Bell & Sons. 1865.
This writer endeavours to give the results of learning in such a manner
that working men may understand them. He says many good things.

1053 MAJOR (J. R., M.A.) Luke, with English Notes. 8vo. *Lond.*, 1826.
Notes compiled with a view to the divinity examinations at Cambridge, containing
a considerable amount of information.

1054 **THOMSON** (JAMES, D.D.) Exposition of Luke, in a
Series of Lectures. 3 vols., 8vo. *Edinb.*, A. & C. Black;
Lond., Longmans. 1849.
*Eminently instructive. Clear good sense, freshness, and earnest-
ness are well combined. We have had great pleasure in examining
these lectures.*

1055 **VAN DOREN** (W. H., *of Chicago*). Suggestive Commentary on the New Testament, on an original plan
[Luke, 2 vols., cr. 8vo., *Lond.*, Dickinson. 1871.
*Well named "suggestive"; it is all suggestions. It teems and
swarms with homiletical hints.*

JOHN.

1056 ANDERSON (ROBERT. 1792—1843). Practical Exposition of John. 2 vols., 12mo. *Lond.*, 1841.

By an evangelical clergyman : sound, but not very original.

1057 AUGUSTINE. Commentary on John. 2 vols. of *Works of Augustine*, now in course of issue by T. & T. Clark. *Edinb.*

1058   „   Homilies on the Gospel and First Epistle of John. 2 vols. of the *Library of the Fathers*, *Lond.* and *Oxf.*, Jas. Parker & Co.

To the wise a mine of treasure. *Augustine* is often fanciful ; but even his fancies show a master-mind. Much that passes for new is stolen from this prince of theologians.

1059 BEITH (ALEXANDER, D.D.) Expository Discourses. Cr. 8vo. *Lond.*, Nisbet. 1857.

Discourses which must have been very profitable to the hearers. Students will do better with works which are more condensed.

1060 BESSER (RUDOLPH, D.D.) Biblical Studies on John. Translated from the German by M. G. Huxtable. 2 vols. cr. 8vo. *Edinb.*, T. & T. Clark. 1861—62.

"The character of this commentary is practical and devotional. There are often very exquisite devotional passages, and a vein of earnest piety runs through the whole work."—*Literary Churchman.*

1061 BROWN (GEORGE J., M.A.) Lectures, forming a Continuous Commentary. 2 vols., 8vo. *Lond.*, Rivingtons. 1863.

The plan of this work will prevent its being widely used ; but its execution strikes us as being uncommonly able. It is a gathering up of other men's materials and an amalgamation of them. It is intensely Episcopalian, even to Baptismal Regeneration, yet it brings a good deal of light to bear on the Gospel of John, and, if to be met with at a very low figure, it is not to be passed by.

1062 DRUMMOND (D. T. K., B.A.) Exposition of the Last Nine Chapters of John. 12mo. Seeleys. 1850.

Good, but not very striking.

1063 DUNWELL (FRANCIS HENRY, B.A.) Commentary on the Authorised Version of John, compared with the Sinaitic, Vatican, and Alexandrian Manuscripts, and also with Dean Alford's revised translation. 8vo. *Lond.*, J. T. Hayes. 1872.

The notes from various authors are good, and the various readings are useful ; but we fail to see any very special value in the volume. The interpretation of the Third of John is eminently unsatisfactory ; *Mr. Dunwell* teaches Baptismal Regeneration.

1064 FAWCETT (JOHN, A.M. 1769—1851). Exposition of John. 3 vols., 8vo., *Lond.*, Hatchards. 1860.

Good, evangelical sermons.

1065 HENGSTENBERG (E. W., D.D.) Commentary on John.
2 vols., 8vo. *Edinb.*, Clark. 1868.
Like others of this author's works : solid, but dry.

1066 **HUTCHESON** (GEORGE). Exposition of John. Folio.
Lond., 1657. Reprinted, roy. 8vo. *Lond.*, Ward. 1841.

*Excellent; beyond all praise. It is a full-stored treasury of
sound theology, holy thought, and marrowy doctrine.*

1067 MEYER (H. A. W., D.D.) *See No.* 928.

1068 O'CONOR (W. A.) Commentary. Cr. 8vo. *Lond.*, Longmans. 1872.
In this translation the first verse runs thus : " In origin the Word was, and the
Word was the Deity, and the Word was Deity." Who likes this, or understands it ?
The notes do not charm us.

1069 SHEPHERD (R., D.D.) Notes on the Gospel and Epistles of John. 4to.
Lond., 1796. Imp. 8vo. *Lond.*, Murray. 1841.
Though the author opposed Socinianism, we cannot but regard his views as an
introduction to that heresy. The spirit of the book is vicious.

1070 **THOLUCK** (AUGUSTUS F., D.D., Ph.D.) Commentary.
8vo. *Edinb.*, T. & T. Clark. 1860.
*More spiritual than is usual with German theologians, and quite
as scholarly as the best of them.*

1071 TITTMANN (K. C., *Theol. Prof.* 1744—1820). Commentary.
2 vols., cr. 8vo. *Bib. Cab. Edinb.*, T. Clark. 1844.
Horne, in speaking of this work in the German, without endorsing all
Tittmann's opinions, declares it to be the most valuable commentary on
John extant in so small a form. Our judgment is less commendatory.

1072 TRAHERON (BARTHOLOMEW. *Died* 1716.) An Exposition of a Parte
of S. Johannes Gospel made in sondrie readinges in the English Congregation. 12mo. 1558. *Very rare,*
A little quaint old book. Not intrinsically worth the price, nor a tenth of it.

1073 **VAN DOREN** (W. H., D.D.) Suggestive Commentary
on John, Vol. I., containing chap. I.—IX. Cr. 8vo.
nett. Vol II. in the press. *Lond.*, Dickinson. 1872.
*If men who read this volume do not preach the better for so doing,
it is not Mr. Van Doren's fault; they must be Van Dolts by nature,
though they may ignore the family name.*

PARTS OF JOHN.

[A selection of authors is all we can give.]

1074 **HILDERSHAM** (ARTHUR). Lectures on John IV.
Folio. *Lond.*, 1628 and 1656.
A mass of godly teaching; but rather heavy reading.

1075 TURNER (SAMUEL, H., D.D.) Essay on our Lord's Discourse at Caper-
naum, recorded in John VI. Cr. 8vo. *New York,* 1851.
Written with the immediate view of combating the errors of *Dr.,* afterwards
Cardinal, Wiseman, who appeals to this chapter for proofs of " the real presence."

1076   PATTERSON (JOHN B., *of Falkirk*).   Lectures on John XIV,
       XV, and XVI.   Cr. 8vo.   *Edinb.*, T. Clark.   1859.
   Solid discourses, containing much thought happily expressed.   Yet
withal somewhat laborious reading.

1077   **ALEXANDER** (THOMAS, D.D.)   Great High Priest
       within the Vail.   John XVII.   18mo.   *Lond.*, 1857.
   Sound theology and honest exposition.   Multum in parvo.

1078   **BROWN** (JOHN, D.D.)   Exposition of John XVII.   8vo.
       Lond., Hamilton, 1850.
   Dr. Brown is always deep, full, and overflowing.

1079   **BURGESS** (ANTHONY).   One Hundred and Forty-five
       Sermons on John XVII.   Folio.   *Lond.*, 1656.
   A standard work by a great Puritan.   Somewhat prolix.

1080   LANDELS (WILLIAM, D.D.)   The Saviour's Parting Prayer for
       his Disciples.   12mo.   *Lond.*, Elliot Stock.   1872.
   Sermons of a high order: style admirable, but rather diffuse.   To be
estimated rather from a homiletical than an expository point of view.

1081   **NEWTON** (GEORGE.   1602—1681).   John   XVII.
       Unfolded.   Folio.   *Lond.*, 1660.   Reprinted in Nichol's
       Commentaries.   Cr. 4to.   *Lond.*, Nisbet.   1867.
   *If not one of the chief of the Puritans, Newton was but little
behind the front rank in ability.   Joseph Alleine was his assistant
minister at Taunton.   His writings are plain and profitable.*

1082   **PIERCE** (SAMUEL EYLES).   Exposition of the Lord's
       Prayer, in John XVII.   8vo.   1812.
   Always sweet as honey to those of strong Calvinistic views.

ACTS OF THE APOSTLES.

[*See* also under *Gospels.*]

1083   **ALEXANDER** (JOSEPH ADDISON, D.D.)   The Acts
       Explained.   2 vols., 8vo.   *Lond.*, Nisbet.   1869.
   In all respects a work of the highest merit.

1084   **ALFORD** (HENRY, D.D.)   Homilies on the former part
       of the Acts of the Apostles.   Ch. I.—X.   8vo.
       Lond., Rivingtons.   1858.
   *Not so good as his critical notes; but such an author always
deserves attention.*

1085   **ARNOT** (WILLIAM, D.D.)   The Church in the House.
       Post 8vo.   *Lond.*, Nisbet.   1873.
   *Intended to be read in families on Sabbath afternoons; but all
who are acquainted with Dr. Arnot will know that even his
simplest expositions are rich and full.   He hath dust of gold.*

1086 BAUMGARTEN (M., Ph.D.) Apostolic History. 3 vols., 8vo. *Edinb.*, T. & T. Clark. 1854.

" An exposition at once profoundly scientific and sublimely Christian, one of the most pressing wants of our times."—*Eclectic Review.* *Alford* calls it excellent, though somewhat fanciful.

1087 BENNETT (JAMES, D.D.) Lectures on the Acts. 8vo. *Lond.*, 1847.

A good specimen of plain and popular pulpit exposition. *Dr. Bennett* fights very earnestly for the Congregationalist view of Baptism, for which we do not blame him; for common humanity leads us to admire a man who struggles for a weak cause.

1088 BENSON (GEORGE, D.D. 1699—1763). History of the first planting of the Christian Religion. 3 vols., 4to. *Lond.*, 1756.
Dull, but displaying considerable research. *Benson* was an Arian.

1089 **BONAR** (H., D.D.) Light and Truth. Vol. III. (*See No. 6.*)

1090 BOUCHIER (BARTON, A.M.) Manna in the House; or, Daily Expositions of the Acts. 12mo. *Lond.*, 1858.

Superior family reading. *Bouchier* did not write for students, but for households, yet even the more advanced may learn from him.

1091 BREWSTER (JOHN, M.A.) Lectures on the Acts. 8vo. 1830.
A sip of *Howson* or *Hackett* is worth a barrel of these weak and watery prelections.

1092 **CALVIN** (JOHN). Commentaries upon the Acts.
Reprint of C.T.S. edition, 2 volumes $7.00. Eerdmans.
This forms the basis of the Calvin Translation Society's edition.

1093 COOK (F. C., M.A., *Canon of Chester*). The Acts, with a Commentary. 8vo. *Lond.*, Longmans. 1866.
Contains many useful notes, instructive to fairly educated readers.

1094 CRADOCK (Samuel, B.D.) The Apostolical History, containing the Acts, Labours, Travels, Sermons, &c., of the Apostles. Folio. *Lond.*, 1762.
Tillotson, Reynolds, Doddridge, and others highly commend the works of this Puritan writer. The style in which the "Apostolical History" is got up is most uninviting; the book is nearly all italics. Many modern works far excel it.

1095 **DENTON** (W., M.A.) Commentary on the Acts. 2 vols., 8vo. *Lond.*, G. Bell. 1874.
A complete list of all authors upon the Acts will be found in this very learned and exhaustive work. We do not always agree with the author, but he has done his work thoroughly well.

1096 DICK (JOHN, D.D. 1764—1833). Lectures on the Acts. Sm. 8vo. *Glasg.*, 1848.

Interesting lectures upon selected portions of the Acts. This work has been reprinted in America, whence we obtained a copy of the second edition; this shows that it has been highly esteemed.

1097 DU VEIL (C. M., D.D. *A learned converted Jew. Died about*
       1700). Explanation of the Acts. 8vo. *Lond.*, 1685. Reprinted
       by *Hansard Knollys Society*. 8vo. 1851.
Claude's prefatory letter highly commends this work. The author
defends the immersion of believers with earnestness.

1098 **FAWCETT** (JOHN, M.A.) Exposition of the Acts.
       3 vols., 8vo.   *Lond.*, Hatchards. 1860.
A fine series of expository discourses. Sometimes we differ.

1099 FORD (J., M.A.) The Acts, illustrated from Ancient and
       Modern Authors. 8vo.   *Lond.*, Masters. 1856. (*See No.* 955.)

1100 **GLOAG** (PATON J., D.D.) Commentary on the Acts.
       2 vols., demy 8vo,   *Edinb.*, T. & T. Clark. 1870.
*Dr. Hackett says of Dr. Gloag's work: "I have examined it with
special care. For my purposes I have found it unsurpassed by any
similar work in the English language. It shows a thorough
mastery of the material, philology, history, and literature pertaining
to this range of study, and a skill in the use of this knowledge,
which places it in the first class of modern expositions."*

1101 GUALTHERUS (RODULPHUS. 1529—1586). A Hundred
       Threescore and Fifteen Homelyes or Sermons vppon the Actes
       of the Apostles, made by Radulphe Gualthere, of Tigurine, and
       Translated out of Latine [by John Bridges, Vicare of Herne].
       Folio. *Black Letter. Lond.*, 1572.
Full of Protestantism. The author judged that, as Luke who wrote
the Act was a physician, his book was meant to be medicine to the Church.

1102 **HACKETT** (HORATIO B., D.D.) American Commentary—
       Hackett on Acts with Arnold and Ford on Romans in one
       volume. $3.50. Judson.
*Hackett occupies the first position among commentators upon the
Acts. The Bunyan Library edition omits some of his most
valuable critical observations.*

1103 HODGSON (ROBERT, D.D., *Dean of Carlisle*). Lectures upon the first
       Seventeen Chapters of the Acts. 8vo. *Lond.*, 1845.
Deficient in Gospel clearness, and in every other respect, except ardent churchism.

1104 HUMPHRY (WILLIAM GILSON, B.D.) Commentary on the Acts. Second
       edition. 8vo. *Lond.*, J. W. Parker & Son. 1854.
Exegetical remarks upon the Greek text. Very good from a philological point of
view, but professedly of an elementary character.

1105 KELLY (W.) Lectures Introductory to the Study of the Acts, Catholic
       Epistles, and Revelation. Cr. 8vo.   *Lond.*, Broom. 1870.
By a man "who, born for the universe, narrowed his mind" by Darbyism.

1106 LANGE (J. P.) Commentary: Edited by Dr. P. Schaff.
       $3.95. Zondervan.
       (*See page* 19.)
Adds nothing to our knowledge of the Acts; but the homiletical
hints are useful.

1107 LIGHTFOOT (JOHN, D.D. 1602—1675). Commentary. Edited by J. R. Pitman, A.M. 8vo. 1823. [Vol. VIII. of Lightfoot's Works.]

Few now-a-days will care for this author, whose learning ran mostly in Talmudical channels. He was profound, but not always discreet.

1108 MACBRIDE (JOHN DAVID, D.D.) Lectures on the Acts and Epistles. 8vo. *Oxf.*, 1858.

This author simply gives a continuous narrative. He has also written on the Gospels. We mention him that the student may not purchase his work as a Commentary.

1109 MASKEW (T. R., B.A.) Annotations on the Acts. With College and Senate-House Examination Papers. 12mo. *Camb.*, 1847.

A handbook to the Acts, viewing it simply as a Greek book ; prepared for the use of students passing through the university.

1110 MIMPRISS (R.) The Acts and Epistles, according to Greswell's Arrangement. 8vo. 1837.

A handy book for teachers.

1111 NEANDER (J. A. W.) History of the Planting and Training of the Christian Church by the Apostles. Translated by J. E. Ryland. 2 vols., cr. 8vo. *Lond., Bohn's Library*, Bell & Sons. 1851. Also in *Cabinet Library*.

The work rather of an historian than of a commentator. Bold, devout, learned, and, on the whole, sound. The result of wide research, and deep learning.

1112 NORRIS (J. P., M.A.) Key to the Acts. Sm. 8vo. *Lond.*, Rivingtons. 1871.

A well-executed sketch of the Acts of the Apostles, giving the student a clear idea of the run of the book. Like the same author's " Key to the Gospels " (*No.* 963), it would be most useful in Bible classes.

1113 OLSHAUSEN (H., D.D.) *See No.* 964.

Denton says that " this is a brief, hasty, and not well-digested supplement to *Olshausen's* volumes on the Gospels." He thinks all the German writers to be much overrated, and we are much of his mind.

1114 PYLE (T., M.A. 1674—1756). Paraphrase. 2 vols., 8vo. 1795.

This pile of printed paper may safely be left on the bookseller's shelves.

1115 **STIER** (RUDOLPH, D.D.) The Words of the Apostles. 8vo. *Edinb.*, T. & T. Clark. 1869.

Devout, scholarly, full of thought. To be used discreetly.

1116 **STOCK** (EUGENE). Lessons on the Acts. For Sunday School Teachers and other Religious Instructors. 8vo. *Lond.*, Ch. of England S. School Institute. 1874.

For half-a-crown the teacher may here obtain one of the most useful books known to us. Though produced for members of the Church of England, we recommend it heartily to ministers and others who are preparing addresses to the young.

1117 THOMAS (DAVID, D.D.) Homiletic Commentary on the Acts. 8vo. *Lond.*, Dickinson. 1870.

Many of the homiletic outlines strike us as " much ado about nothing "; still, if a man should read this work and get no help from it, it would be his own fault.

1118 THOMSON (JAMES, D.D.) Exposition of the Acts. 8vo. *Lond.*, A. Hall, Virtue, & Co. 1854.
We fail to see much here of service to a preacher.

1119 TROLLOPE (W., M.A.) Commentary on the Acts, with Examination Questions, for the B.A. Degree. 12mo. *Camb.*, 1854.
Well adapted to accomplish the design indicated in the title.

1120 **VAUGHAN** (CHARLES J., D.D.) Lectures. 3 vols. Fcap. 8vo. *Lond.*, Macmillan. 1864, etc.
Not only does Dr. Vaughan expound his texts in the ablest manner, but he introduces passages of Scripture so aptly that he suggests discourses. Bating his Churchianity, we cannot too highly commend him.

LIVES OF THE APOSTLES, &c.

1121 **KITTO** (JOHN, D.D.) "The Apostles and the Early Church." *Daily Bible Illustrations.* (See No. 41.)

1122 BAUR (FERDINAND CHRISTIAN, D.D.) Paul, his Life and Works. From the German. 2 vols., 8vo. *Lond.*, William & Norgates. 1873—75.
Of the very Broad Church school. Not at all to our mind.

1123 BEVAN (JOSEPH GURNEY). Life of Paul. 8vo. *Lond.*, 1807.
For the Society of Friends. Contains nothing which adds to our information upon the life of Paul. It may have been useful in its day, but it is superseded.

1124 BINNEY (THOMAS, D.D.) Paul : his Life and Ministry. Cr. 8vo. *Lond.*, Nisbet. 1870.
Mr. Binney says, "This work is strictly an outline of the life of St. Paul, and it is nothing more." It is a capital preparation for reading *Lewin* and *Conybeare* and *Howson.*

1125 BLUNT (HENRY, A.M.) Lectures upon the History of St. Paul. 2 vols., 12mo. Sixth edition. *Lond.*, 1835.
Printed in such large and widely-leaded type that a very little matter goes a long way. Very good, but not striking.

1126 **CONYBEARE** (W. J., M.A.) and **HOWSON** (J. S., D.D., *Dean of Chester*). Life and Epistles of St. Paul.
One volume edition, unabridged. $5.00. Eerdmans.

Far superior to any other work on the subject. It stands like some o'ertopping Alp, a marvel among Scriptural biographies. We have not space to mention Howson's minor works connected with Paul, but they are all good.

1127 **EADIE** (JOHN, D.D., LL.D.) Paul, the Preacher. An Exposition of his Discourses and Speeches, as recorded in the Acts. Cr. 8vo. *Lond.*, Griffin. 1859.
Designed to give ordinary readers a juster and fuller conception of the doctrine and life-work of the apostle. An able work.

1128 LEWIN (Thomas, M.A., F.S.A., *Barrister-at-Law*). Life and Epistles of St. Paul.   Second edition, much enlarged. 2 vols., demy 4to.   *Lond.*, G. Bell & Sons.   1875.

Dr. Gloag in his Commentary on the Acts says: " Two works are especially instructive, and deserve careful perusal. The Life and Epistles of St. Paul, by Lewin, and the classical work on the same subject by Conybeare and Howson.   In the former the historical connections of the Acts are chiefly stated, and in the latter its geographical relations."

1129 LYTTLETON (George, Lord).   Observations on the Conversion and Apostleship of St. Paul.   In a letter to Gilbert West, Esq.   8vo.   *Lond.*, 1747.   [Numerous editions.   The Tract Society's edition.   Fcap. 8vo.

Gilbert West and his friend *Lord Lyttleton*, both men of acknowledged talents, had imbibed the principles of infidelity from a superficial view of the Scriptures.   Fully persuaded that the Bible was an imposture, they were determined to expose the cheat.   *Mr. West* chose the Resurrection of Christ, and *Lord Lyttleton* the Conversion of St. Paul, for the subject of hostile criticism.   Both sat down to their respective tasks, full of prejudice, and a contempt for Christianity.   The result of their separate attempts was that they were both converted by their endeavours to overthrow the truth of Christianity !   They came together, not as they expected, to exult over an imposture exposed to ridicule, but to lament their folly, and to congratulate each other on their joint conviction, that the Bible was the word of God.   Their able enquiries have furnished two most valuable treatises in favour of revelation ; one, entitled "Observations on the Conversion of St. Paul," and the other, "Observations on the Resurrection of Christ."

1130 MACDUFF (J. R., D.D.)   St. Paul in Rome.   Cr. 8vo. *Lond.*, Nisbet.   1871.

Sermons preached in Rome, into which are ably introduced eloquent mention of the existing traditions and remains which associate the Apostle with that great city.

1131 BISCOE (Richard, M.A., *Preb. of St. Paul's.   Died* 1748). History of the Acts of the Apostles.   Confirmed from other Authors, and considered as full evidence of the Truth of Christianity.   8vo.   *Oxf.*, 1840.

1132 PALEY (William, D.D.   1743—1805).   Horæ Paulinæ. Numerous editions.   The Religious Tract Society publishes the Horæ Paulinæ, with Notes, and Horæ Apostolicæ, by Rev. T. Birks.   12mo.

1133 TATE (James, *Canon of St. Paul's*).   The Horæ Paulinæ carried out and illustrated.   8vo.   *Lond.*, 1840.

Though not commentaries, the three works just mentioned are sources of information not to be neglected by the student of the Acts.

1134 RIVINGTON (Francis).   Life and Writings of St. Paul.   Cr. 8vo.   *Lond.*, Sampson Low & Co.   1874.

Nobody possessing *Conybeare* and *Howson* will need this work, though in the absence of better this would have been serviceable.

1135 SMITH (Thornley).   Saul of Tarsus.   *Lond.*, J. Blackwood & Co.

Thornley Smith always deserves attentive reading.

1136 BLUNT (HENRY, A.M.) Lectures upon the History of St. Peter. 12mo. *Lond.*, 1830.   (*For remarks, see No.* 1125).

1137 **GREEN** (SAMUEL G., D.D., *President of Rawdon College*). The Apostle Peter : his Life and Lessons. 12mo. *Lond.*, S. School Union. 1873.

Contains a large amount of needful information, condensed and well arranged. Dr. Green is the writer on Peter's biography.

1138 KRUMMACHER (F. W., D.D.) St. John the Evangelist. 12mo. *Bib. Cabinet. Edinb.*, T. & T. Clark.

The author's name is a sufficient guarantee. He has also written on Cornelius and Stephen.

1139 GOULBURN (EDWARD MEYRICK, D.D., *Dean of Norwich*). Acts of the Deacons : Lectures on Acts VI.—IX. Sm. 8vo. *Lond.*, Rivingtons. 1869.

An interesting topic well handled.

THE APOSTOLICAL EPISTLES.

1140 BENSON (GEORGE, D.D. 1699—1763). Paraphrase and Notes on 1 & 2 Thessalonians, 1 & 2 Timothy, Philemon, Titus, and the Seven Catholic Epistles. 2 vols., 4to. 1734.

Benson has closely followed *Locke's* method, though scarcely with equal footsteps, and has paraphrased those Epistles which *Locke* did not live to complete. In the consecutive reading of an Epistle *Locke* and *Benson* are great assistants, but as *Benson* was an Arian he must be read with great caution. (*See No.* 1148).

1141 DENTON (W.) Commentaries on the Epistles for Sundays and Holy Days. 2 vols., 8vo.   *Lond.*, G. Bell & Co. 1869—71.

Will be a treasure to Churchmen. *Denton* is a good author.

1142 **DICKSON** (DAVID). Exposition of all the Epistles. Folio. *Lond.* 1659.

Dickson is a writer after our own heart. For preachers he is a great ally. There is nothing brilliant or profound ; but everything is clear and well arranged, and the unction runs down like the oil from Aaron's head. In this volume the observations are brief.

1143 **ELLICOTT** (CHARLES J., D.D., *Bp. of Gloucester and Bristol*). Commentary on St. Paul's Epistles. 5 vols., 8vo. Galatians,   Ephesians,   Pastoral Epistles, Philippians, Colossians, and Philemon, Thessalonians,   *Lond.*,Longmans. 1861—64.

Dr. Eadie says, "Ellicott is distinguished by close and uniform adherence to grammatical canon, without much expansion into exegesis." Dr. Riddle thinks Ellicott to be in many respects without an English rival. For scholars only.

1144 **FERGUSON** (JAMES). Exposition of the Epistles to the Galatians, Ephesians, Philippians, Colossians, and Thessalonians. 8vo. *Edinb.*, 1659—74. Reprinted, 1 vol., large 8vo. *Lond.*, 1841.

He who possesses this work is rich. The author handles his matter in the same manner as Hutcheson and Dickson, and he is of their class—a grand, gracious, savoury divine.

1145 **GLOAG** (PATON J., D.D.) Introduction to the Pauline Epistles. 8vo. *Edinb.*, T. & T. Clark. 1874.

Not an exposition, but an exceedingly valuable introduction, illustrating the design, date, and circumstances of the inspired letters.

1146 JOWETT (BENJAMIN, M.A., *Regius Professor, Oxford*). Epistles to the Thessalonians, Galatians, and Romans [Greek and English]; with Critical . Notes. 2 vols., 8vo. *Lond.*, Murray. 1859.

Professor Jowett's most unseemly attack on Paul, as an apostle, as a thinker, as a writer, and as a man, only proves his own incapacity for forming a just judgment either of the apostle or of himself.

1147 KELLY (WILLIAM). Lectures Introductory to the Study of Paul's Epistles. Demy 8vo. *Lond.*, G. Morrish. 1869.

Of the same character as *Mr. Kelly's* other works. (*See No.* 1220).

1148 LOCKE (JOHN, M.A. 1632—1704). Paraphrase and Notes on the Epistles to the Galatians, Corinthians, Romans, and Ephesians. 4to. *Lond.*, 1733. Also 8vo. editions.

Anything from such a man is worthy of attention, and this piece, as a protest against rending texts from their connection, is most judicious. The paraphrase, though open to criticism, is executed with great candour, and really illuminates the text. (*See Benson, No.* 1140).

1149 LYTH (JOHN, D.D.) The Homiletical Treasury. Romans to Philippians. Cr. 8vo. *Lond.*, Elliot Stock. 1869.

The plan of this book is surpassingly useful, but *Dr. Lyth* does not carry it out to our satisfaction. It is easy to divide an egg by letting it drop on the floor, and in this fashion this author divides texts.

1150 MACKNIGHT (J., D.D. 1721—1800). Translation with Commentary and Notes. 6 vols., 8vo., 1816; also 4 vols., 8vo., and 1 vol., royal 8vo.

To be read with great caution. We do not admire this author.

1151 MARSTON (CHARLES DALLAS, M.A.) Expositions on the Epistles. 12mo. *Lond.*, J. F. Shaw & Co. 1868.

Expositions of each Epistle as a whole. An admirable method of instruction. To do this in a popular style is as praiseworthy as it is difficult. *Mr. Marston* has succeeded.

1152 PAGET (ALFRED T., M.A.) On the Unity and Order of the Epistles of St. Paul. 8vo. *Lond.*, Rivingtons. 1851.

Suggests a rich vein for the student's own working. Few, we fear, will carry it out, but these will prize the Epistles more than others.

1153 PEILE (T. W., D.D.) Annotations on the Apostolical Epistles, for the use of Students of the Greek Text. 4 vols., 8vo. *Lond.*, 1848—52.

Anticalvinistic in doctrine, and in style involved, obscure, and terribly parenthetical. The purchase of the volumes would be a heavy investment.

1154 PRICHARD (C. E., M.A.) Commentary. Ephesians, Philippians, and Colossians. *Lond.*, Rivingtons. 1865.

Not too diffuse : among the notes are some admirable hints which may be worked out. The book is a small one for so large a subject.

1155 SLADE (JAMES, M.A.) Annotations on the Epistles. For the use of Candidates for Holy Orders. 2 vols., 8vo. *Lond.*, 1836.

This is practically a continuation of *Elsley's* work (*No.* 954), which closed with the Acts. Notes dry and sapless, but from a literary point of view respectable.

ROMANS.

[Our space does not permit us to repeat the names of authors mentioned under *Acts* and *Apostolical Epistles*, but we urge the student carefully to refer thereto.]

1156 ADAM (THOMAS). Paraphrase on Romans I. to XI. 8vo. 1774 ; 12mo. 1805.

A poor paraphrase ; very correct and evangelical, but thin as Adam's ale. We are disappointed, for the " Private Thoughts" of the same author are highly esteemed.

1157 ANDERSON (ROBERT, *of Brighton.* 1792—1843). Exposition of Romans. 12mo. *Lond.*, 1837.

After the manner of *Charles Bridges.* Full of holy unction and devout meditation.

1158 BROWN (JOHN, *of Wamphray*). Exposition of Romans. 4to. *Edinb.*, 1766.

By a Calvinist of the old school. Heavy, perhaps ; but precious.

1159 **BROWN** (JOHN, D.D., *Edinb.*) Analytical Expositions of Romans. Large 8vo. *Edinb.*, W. Oliphant & Co. 1857.

Dr. Brown's work must be placed among the first of the first-class. He is a great expositor.

1160 **CALVIN** (JOHN). Commentary on Romans. Translated by Christopher Roodell. Reprint of C.T.S. edition. $4.50. Eerdmans.

1161 CHALLIS (JAMES, M.A., F.R.S., F.R.A.S.) Translation of Romans, with Notes. 8vo. *Lond.*, G. Bell & Sons. 1871.

The translation is made in the current language of the day. The notes are mainly critical.

1162 CHALMERS (T., D.D.) Lectures on Romans. 4 vols., 8vo. 1827. 4 vols., 12mo. *Edinb.*, Edmonston & Co. 1854.

Our preferences as to expositions lie in another direction ; but we cannot be insensible to the grandeur and childlike simplicity which were combined in *Chalmers.*

1163 EDWARDS (TIMOTHY, A.M.) Paraphrase, with Annotations, on Romans and Galatians. 4to. *Lond.*, 1752.

Watt calls this a judiciously compiled work from the best comments. We judge it to be poor as poverty itself.

1164 EWBANK (W. W.) Commentary, with Translation and Notes. 2 vols., post 8vo. *Lond.*, J. W. Parker. 1850.

A sound evangelical comment, very good and gracious. In condensed thought this work is not rich: it is adapted for general reading.

1165 FORD (J., M.A.). Romans. Illustrated from Ch. of England Divines. 8vo. Masters, 1862. (*See No.* 955).

1166 **FORBES** (JOHN, LL.D.) Analytical Commentary, tracing the Train of Thought by the Aid of Parallelism, with Notes, &c. 8vo. *Edinb.*, T. & T. Clark. 1868.

We think Dr. Forbes carries the idea of parallelism further than it should go. It can only be applied strictly to poetical books, which Romans is not. He tries to bring out the other side of the truths taught in Hodge, Edwards, and Calvin; but we confess our preference of those authors to himself. The work will greatly edify those whom it does not confuse.

1167 FRY (JOHN, B.A.) Lectures. 8vo. *Lond.*, 1816.

Having no theory to serve in this instance, *Fry* writes to edification.

1168 GODWIN (JOHN H., *Hon. Prof., New Coll., Lond.*) New Translation, with Notes. 8vo. *Lond.*, Hodder & Stoughton. 1873.

Such a book as students need while studying the Greek text in college.

1169 **HALDANE** (R. 1764 — 1842). Exposition: with Remarks on the Commentaries of Macknight and others. 8vo. *Edinb.*, W. Oliphant & Co. 1874.

Dr. Chalmers styled this "a well-built commentary," and strongly recommended it to students of theology. In his "Sabbath Readings" he writes: "I am reading 'Haldane's Exposition of the Epistle to the Romans,' and find it solid and congenial food."

1170 HINTON (J. HOWARD.) Exposition. 8vo. *Lond.*, 1863.

Not believing in the constant parallelism of the Epistles, we care very little for this treatise, much as we esteem the author.

1171 **HODGE** (CHARLES). Commentary. Revised unabridged edition. $5.00. Eerdmans.

Hodge's method and matter make him doubly useful in commenting. He is singularly clear, and a great promoter of thought.

1172 KELLY (WILLIAM). Notes. 12mo. *Lond.*, G. Morrish. 1873.

Many of the remarks are admirable, but the theories supported are untenable.

1173 KNIGHT (ROBERT). Commentary. 8vo. *Lond.*, 1854.

Not at all to our mind. The author often seems to us rather to becloud the text than to explain it.

1174 **LANGE** (J. P., D.D.) and **FAY** (F. R.) Commentary on Romans. (*See page* 19, *and No.* 923).

1175 MARTYR (PETER. 1500—1562). A most learned and fruitful Commentary on Romans. Folio. 1568.

Being in *black letter*, and very long, few will ever read it; but it contains much that will repay the laborious book-worm.

1176   OLSHAUSEN (H., D.D.) Commentary on Romans. 8vo.
       Edinb., T. & T. Clark. 1850.

Nobody seems very enthusiastic as to *Olshausen*, but some authors
have borrowed from his pages more than they have confessed. Personally
we do not care for him, but many prize and all respect him.

1177   **PARR** (ELNATHAN, B.D.) A Short View of the Epistle
       to the Romans. [Chap. I.; II., 1, 2; and VIII. to XVI.]
       This Exposition forms nearly the whole of "*The Workes*"
       of Parr. Fourth edition. Small folio. 1651.   The
       quartos do not contain the Exposition of Chap. I. and II.

*The style is faulty, but the matter is rich and full of suggestions.
We regret that the work is not complete, and is seldom to be met
with except in fragments.*

1178   PLUMER (WILLIAM S., D.D., LL.D.) Commentary, with
       Introduction on the Life, Times, Writings, and Character of
       Paul. Imp. 8vo.   *Edinb.*, W. Oliphant. [N. D.]

Plumer is a laborious compiler, and to most men his works will be of
more use than those of a more learned writer.

1179   PRIDHAM (ARTHUR). Notes. Cr. 8vo.   *Lond.,* Yapp. 1862.
       Sound and gracious, but somewhat dull.

1180   PURDUE (E., A.M.) Commentary on Romans. 8vo. *Dub.*, 1855.
       Not important.

1181   **ROBINSON** (T., D.D.) Suggestive Commentary on
       Romans. [*Van Doren* Series of Commentaries.] 2 vols.,
       cr. 8vo.   *Lond.*, Dickinson & Higham. 1871.

A good book in a good style. Worth any amount to preachers.

1182   STEPHEN (JOHN, A.M.) Expositions on Romans. A Series
       of Lectures. 12mo. *Aberd.*, 1857.
       Sound in doctrine, practical in tone; above mediocrity.

1183   STUART (MOSES.) Commentary on Romans. 8vo.   *Lond.,*
       W. Tegg & Co.

Moses Stuart is judged to have been at his best in Romans and
Hebrews.   The present work is in some points unsatisfactory, on
account of certain philosophico-theological views which he endeavours
to maintain.   *Mr. Haldane* denounced him as by false criticism "misrepresenting the divine testimony in some of the most momentous
points of the Christian scheme."   The charge was too true.

1184   TERROT (C. H., A.M., *Bp. of Edinburgh*). Romans [in Greek], with
       Introduction, Paraphrase, and Notes. 8vo. *Lond.*, 1828.
       Anti-Calvinistic.   Why do not such writers let Romans alone?

1185   THOLUCK (A. F.) Exposition of Romans. 2 vols., fcap.
       8vo.   *Bib. Cabinet Series. Edinb.*, T. Clark. 1842.

Moses Stuart confesses his great obligations to this eminent divine,
who far exceeds the most of his German brethren in spirituality, and is
not behind them in scholarship; yet even he is none too orthodox nor
too reverent in his treatment of Holy Scripture.

1186 **VAUGHAN** (CHARLES JOHN, D.D.) Romans. The Greek Text, with English Notes. Cr. 8vo. *Lond.,* Macmillan & Co. 1874.

Very valuable to students of the Greek. The result of independent study and honest labour.

1187 WALFORD (W.) Curæ Romanæ. 12mo. *Lond.,* 1846.

Walford makes comments of considerable value; he does not stand in the front rank, but his mediocrity is respectable.

1188 WARDLAW (RALPH, D.D.) Lectures on Romans. 3 vols., cr. 8vo. *Lond.,* Fullarton & Co. 1861.

Wardlaw interprets with great sobriety and spirituality, and we never consult him in vain, though we do not always agree with him.

1189 WILLET (ANDREW). Hexapla: that is, a Sixfold Commentary upon Romans. Folio. 1611. *(See No. 142.)*

1190 WILLIAMS (H. W., *Wesleyan Minister*). Exposition. Cr. 8vo. *Lond.,* 66, Paternoster Row. 1869.

This epistle has a fascination for Arminian writers; it affords them an opportunity for showing their courage and ingenuity. *Mr. Williams's* book is instructive.

1191 WILSON (THOMAS. *Puritan. Died* 1621). Commentary on Romans. 4to. *Lond.,* 1614. Folio, 1627 and 1653.

Intended for the less-instructed among the preacher's hearers, and put into the form of a dialogue. It is very solid, but does not contain much which is very striking or original.

1192 **SCLATER** (W., D.D. *Died* 1626). A Key to the Key of Scripture; or an Exposition, with Notes, upon the Romans, Chap. I., II., III. 4to. 1611 and 1629.

An antique, but precious book.

1193 MORISON (JAMES, D.D.) Exposition of the Third Chapter of Romans. 8vo. *Lond.,* Hamilton. 1866.

A scholarly and exhaustive exposition. When we do not agree with *Dr. Morison,* we pay homage to his great learning and critical skill.

1194 **FRASER** (JAMES. 1700—1796). The Doctrine of Sanctification. Explication of Romans VI. to VIII. 1—4. 8vo. *Edinb.,* 1830.

Dr. John Brown says: "Fraser's Scripture Doctrine of Sanctification is well worth studying. The old Scotch divine is rude in speech, but not in knowledge."

1195 **ELTON** (EDWARD, B.D.) Sundry Sermons upon Romans VII., VIII., and IX. Folio. *Lond.,* 1653.

The style is plain and homely, but the matter is of the choicest kind. This old folio is like an old skin bottle, with a rough exterior, but filled within with the product of the rarest vintage. Such books as this we never tire of reading.

1196   KOHLBRÜGGE (H. F., D.D., *of Elberfeld*).   Romans VII., paraphrased.   12mo.   *Lond.*, 1854.

An instructive rendering of this deeply experimental chapter.

1197   **BINNING** (HUGH.   1627—1653).   The Sinner's Sanctuary.   Forty-eight Sermons on Romans VIII.   4to.   1670. Also Vols. I. and II. of his *Works.*   3 vols., 12mo.   *Edinb.*, 1839.

The writer of Binning's Memoir says : " There is a pure stream of piety and learning running through the whole, and a very peculiar turn of thought, which exceeds the common rate of writers on this choice part of the Holy Scriptures."

1198   **HORTON** (THOMAS, D.D.)   Forty-six Sermons on Romans VIII.   *Lond.*   Folio.   1674.

Full of matter, well, but rather too formally, arranged.   The sermons are very prim and orderly.

1199   WINSLOW (OCTAVIUS, D.D.)   No Condemnation in Christ. [On Romans VIII.]   Cr. 8vo.   *Lond.*, Shaw.   1860.

Dr. Winslow is always sound and sweet ; but his works are better adapted for general readers than for students.   He is extremely diffuse.

I. & II. CORINTHIANS.

[*See* also under *Apostolical Epistles.*]

1200   BILLROTH (DR. GUSTAV.   1808—1836).   Commentary on the Epistles to the Corinthians.   2 vols., 12mo.   *Bib. Cabinet Series.   Edinb.*, T. & T. Clark.

To be prized for its criticism.   The author tries to bring forth from each passage the sense which the Apostle intended it to convey. Observations and reflections there are none ; but we are not among those who throw away "the dry bones of criticism"—bones are as needful as meat though not so nourishing.

1201   **CALVIN** (JOHN).   Commentarie upon Corinthians. Reprint of C.T.S. edition, 2 volumes $7.00.   Eerdmans.

Tymme seems to have been constantly occupied in translating the Reformers, and to have done his work well.

1202   **HODGE** (CHARLES, D.D.)   Exposition of I. Corinthians. $4.00. Eerdmans.   Exposition of II. Corinthians. $3.50. Eerdmans.

The more we use Hodge, the more we value him.   This applies to all his commentaries.

1203   **LANGE** (J. P.)   Commentary on I. and II. Corinthians, by C. F. Kluig, D.D.   (*See page* 19.)

1204   LOTHIAN (W.)   Lectures on I. & II. Corinthians.   8vo.   *Edinb.*, 1828.

This work must have done good service in its day, as in some degree an antidote to *Macknight ;* it is good and sound ; but the student need not distress himself if he cannot procure it, for it is not indispensable.

1205 OLSHAUSEN (H., D.D.) Commentary on I. and II. Corinthians. 8vo. *Edinb.*, T. & T. Clark. 1851.

Dr. Lindsay Alexander says that this comment is highly esteemed for
its happy combinations of grammatico-historical exegesis, with spiritual
insight into the meaning of the sacred writers.

1206 PRIDHAM (ARTHUR). Notes and Reflections on I. and II.
Corinthians. 2 vols., cr. 8vo. *Lond.*, Nisbet. 1866.

We do not always agree with *Mr. Pridham,* but we always admire
the quiet, candid, and unaffected manner in which he writes.

1207 ROBERTSON (FREDERICK W., M.A. 1816—1853). Expository Lectures. 12mo. *Lond.*, King. 1872.

Robertson's doctrinal vagaries are well known; yet he is a great thinker
and a prompter of thought in other men. Read with discretion.

1208 STANLEY (ARTHUR PENRHYN, D.D., F.R.S., *Dean of Westminster.*) Corinthians. 8vo. *Lond.*, Murray. 1876.

We do not advise the purchase of these volumes; for although *Dean
Stanley* is an instructive writer, our perusal of his notes does not impress
us with any sense either of their value or soundness.

1209 COLET (JOHN, D.D., *Dean of St. Paul's.* 1466—1519). Treatise on
I. Corinthians. With Translation. Demy 8vo. *Lond.*, G. Bell &
Sons. 1874.

A curiosity and nothing more. This same ancient *Dean Colet,* the friend of
Erasmus, wrote also on the Romans.

1210 PEARCE (ZACHARY, D.D.) Translation of I. Corinthians, with
Paraphrase and Notes. In Vol. II. of Commentary. (*No.* 966.)

We ought to value this work greatly, for the author was a renowned
scholar; but we confess we do not think much of his productions.

[The writers on small portions of these Epistles are too numerous to
be mentioned in our short Catalogue. *Burgess, Branston, Thomas
Fuller, Sibbes, Manton, Watson,* and other masterly writers have all left
a contribution to the expository stores of the Church of Christ.]

GALATIANS.

[Do not forget to consult works from No. 1140 to 1155.]

1211 BAGGE (HENRY T. J., B.A.) Galatians. 8vo. *Lond.*, 1856.

Simply a revised text and critical notes.

1212 **BAYLEY** (SIR E.) Commentary on Galatians. Thick
post 8vo. *Lond.*, Nisbet. 1869.

*Upon each portion there is a commentary, a paraphrase, and a
sermon, and thus the author conveys a considerable amount of
instruction. He is thoroughly evangelical, and his style clear.*

1213 **BROWN** (JOHN, D.D. *Edinburgh*). Exposition of
Galatians. 8vo. *Edinb.*, 1853.

*Brown is a modern Puritan. All his expositions are of the
utmost value. The volume on Galatians is one of the scarcest books
in the market.*

1214 **CALVIN** (JOHN). Forty-two Sermons on Galatians. 4to. *Lond.,* 1574. [A different work from his Commentary.]

1215 **EADIE** (JOHN, D.D.) Commentary on the Greek Text of Galatians. 8vo. *Edinb.,* Clark. 1869.

This is a most careful attempt to ascertain the meaning of the Apostle by a painstaking analysis of his words. The author is not warped by any system of theology, but yet he does not deviate from recognized evangelical truth. As a piece of honest grammatical exegesis the value of this commentary is very great, though there is room to differ from it here and there.

1216 EDMUNDS (JOHN, M.A.) Galatians. With Explanatory Notes. Crown 8vo. *Edinb.,* Oliver & Boyd. 1874.

Thoroughly ritualistic. See remarks on this author's work on Thessalonians.

1217 GODWIN (JOHN H.) Galatians. Translation, with Notes and Doctrinal Lessons. Cr. 8vo. *Lond.,* Hodder. 1871.

A helpful translation, with good textual notes.

1218 HALDANE (JAMES ALEXANDER. 1768—1851). Exposition of Galatians. 12mo. 1848.

This work has never been popular, because the author in the third chapter discusses the question of baptism. This is a fault of which we may say as the Papist said of venial sin : " It deserved to be forgiven."

1219 HAWKER (JOHN, M.A.) Bible Thoughts in Quiet Hours. Commentary on Galatians. *Lond.,* Yapp & Hawkins. 1874.

These " thoughts " are sound and edifying. The book does not profess to be a thorough exposition.

1220 KELLY (WILLIAM). Lectures on Galatians. 12mo. *Lond.,* G. Morrish. [N.D.]

Mr. Kelly's authoritative style has no weight with us. We do not call these lectures expounding, but confounding.

1221 **LANGE** (J. P.) Commentary on Galatians, by Otto Schmoller, Ph.D. Ephesians, Philippians, and Colossians, by Karl Braune, D.D. (*See page* 19.)

1222 **LIGHTFOOT** (J. B., D.D., *Canon of St. Paul's*). Galatians. Revised Text, with Introductions, Notes, and Dissertations. $3.50. Zondervan.

The Spectator says: " There is no commentator at once of sounder judgment, and more liberal, than Dr. Lightfoot."

1223 LUSHINGTON (THOMAS. *Died* 1661). The Justification of a Sinner : the Main Argument of the Epistle to the Galatians. Folio. 1650.

A translation from *Crellius,* a Socinian divine, made by *Lushington,* who was far gone towards the same error. We mention the book to warn our readers of its character ; for bad works of the Puritan period are few.

1224 **LUTHER** (MARTIN). Commentary on Galatians. Unabridged $5.00 Revell; Graebner abridged $2.50. Zondervan.

" I prefer this book of Martin Luther's (except the Bible) before all the books that I have ever seen, as most fit for a wounded conscience."—Bunyan. This is a great historic work, and is beyond

criticism, on account of its great usefulness. As a comment its accuracy might be questioned; but for emphatic utterances and clear statements of the great doctrine of the Epistle it remains altogether by itself, and must be judged per se.

1225 OLSHAUSEN (H., D.D.) Commentary on Galatians, Ephesians, Colossians, and Thessalonians. 8vo. *Edinb.*, T. & T. Clark. 1851 *(For remarks, see No. 964.)*

1226 PEARSON (SAMUEL, *Minister of Gt. George St. Chapel, Liverpool*). Sermons on Galatians. Cr. 8vo. *Lond.*, Clarke. 1874.

Discourses worthy of the successor of *Spencer* and *Raffles*.

1227 PERKINS (WILLIAM. 1558—1602.) Commentarie on the First Five Chapters of Galatians, with a Supplement on the Sixth Chapter, by Ralfe Cudworth. Thick 4to. 1604.

Perkins was justly esteemed by his cotemporaries as a master in theology. This commentary is deeply theological, and reads like a body of divinity : truth compels us to confess that we find it dull.

1228 PRIDHAM (A.) Galatians. Cr. 8vo. *Lond.*, Nisbet. 1872.

Pridham is, we suppose, of the moderate *Brethren* school, but he is not carried away by any theory, being essentially a man of sober mind.

EPHESIANS.

[See also under *Apostolical Epistles.*]

1229 BAYNE (PAUL, A.M. *Puritan. Died* 1617). Commentary on Ephesians. Folio. 1643, &c. [Reprinted in *Nichol's Commentaries.* Cr. 4to. *Lond.*, Nisbet. 1866.]

Sibbes says of this work : " The greatest shall find matter to exercise themselves in ; the meaner, matter of sweet comfort and holy instruction ; and all confess that he hath brought some light to this Scripture."

1230 CALVIN (JOHN). Sermons on Ephesians, Translated by A. Golding. *Black Letter.* 4to. *Lond.*, 1577.

Not the same as the exposition. The Sermons are priceless.

1231 EADIE (JOHN, D.D.) Commentary on the Greek text of Ephesians. 8vo. *Lond.*, Griffin. 1861.

" *This book is one of prodigious learning and research. The author seems to have read all, in every language, that has been written upon the Epistle. It is also a work of independent criticism, and casts much new light upon many passages.*"

1232 GRAHAM (WILLIAM, D.D., *of Bonn, Prussia*). Lectures on Ephesians. Cr. 8vo. *Lond.*, Partridge & Co. 1870.

Dr. Graham is an earnest opponent of the German Neologians and frequently writes with their negations before his eye. He is a commentator of considerable learning and much spirituality of mind.

1233   HEMMINGE (NICHOLAS, D.D.) Commentary on Ephesians, translated. 4to. *Lond.*, 1581. (*See No.* 553.)

1234   **HODGE** (CHARLES, D.D.)   Commentary on Ephesians. $4.00.   Eerdmans.

Most valuable.   With no writer do we more fully agree.

1235   KELLY (W.) Lectures. 12mo.   *Lond.*, G. Morrish. (*See No.* 1256).

1236   LATHROP (JOSEPH, D.D., *of America.* 1731—1820).   Exposition of the Epistle to the Ephesians, in a Series of Discourses. Thick 8vo.   *Philadelphia*, 1864.

These discourses are sure to be of the highest class.   We have not been able to procure a copy.

1237   M'GHEE (R., A.M., M.R.I.A.) Lectures on Ephesians. 2 vols., 8vo. Fourth edition. *Lond.*, Saunders & Otley. 1861.

Lively, warmhearted, extemporaneous sermons, full of good teaching. The preacher aimed to edify the many, rather than to write a critical work for the few, and he has succeeded.

1238   NEWLAND (HENRY, M.A)   A New Catena of St. Paul's Epistles.   Commentary on Ephesians, in which is exhibited the Results of the most learned Theological Criticisms, from the Age of the Early Fathers down to the Present Time. 8vo. *Lond.*, J. Parker & Co. 1866.

Used discreetly, this Catena of patristic, mediæval, and modern Church interpreters, may be very helpful ; without discretion it will mislead.

1239   **PATTISON** (R.E., D.D., *late Pres. of Waterville Col.*) Commentary on Ephesians. 8vo. *Boston, U.S.* 1859.

A book to instruct intelligent, experienced believers.   It is a model for a class-book, plain and yet profound.

1240   PERCEVAL (A. P.) Lectures on Ephesians. 12mo. *Lond.*, 1846.
Good, but not likely to produce headache by overloading the brain with thought.

1241   PRIDHAM (A.) Ephesians. 12mo.   *Lond.*, Yapp.
Style heavy, matter weighty.

1242   PULSFORD (JOHN).   Christ and his Seed; Central to all things: being a Series of Expository Discourses on Paul's Epistle to the Ephesians. 4to.   *Lond.*, Hamilton, Adams & Co. 1872.

Contains a great deal of deep thought, but is too mystical and often too cloudy to be of much service to those who wish to explain Scripture.

1243   RIDLEY (LANCELOT. *About* 1540.) Commentaries on Ephesians, Philippians, and part of Jude. [Reprinted in *Richmond's Fathers.*]
John Bale wrote in 1543 : "The Commentary which that virtuous, learned man, *Master Lancelot Ridley*, made upon St. Paul's Epistle to the Ephesians, for the true erudition of his Christian brethren, hath my *Lord Bonner* here also condemned for heresy.   But what the cause is I cannot tell, unless it be for advancing the Gospel as the thing whereby we are made righteous."   Our author is equally fierce against Anabaptists and Papists, but is not much of a commentator.

1244   TURNER (SAMUEL H., D.D.) Ephesians, in Greek and English ; with Analysis and Commentary. 8vo. *New York*, 1856.

A learned American work ; good, but not very attractive.

1245 EVANS (JAMES HARRINGTON, A.M. 1785—1849). Christian
      Solicitude, as exemplified in Ephesians III. 16mo. *Lond.*,
      J. F. Shaw. 1856.
Harrington Evans was a great teacher. A more sound, earnest, and
instructive divine never lived. This book consists of notes of sermons
preserved by a hearer. It is well worthy of study. His Memoir
contains fragmentary remarks upon Ephesians I.

1246 ROLLOCK (ROBERT. 1855—1598). An Exposition of part
      of the fift and sixt chapters of S. Pavle's Epistle to the
      Ephesians. 4to. *Lond.*, 1630. [In a volume containing sundry
      fragments of Expositions.]
This renowned Scotchman's writings generally come to us as translations from the Latin, and have been made preternaturally dull in the
process of interpretation ; but this appears to have been written in English
by himself. It is practical to a high degree, and goes into minute details
of the married life, &c. It will not be much appreciated in these days,
though *Dr. McCrie* styles *Rollock's* works "succinct and judicious."

PHILIPPIANS.

[See also under *Epistles.*]

1247 ACASTER (J.) Expository Lectures on Philippians. 8vo. *Lond.*, 1827. 2/-
Useful in showing the preacher how *not to do it.* By a violent effort we forced
ourselves to read one lecture ; but we have done nothing to deserve to read another.
The author was domestic chaplain to an earl, meant well, and did his little best.

1248 AIRAY (HENRY. 1559—1617). Lectures on Philippians. 4to.
      Lond., 1618. [Reprinted, with *Cartwright* on Colossians,
      in *Nichol's Commentaries.* Cr. 4to. *Lond.*, Nisbet. 1864.]
Mr. Grosart says : "You will look in vain in this commentary for
erudite criticism or subtle exegesis in the modern sense : but there
seems to us to be an instructively true following up of the Apostolic
thoughts, and a quick insight into their bearings and relative force.

1249 CALVIN (JOHN). Commentarie on Philippians. Translated
      by Wm. Becket. 4to. *Lond.*, 1584.

1250 CALVIN AND STORR. Expositions of Philippians and Colos-
      sians. By J. Calvin and Gottlob Storr. Translated by R. John-
      ston. 12mo. *Bib. Cabinet. Edinb.*, Clark. 1842.
A sort of sandwich, with *Calvin* for the meat, and *Storr* for very hard
black bread. Students who can enjoy both spiritual exposition and
stern criticism with equal relish will make fine expositors.

1251 DAILLÉ (JEAN. 1594—1670). Exposition of Philippians.
      Translated by Rev. James Sherman. Imp. 8vo. *Lond.*, 1841.
      [This Exposition, together with *Daillé* on Colossians, and
      Jenkyn on Jude, have been issued in one thick volume by *Mr.*
      Nichol of Edinburgh. *Lond.*, Nisbet. 1863.]
Written in a deliciously florid style. Very sweet and evangelical :
after the French manner.

1252 **EADIE** (JOHN, D.D.) Commentary on the Greek text of Philippians. 8vo., *Lond.*, Griffin. 1859.
A standard work. Essential to the scholarly student.

1253 EASTBURN (M.) Lectures. 8vo. *New York,* 1853.
Designed for family reading. Moderately good.

1254 HALL (ROBERT, A.M. 1764—1831). Exposition of Philippians, in twelve Discourses. 8vo. *Lond.,* 1843.
Robert Hall does not shine so much upon the printed page as he did when he blazed from the pulpit. These discourses were published after his death, from the notes of a hearer. They are good as sermons, but not remarkable as expositions.

1255 **JOHNSTONE** (ROBERT, LL.B., *of Glasgow*). Lectures on Philippians, with revised Translation, and Notes on the Greek text. 8vo. *Edinb.*, Oliphant. 1875.
A noble volume. A real boon to the man who purchases it.

1256 KELLY (W.) Philippians and Colossians. 12mo. *Lond.*, Morrish. 1869.
Much that is excellent placed in "darkness visible."

1257 **LANGE** (J. P.) *See No.* 923, *and also page* 19.

1258 **LIGHTFOOT** (J. B., D.D.) A revised text, with Notes. &c. $3.50. Zondervan.
Deservedly regarded as a standard work. The more instructed student will appreciate it.

1259 MEYER (DR. H. A. W.) Critical and Exegetical Handbook to the Epistles to the Philippians and Colossians. (*See No.* 928).
No doubt wonderfully learned, but we cannot get on with it. Quotations from heretics we have happily never heard of before are of no great use to simple believers like ourselves.

1260 NEAT (CHARLES). Discourses from Philippians. Sm. 8vo. *Lond.,* 1841.
Strongly Calvinistic, and correct to a hair ; but utterly devoid of originality either of thought or expression.

1261 NEANDER (JOHANN AUGUST WILHELM. 1789—1850). Philippians and James, practically and historically explained. Post 8vo. *Edinb.,* T. & T. Clark. 1851.
Without dwelling upon the wording of the Epistle, *Neander* reproduces its spirit in other language, and so expounds it. The little work will be greatly appreciated by a certain order of minds.

1262 NEWLAND (H., M.A.) New Catena. Philippians. 8vo. J. Parker. 1860. (*See No.* 1238).

1263 PEIRCE (JAMES. *Died* 1726). Paraphrase on Philippians, Colossians, and Hebrews. 4to. *Lond.*, 1733.
Had he but known the Lord, his writings would have been admirable. He conceals his *Arianism*, but it is fatal to his acceptance with believers. He wrote after the manner of *Mr. Locke.*

1264 ROBERTSON (J. S. S., M.A.) Lectures on Philippians. 12mo. *Lond.,* 1849.
Lectures which will never set the Thames on fire.

1265 TODD (James F., M.A.) Apostle Paul and the Church at Philippi. Acts XVI. and Philippians. 8vo. *Lond.*, Bell & Daldy. 1864.

A respectable work. The author is sound in doctrine and valorous in controverting error, and he says many good things; but he rather *uses* the text than expounds it. He deserves a reading; but men with whom money is scarce need not purchase this book.

1266 TOLLER (Thomas). Discourses on Philippians. 12mo. *Lond.*, 1855.

A very favourable specimen of plain, popular exposition. Nothing either deep, or new, or critically accurate; but sensible and practical.

1267 **VAUGHAN** (C. J., D.D.) Lectures on Philippians. Extra Fcap. 8vo. *Lond.*, Macmillan. 1864, &c.

Deservedly esteemed. Dr. Vaughan gives a literal translation of his text from the original Greek, and then expounds it, believing it, as he says, " to be the duty of every Christian teacher to assist his congregation in drinking, not of the stream only, but at the spring of revealed truth."

1268 WIESINGER (Lic. August). Commentary on Philippians, Titus, and 1 Timothy; in continuation of the work of Olshausen. 8vo. *Edinb.*, T. & T. Clark. 1857.

Many mistake this for *Olshausen's.* It is of the critical and grammatical school, and bristles all over with the names of the German band. We prefer the Puritanic gold to the German silver which is now in fashion.

COLOSSIANS.

1269 **BAYNE** (Paul, A.M.) Commentary on Colossians I. and II. 4to. *Lond.*, 1634.

On the two first chapters only. Edifying and very rare.

1270 **BYFIELD** (Nicholas, *Puritan.* 1579—1622.) Exposition upon Colossians; being the Substance of near seven years' week-day sermons. Folio. 1615 and 1617. [Reprinted in *Nichol's Commentaries.* Cr. 4to., *Lond.*, Nisbet. 1869.]

The author lived in intense pain, and died at 44, yet he produced quite a mountain of literature. He writes like an earnest, faithful man, resolved to keep back nothing of the counsel of God; but he too little studies brevity, and consequently he wearies most readers. He is always worth consulting.

1271 CALVIN. (*See Nos.* 1249, 1250).

1272 CARTWRIGHT (Thomas, B.D. *Puritan.* 1535—1603). Commentary on Colossians. 4to. *Lond.*, 1612. [Reprinted in *Nichol's Commentaries. See No.* 1248.]

This is but a small affair, consisting of scanty and second-rate " notes " by a hearer. Yet what there is of it has the true ring, and is rich in spirituality.

1273 DAILLÉ (J.) (*See No.* 1251).

1274 **DAVENANT** (JOHN, *Bp. of Salisbury.* 1572—1641.)
      Exposition of Colossians.   Translated from the Latin,
      by Josiah Allport. 2 vols., 8vo. *Lond.,* 1831.
"*I know no exposition upon a detached portion of Scripture
(with the single exception of Owen on the Hebrews) that will compare
with it in all points. Leighton is superior in sweetness, but far
inferior in depth, accuracy, and discursiveness.*"—*C. Bridges.*

1275 **EADIE** (JOHN, D.D.) Commentary on the Greek text
      of Colossians.   8vo.,   *Lond.,* Griffin.   1856.
Very full and reliable.   A work of the utmost value.

1276 **ELTON** (EDWARD, B.D.)   Exposition of Colossians.
      Third edition.   Folio.   *Lond.,* 1637.
A Puritan work; strongly Calvinistic, popular, and very full.

1277 GISBORNE (THOMAS, *Prebendary of Durham.* 1758—1846).
      Exposition of Colossians.   12mo.   *Lond.,* 1816.
Sermons which very much remind us of those of *Henry Melvill,* but
with less of the Gospel in them. *Gisborne* was a preacher of considerable
repute, but he was more at home upon moral than spiritual topics.

1278 GUTHRIE (THOMAS, D.D.)   Christ the Inheritance of the
      Saints.   Discourses from Colossians. $2.50. Zondervan.

Not so much an exposition as a series of brilliant discourses, or
prose poems. *Dr. Guthrie* has only touched upon the first chapter.

1279 **LIGHTFOOT** (J. B., D.D.)   Colossians and Philemon.
      A revised Text, with Introductions, Notes, &c.   8vo.,
      Macmillan & Co.   1875.
For remarks, see No. 1258. *Lightfoot writes for scholars.*

1280 MILNER (JOSEPH, M.A.) Sermons on Colossians, 1 Thessa-
      lonians V., and. James I.   8vo.   *Lond.,* 1841.
Respectable sermons by the Church historian.

1281 ROLLOCK (R.) Lectures on Colossians. 4to. *Lond.,* 1603.
It is said that when this great divine died the entire population of
Edinburgh attended his funeral.   His Lectures on Colossians were once
very popular, but are now extremely scarce.   The style is very simple
and colloquial, and the matter far from profound.

1282 **SPENCE** (JAMES, D.D.)   Discourses on Colossians.   Cr.
      8vo.   *Lond.,* Hodder.   1875.
*A good specimen of honest, popular expounding.   Intended for a
congregation, but useful to the student.*

1283 WATSON (THOMAS, B.A.) Discourses on Colossians. 8vo. *Lond.,* 1838.
Thoroughly evangelical and remarkably commonplace.

1284 WILSON (DANIEL, D.D., *Bp. of Calcutta*). Explanatory Lectures
on Colossians. 8vo. *Lond.*, 1845.
By a famous modern evangelical, who shows much ability in wielding
this Scripture against Tractarians and others. The work contains little
original exegesis.

1285 **LOCKYER** (NICH., *Puritan.* 1612—1684-5). England
Faithfully Watcht with in her Wounds. [Lectures on
Colossians I.] 4to. *Lond.*, 1646.
Rich, full, simple. A fair specimen of plain Puritan preaching.

I. & II. THESSALONIANS.

1286 EDMUNDS (J., M.A.) Commentary on 1 and 2 Thessalonians. Cr. 8vo.
Lond., Bell & Daldy. 1858.
For school Teachers. The author's notion of a Commentary, which he fully
carries out, is contained in his preface. "My idea of the Middle-class Commentary
is, that it should be in strict accordance with the doctrine and ritual of the Church,
should illustrate her ritual, and should recommend her to the esteem and affection of
her children, by proving her adherence to the Word of God."

1287 JEWEL (JOHN, *Bp. of Salisbury.* 1522—1571). Expositions
upon I. & II. Thessalonians. Sm. 8vo. *Black Letter. Lond.*,
1583. Reprinted 1811 and 1841. Also in his *Works.*
Hooker calls *Jewel* "the jewel of bishops." This work is in the usual
style of the first Reformers, but rather more lively than most of them.
Many of the topics touched upon were peculiar to the times in which the
exposition was written. It will serve as a good specimen of the
preaching of the Fathers of the English Church.

1288 **LANGE** (J. P.) Commentary on Thessalonians, by Drs.
Auberlen and Riggenbach. Translated by Dr. Lillie.
Timothy, Titus and Philemon, by Prof. Von Oosterzee.
Hebrews, by Dr. C. B. Moll. Edited by Dr. Schaff.
$3.95. Zondervan.
" *Lillie's Thessalonians will be found to be one of the best
executed portions of the American edition of Lange. The translation is remarkably accurate and elegant, and the additions from
his own researches, and the best English Commentaries, are carefully selected and valuable.*"—*Dr. P. Schaff.*

1289 **LILLIE** (JOHN, D.D., *Kingston, New York.* 1812—1867).
Lectures on Thessalonians. Large 8vo.   *Edinb.*,
W. Oliphant & Co. 1863.
Remarks on the preceding will apply here.

1290 ROLLOCK (ROBERT). Lectures on the Epistles to the
Thessalonians, preached by R. R. 4to. *Edinb.*, 1606.
For remarks, *see No.* 1246.

1291 SCLATER (WILLIAM, D.D.) Exposition upon 1 and 2
Thessalonians. 4to. *Lond.*, 1627.
Sclater is antique ; but, in the usual Puritanic manner, he gives very
instructive disquisitions upon a vast variety of topics suggested by the text.

1292 PATTERSON (ALEXANDER SIMPSON, D.D., *Glasgow*). Com-
      mentaries on 1 Thessalonians, James, and 1 John. 12mo.
      Edinb., 1857.
   Notes of discourses, with much in them. Hints may be gleaned here
in abundance by students who open their eyes.

1293 PHILLIPS (J.) The Greek of Thessalonians explained. 4to. *Lond.*, 1751.
      Short, but not particularly sweet. *Very scarce.*

1294 BRADSHAW (W., *Puritan.* 1571—1618). A Plaine and Pithy Exposition of
      2 Thessalonians; published since his decease by T. Gataker. 4to. 1620.
   As we cannot get a sight of this, perhaps some reader will present us with a copy.

1295 **MANTON** (THOMAS, D.D.) Eighteen Sermons on 2
      Thessalonians II., concerning Antichrist. 8vo. 1679.
   *Here Manton smites heavily at Popery. Richard Baxter wrote
a commendatory preface to this valuable exposition.*

1296 SQUIRE (JOHN, M.A.) A Plaine Exposition on 2 Thessa-
      lonians II., 1—13, proving the Pope to be Antichrist. 4to.
      Lond., 1630.
   Squire works out the point of the Pope's being Antichrist with very
great cogency of reasoning.   The exposition of the Epistle is lost in
the point aimed at ; but that point is of the utmost importance.

PASTORAL EPISTLES;

Or, the Epistles of Timothy, Titus, and Philemon.

1297 **CALVIN** (JOHN).   C Sermons on the Epistles of S.
      Paule to Timothie and Titus, translated out of the
      French, by L. T. 4to. *Lond.*, 1579.
   Quite a different work from Calvin's Commentaries.

1298 **FAIRBAIRN** (PATRICK, D.D.) The Pastoral Epistles,
      Greek Text, Translation, Introductions, Expository Notes,
      &c. Cr. 8vo.   *Edinb.*, T. & T. Clark. 1874.
   *What with a good translation, full defence of the Apostolic
authorship of the Epistles, fruitful comments, and profitable dissertations, this volume is about as complete a guide to the smaller
epistles as one could desire.*

I. & II. TIMOTHY.

[See also under *Pastoral Epistles.*]

1299 BICKERSTETH (E.) (*See No.* 1386).

1300 PATTERSON (ALEX. S., D.D.) Commentary on Timothy and
      Titus. 18mo. 1848. (*See our remarks on No.* 1292.)

1301 SLADE (HENRY RAPER, LL.B.) Pulpit Lectures on the Epistles to Timothy.
      Cr. 8vo. 1837.
      Utter rubbish. Dear at a gift.

1302 WIESINGER (L. A.)   (*See No.* 1268).

1303 PINDER (JOHN H., M.A.)   The Candidate for the Ministry.   Lectures on
      1 Timothy. 12mo. *Lond.*, 1837.
      Of no consequence.

1304 **BARLOW** (JOHN. *Puritan.*)   Exposition of 2 Timothy,
      I. and II. Folio. *Lond.*, 1632.
      By a master in Israel.   Thoroughly practical, deeply experi-
      mental, and soundly doctrinal.

1305 **HALL** (THOMAS).   Commentary on 2 Timothy III. and
      IV. Folio. *Lond.*, 1632—1658.
      Hall is often found in union with Barlow, completing the
      Commentary on 2 Timothy, as he completed Amos, (No. 840.*)   He*
      is a masterly expositor, of the old-fashioned school.

TITUS.

[See also under *Pastoral Epistles.*]

1306 GRAHAM (W., D.D.) Titus. 12mo.   *Lond.*, Nisbet. 1860.
      Dr. Graham endeavours to make criticism intelligible, and the results
of learning really edifying.   We have our doubts as to some of his
criticisms, and he is quite dogmatic enough, but on the whole good.

1307 **TAYLOR** (THOMAS, D.D. *Puritan.* 1579—1632).   Com-
      mentarie upon Titus. 4to. *Camb.*, 1619.
      Folio. 1668.   Also in *Works.*
      The title-page calls Thomas Taylor " a famous and most elabo-
      rate divine."   He was a preacher at Paul's Cross during the
      reigns of Elizabeth and James I., and a voluminous writer.   This
      Commentary will well repay the reader.

PHILEMON.

1308 **ATTERSOLL** (WILLIAM. *Puritan*).   Commentary upon
      Philemon. Second Edition. Folio. *Lond.*, 1633.
      A long comment upon a short epistle.   The pious author labours
      to keep to his text, and succeeds in bringing out of it a mass of
      quaint practical teaching.

1309 **COX** (SAMUEL).   Philemon. In " The Private Letters of
      St. Paul and St. John." 12mo.   *Lond.*, Miall. 1867.
      Such exposition as this adds interest to the epistles, and makes
      their writers live again before our eyes.   Mr. Cox delivered this
      work in public on certain week evenings.   Happy are the people
      who are thus instructed.

1310   DYKE (Daniel, B.D. *Puritan. Died about* 1614). A most
fruitful Exposition upon Philemon. *Lond.* 4to. 1618.

Dyke's remarks are memorably practical and full of common sense·
He abounds in proverbs.   The work is not very valuable as an exposition of the words, but excels in making use of them.

1311   **JONES** (William, D.D., *of East Bergholt.*) Commentary upon Philemon, Hebrews, and 1 and 2 John.   Folio.
Lond., 1636.

*Very lively, sprightly, colloquial lectures, by a Suffolk divine,
who thinks the Brownists and Dissenters were not persecuted.
" Christ was whipped, that was persecution ; Christ whipped some
out of the temple, that was no persecution." Despite his intolerance
he says some uncommonly racy things.*

1312   **LIGHTFOOT** (J. B., D.D.)   *See No.* 1279.

HEBREWS.

1313   **BROWN** (John, D.D.)   Exposition of Hebrews.   2 vols.,
8vo.   *Edinb.,* 1862.

*Dr. David Smith says of this work: " There is not a single
instance of carelessness in investigating the true meaning of a text,
or of timidity in stating the conclusion at which the author had
arrived." What more could be said in praise of any exposition ?*

1314   **CALVIN** (John).   Commentary on Hebrews, translated
by Clement Cotton.   Reprint of C.T.S. edition. $3.50.
Eerdmans.

1315   DALE (R. W., M.A.)   The Jewish Temple and the Christian
Church.   Discourses on Hebrews.   Cr. 8vo.   *Lond.,* Hodder & Stoughton.   1871.

Among modern divines few rank so highly as *Mr. Dale.* Daring and
bold in thought, and yet for the most part warmly on the side of orthodoxy, his works command the appreciation of cultured minds.

1316   DELITZSCH (F., D.D.)   Commentary on Hebrews.   2 vols.,
$7.00.   Eerdmans.

Remarks formerly made upon *Delitzsch* apply here also.   (*Nos.* 412,
and 724.)

1317   **DICKSON** (David.)   Short Explanation of Hebrews.
8vo.   *Aberd.,* 1635 ; *Camb.,* 1649 ; and *Lond.,* 1839.

*This is generally to be found in connection with the author's
" Brief Exposition on Matthew." (No.* 1033.)   *We need say no
more than—get it, and you will find abundance of suggestions
for profitable trains of thought.*

1318 DUNCAN (Robert, *of Tillicultry.* 1699—1729). Exposition of Hebrews. 8vo. 1731. 3/6. New edition, cr. 8vo.
Edinb., Ogle & Murray.

"An excellent condensation of *Dr. Owen's* valuable work, and giving the pith and marrow of the great commentator."

1319 EBRARD (John H. A., *Prof. Theol. Erlangen*). Commentary on Hebrews. 8vo. *Edinb.,* T. &. T. Clark. 1853.

This is intended as a continuation of *Olshausen,* but it is an improvement thereon. *Ebrard* is at once learned and spiritual, and we prefer him to almost any other author whose works the Messrs. Clark have issued.

1320 **GOUGE** (William, D.D. *Puritan.*) Commentary on Hebrews. 2 vols. Folio. *Lond.,* 1655. [Reprinted in *Nichol's Commentaries.* 3 vols., Cr. 4to. *Lond.,* Nisbet. 1866-7.]

We greatly prize Gouge. Many will think his system of observations cumbrous, and so, perhaps, it is ; but upon any topic which he touches he gives outlines which may supply sermons for months.

1321 **HALDANE** (James Alex. 1768—1851.) Notes on Exposition of Hebrews. 12mo. *Lond.,* Nisbet. 1860.

A posthumous work, and issued, not as a finished exposition, but as "Notes of an intended Exposition." Very valuable for all that.

1322 HOWARD (J. E.) Hebrews. A Revised Translation, with Notes. Demy 12mo. *Lond.,* S. W. Partridge & Co. 1872.
Contains a few suggestive observations ; but is a small affair in all respects.

1323 JONES (W., D.D.) *See No.* 1311.

1324 JONES (W., M.A. 1726—1800). Four Lectures on the Relation between the Old and New Testaments as set forth in Hebrews. 8vo. 1811.
Very little of it, and bound up with a work of an ingenious, but fanciful character

1325 KNOX (J. Spencer, A.M.) The Mediator of the New Covenant. Sermons on Hebrews. 8vo. *Dublin,* 1834.
Thirteen Sermons on select passages. Mediocrity highly polished.

1326 **LANGE** (J. P.) *See No.* 1288.

1327 LAWSON (G.) Exposition of Hebrews. Wherein the Socinian Comment is examined. Folio. *Lond.,* 1662. *Scarce.*

Richard Baxter says : " I must thankfully acknowledge that I learned more from *Mr. Lawson* than from any divine that ever I conversed with."

1328 **LINDSAY** (W., D.D., *Prof. Theol. Glasgow.*) Lectures on Hebrews. 2 vols. Demy 8vo. *Edinb.,* Oliphant. 1867.

One of those great expository works with which the Scotch ministry has so frequently enriched the Church. We wonder if any one ever read this excellent exposition through ; we should not like to be sentenced to do so.

1329 [LUSHINGTON (Thomas, M.A.).] The Expiation of a Sinner. Commentary upon Hebrews. Folio. 1646.

This work was published anonymously, and is charged with Socinianism.

1330 M'CAUL (Joseph B., *Hon. Canon of Rochester*). Hebrews. A Paraphrastic Commentary, with Illustrations from Philo, the Targums, &c. 8vo. *Lond.*, Longmans. 1871.

Mr. M'Caul attacks the gentlemen of the higher criticism with great plainness of speech and some asperity. We hardly think his work will attain a great circulation, it has so much Hebrew, Greek, Latin, and German in it, that only men of learning and leisure can use it.

1331 **MACLEAN** (A. 1732—1812.) Paraphrase and Commentary on Hebrews. 2 vols., 12mo. *Lond.*, 1847.

One of the most judicious and solid expositions ever written.

1332 NELSON (Robert). Comments on Hebrews. Cr. 8vo. *Lond.*, Morgan & Scott. 1868.

By a thoughtful and devout man, but we cannot endorse some of his interpretations. The taint of a certain modern school appears in passages such as this : " Had Paul been preaching holiness of life as essential to seeing the Lord, would he not have been advocating the very principle on which the law was based?" We are afraid of this covert Antinomianism ; its presence eats as doth a canker.

1333 [NEWTON (Adelaide L.)] Hebrews compared with the Old Testament. Cr. 8vo. *Lond.*, Nisbet. 1872.

Devout, simple, and instructive. The authoress was an invalid, and died ere she had finished her work. She worked out a good idea with far more of expository matter than could have been expected of her.

1334 **OWEN** (John, D.D.) Exposition of Hebrews. 4 vols. Folio. *Lond.*, 1668-74. Also 7 vols. 8vo. Edited by Dr. Goold. *Edinb.*, T. & T. Clark.

Abridged edition reprinted in one volume entitled Hebrews, the Epistle of Warning. $3.00. Kregel.

Out of scores of commendations of this colossal work we select but one. Dr. Chalmers pronounced it " a work of gigantic strength as well as gigantic size ; and he who hath mastered it is very little short, both in respect to the doctrinal and practical of Christianity, of being an erudite and accomplished theologian."

1335 PARRY (Thomas, M.A., *Bp. of Barbadoes*). Hebrews, in a Series of Lectures. 12mo. *Lond.*, 1834.

So feeble that we wonder how it got through the press. A sermonized paraphrase.

1336 PATTERSON (Alexander Simpson, D.D.) Commentary on Hebrews. 8vo. 10/6. *Edinb.*, T. & T. Clark. 1856.

Lectures delivered in the course of the author's ministrations. Excellent for the public ; the student should consult other authors for learning ; but *Patterson* has savour and spirituality.

1337 PRIDHAM (A.). Hebrews. Cr. 8vo. *Lond.*, Nisbet. 1862.

Rather mystified with expressions peculiar to " dispensational truth." whatever that may mean ; but devout, candid, sober, and sound.

1338 SAMPSON (FRANCIS S., D.D. *Prof. Orient. Lit., Prince Edward, Va.*) Commentary on Hebrews. 8vo. *New York,* 1856.

A respectable production, but we know many which we value far more. As a set of lectures to a college class these comments would be of great value, but the author did well not to print them, although it was natural and fitting that his surviving colleague should do so.

1339 SAMPSON (G. V.) Translation, with Notes. 8vo. *Lond.,* 1828.

Dr. Kendrick says that *Sampson* is candid and sensible, but scarcely grapples with the difficult points of the Epistle. Perhaps he was not strong enough.

1340 SAPHIR (ADOLPH). Lectures on Hebrews. Vol 1. Chapters I-VII. Volume 2. Chapters VIII-XIII. 2 volumes. $4.00. Loizeaux.

Mr. Saphir has always something to say worthy of the attention of spiritual minds. His mind finds a track of its own, but he is never speculative. We always enjoy his remarks, though he is not specially terse or brilliant.

1341 STEWARD (GEORGE). Argument of the Epistle to the Hebrews. 8vo. *Edinb.,* T. & T. Clark. 1872.

Unhappily the author died before he had quite completed this "argument." The work is most helpful.

1342 **STUART** (MOSES, M.A.) Commentary on Hebrews. 8vo. *Lond.,* 1837. Also 1853. Tegg & Co.

We are constantly differing from Moses Stuart, but are bound to consult him. He is one of the greatest of American scholars, and this is one of his best comments.

1343 TAIT (WILLIAM, M.A.) Meditationes Hebraicæ. 2 vols. Cr. 8vo. *Lond.,* Hamilton, Adams & Co. 1855.

A noteworthy series of lectures. If *Gouge, Owen,* and others, had not done all for Hebrews that one could well need, this would have been of first-class value; and though we have much better it is still a worthy companion to them.

1344 THOLUCK (A. F.) Commentary on Hebrews. 2 vols., 12mo. *Biblical Cabinet. Edinb.,* Clark. 1842.

Delitzsch speaks highly of this work ; but, for our part, we understand the Epistle better without *Tholuck* than with him. Clouds of smoke and volleys of hard words destroy our equanimity.

1345 TURNER (SAMUEL H., D.D.) Hebrews, in Greek and English ; with Commentary. 8vo. *New York,* 1852.

Carefully done. Written for those who really wish to understand the Epistle.

1346 WILLIAMS (H. W.) Exposition of Hebrews. Cr. 8vo. *Lond.,* 66, Paternoster Row. 1872.

The author has evidently been a diligent reader and student. Apart from its Wesleyan peculiarities, we can commend this book as edifying and instructive, though we do not place it in the first class.

PARTS OF HEBREWS.

1347 **DEERING** (EDWARD, B.D. *Puritan. Died* 1576). Twenty-seven Lectures upon Hebrews [chap I.—VI.] 4to. 1590.

Mainly aimed at the errors of the Church of Rome, and at the practical questions of the Reformation period. A learned but antiquated set of lectures.

1348 MANCHESTER (GEORGE MONTAGUE, *Duke of).* Horæ Hebraicæ. An Attempt to discover how the Argument of the Epistle to the Hebrews [I.—IV. 11] must have been understood by those therein addressed. Royal 8vo. *Lond.,* 1835.

A peculiar book, altogether *sui generis,* written by a man who did his own thinking. The Duke would be an unreliable guide, but he frequently strikes out new paths, and suggests novel trains of thought.

1349 ANDERSON (JAMES S. M., M.A.) Discourses on the 11th and part of the 12th chapters of Hebrews. 2 vols., 8vo. *Lond.,* 1839-43.
Good Church sermons. Of very slight value for commenting purposes.

1350 **MANTON** (T., D.D.) Sixty-six Sermons on Hebrews XI, in vol. III of Manton's *Works.* Folio edition.

Exhaustive. Manton piles up his matter heaps upon heaps.

1351 PERKINS (WILLIAM). A Cloud of Faithful Witnesses. Commentary on Hebrewes XI. 4to. 1622.   and *Works,* vol. III.

Good in its day, but now superseded. Very many points are discussed which would now be regarded as ridiculous : as for instance, *whether a man may travel in a foreign country.* It is terribly prosy.

1352 ANDREWS (G.). Sermons upon Hebrews XII. 4to. 1711.
Thoroughly Scotch. Sound, but somewhat prolix and commonplace.

1353 PHILLIPS (W. SPENCER, B.D.) The Triumphs of a Practical Faith. [On Hebrews XI.] 12mo. *Lond.,* 1840.
Cloudy discourses on the cloud of witnesses. Will quicken no one's pace.

1354 SYLVESTER (MATTHEW). The Christian's Race and Patience. Sermons on Hebrews XII. 2 vols., 8vo. 1702—1708.
Not of the first class ; yet respectable sermons.

CATHOLIC EPISTLES.

1355 **EBRARD** (J. H. A.) *See No.* 1387.

1356 LANGE (J. P.) Commentary on James, by Prof. Van Oosterzee. Epistles of Peter, by Dr. C. F. Fronmüller. Epistles of John, by Dr. K. Braune. Epistle of Jude, by Dr. C. F. Fronmüller. Edited by Dr. Schaff. $3.95. Zondervan.

In his comment on the First Epistle of John, *Dr. Braune* teaches baptismal regeneration in a very decided manner. This plague-spot of sacramentarianism should put the reader on his guard.

JAMES.

1357 ADAM (JOHN, D.D., *of Aberdeen*). Exposition of James. 8vo. *Edinb.*, T. & T. Clark. 1867.

Good, plain discourses, for which the author acknowledges his indebtedness to various eminent writers who have discussed the Epistle. Our readers had better make similar discourses of their own—*if they can.*

1358 HEMMINGE (NICHOLAS, D.D.) A Learned and Fruitful Commentarie upon James, translated by W. G. *Black Letter.* 4to. 1577.
The price which this book fetches is preposterous. It is hard antique reading.

1359 JACOBI (BERNARD, *of Petershagen, Prussia*). Lectures on James. 12mo. Religious Tract Society. 1838.

A good, simple, practical set of expository Lectures. Safe in doctrine, or the Religious Tract Society would not have issued it.

1360 **JOHNSTONE** (ROBERT, LL.B. *Glasgow.*) Lectures on James. $3.40. Baker.

A very useful, scholarly, and readable book.

1361 **MANTON** (THOMAS, D.D.) Commentary on James. 4to. *Lond.*, 1651 ; 8vo., 1842 ; also in vol. IV. of Manton's *Works*, Nichol's edition.

In Manton's best style. An exhaustive work, as far as the information of the period admitted. Few such books are written now.

1362 MAYER (JOHN, D.D.) Praxis Theologica : or the Epistle of James Resolved, Expounded, and Preached upon. 4to. 1629. (*See pages* 10 *and* 11.)

1363 NEANDER (J. A. W.) James, practically explained. Translated by Mrs. Conant. 12mo. *New York*, 1852.
See also No. 1261.

1364 NELSON (ROBERT). James. Thin cr. 8vo. *Lond.*, Bagsters. 1872.
Setting out with the notion that the epistle is only written to the Jews, this author's remarks are too much warped by this and other theories to be of any value to students.

1365 **STIER** (R., D.D.) *See No.* 972.

1366 PATTERSON (A. S., D.D.) Commentary on James. 18mo. *Paisley*, 1851. (*See remarks on No.* 1292.)

1367 TURNBULL (RICHARD, M.A.) Expositions of James and Jude. Thick 12mo., 1592 ; and 4to., 1605.
Old and occupied with Popish controversies. Good, solid, and tedious.

1368 **WARDLAW** (RALPH, D.D.) Lectures on James. Cr. 8vo. Fullerton & Co. 1862.

The lectures are noteworthy specimens of expository preaching. They were Wardlaw's last work, and are fully up to the mark.

I. & II. PETER.

1369   AMES (WILLIAM, D.D. 1576—1633). Exposition of the Epistles of
       Peter. 4to. *Lond.*, 1641.
   Too much divided and subdivided, chopped up and cut into dice pieces and laid in
order ; for, after all, there is very little meat in it. It is an analysis, and little more.

1370   BENSON (GEORGE.) Epistles of Peter. 4to. 1742.
   The author was an Arian. *"Benson* possessed considerable learning, but no great
portion of genius." This is a paraphrase with notes.

1371   **LILLIE** (JOHN, D.D. *Kingston, N.Y.*)   Lectures on
       1 and 2 Peter. 8vo.   *New York*, 1869. *Lond.*,
       Hodder and Stoughton.
   *Dr. Schaff says :—" Though very different from the immortal
work of Archbishop Leighton on the First Epistle of Peter, these
lectures breathe the same reverential spirit and devotional fervour,
while they are much more full and thorough as an exposition."*

1372   **LUTHER** (MARTIN).   Commentarie upon the Two
       Epistles of St. Peter and that of St. Jude, gathered out
       of the lectures of Martin Luther.   Translated by Thomas
       Newton. 4to. *Lond.*, 1581. *Black letter.*
   *In Luther's racy style. One of his best productions. Copies are
scarce as white elephants, and consequently expensive.*

1373   **NISBET** (ALEXANDER).   Exposition of 1 and 2 Peter.
       8vo. *Edinb.*, 1658.
   *A judicious and gracious Scotch commentary, after the style of
Dickson and Hutcheson.*

I. PETER.

1374   ALLEY (WILLIAM, *Bp. of Exeter. Died* 1571). Exposition of 1 Peter.
       [In "Poore Man's Librarie." Folio. *Lond.*, 1560].   *Very rare.*
   A curious old *Black Letter* Folio. The exposition on Peter is mainly occupied
with the questions and controversies of the Reforming period. Do not buy it.

1375   **BROWN** (JOHN, D.D. *Edinburgh.*) Expository Dis-
       courses on 1 Peter. 3 vols. Cr. 8vo.   *Edinb.*, W.
       Oliphant & Co. 1866.
   *The epistle is divided into paragraphs, and these are made the
themes of discourses. Thus Dr. Brown produced what is sub-
stantially a commentary, and one of the best. It affords us a
grammatical interpretation, together with an exposition, at once
exegetical, doctrinal, and practical. It is a standard work, and the
indices increase its value.*

1376 BYFIELD (NICHOLAS). Commentary upon 1 Peter I. II. III. Folio. 1637.

Byfield is an able and pious divine, but he is not very vivacious, and neither in manner nor matter is he at all original.

1377 KOHLBRÜGGE (H. F., D.D., *of Elberfeld*). Sermons on 1 Peter. 12mo. *Lond.*, 1853.

Strictly orthodox and deeply spiritual. No German neology may be expected from this author. He is very happy in his practical remarks.

1378 **LEIGHTON** (ROBERT, D.D. *Abp. of Glasgow.* 1613 —1684.) Commentary upon 1 Peter. 2 vols. 18mo. Royal edition, with Portrait, Rel. Tract Soc.

Dr. Henry Mills thus wrote of Leighton's works:—" There is a spirit in them I never met with in any other human writings, nor can I read many lines in them without being moved." We need scarcely commend this truly heavenly work. It is a favourite with all spiritual men.

1379 **ROGERS** (JOHN, A.M. *Puritan. Died* 1636.) Fruitful Exposition upon all the First Epistle of Peter. Folio. *Lond.*, 1650. *Very rare.*

Rogers was a true Boanerges. His style is earnestly practical and wisely experimental. This is one of the scarcest and liveliest of the Puritan expositions.

1380 STEIGER (WILHELM, *Prof. Theol. Geneva.* 1809—1836). Exposition of 1 Peter. Translated by Dr. Fairbairn. 2 vols., 12mo. *Biblical Cabinet.* *Edinb.*, T. & T. Clark. 1836

Steiger was a sound German divine. His criticism is good, but like all the Germans he is far too fond of dragging in learned names.

1381 GOMERSALL (R.) Sermons on St. Peter [chap. II. 13—16]. 4to. 1634.

Teaches absolute submission to rulers. Only worth notice from its age.

II. PETER.

1382 **ADAMS** (THOMAS). Commentary upon the 2nd Epistle of Peter. Folio. *Lond.*, 1633. New Edition, revised by Rev. James Sherman, in imp. 8vo., 1839; now included in *Nichol's Commentaries;* *Lond.*, Nisbet. 1862.

Full of quaintnesses, holy wit, bright thought, and deep instruction. We like Adams better in commenting than in preaching. His great work is quite by itself, and in its own way remains unrivalled. We know no richer and racier reading.

1383 SYMSON (ARCHIBALD). Exposition upon the Second Epistle
       Generall of St. Peter.   4to.   *Lond.*, 1632.

   Abundance of matter, pithily expressed.   *Symson* is among the oldest
and rarest of the English divines.

1384 **BROWN** (JOHN, D.D.) Parting Counsels; an Exposition
       of 2 Peter I.   8vo.   *Edinb.*, Oliphant.   1856.

   *We always think of Brown as a Puritan born out of due time.
Everything he has left us is massive gold.   He is both rich and
clear, profound and perspicuous.*

1385 WILSON (WILLIAM, *of Musselburgh*). Second Epistle of Peter.
       12mo.

   "Thoughtful and fresh in its matter, fine and polished in its style,
laying hold of us at once, and tightening its grasp on our sympathies
the longer we read."—*B. and For. Evan. Review.*   [Too laudatory.]

JOHN'S EPISTLES.

1386 BICKERSTETH (EDWARD. 1786—1850). Exposition on the Epistles of
       John and Jude, and of Paul to Timothy. 12mo. *Lond.*, 1853.
       Notes taken by his children of *Mr. Bickersteth's* expositions at family prayer.
   Simple, devout, soundly evangelical, and, we must add, superficial and commonplace.

1387 **EBRARD** (J. H. A.) Commentary on the Epistles of
       St. John.   With an Appendix on the Catholic Epistles.
       8vo.   *Edinb.*, T. & T. Clark.   1860.

   Dr. Candlish, in his Exposition on 1 *John, says:* "*I must
acknowledge my obligation to Dr. Lücke.   But it is Dr. Ebrard
who has helped me most.   Ebrard is especially valuable, and for an
English reader, acquainted with theology, very easily intelligible."*

1388 **HAWKINS** (THOMAS). Commentary on John's Epistles.
       8vo.   *Halifax*, 1808.

   *Very excellent.   The writer has upon every verse something to
say worth the saying.*

1389 LÜCKE (G. C. F.   *Bonn*). Epistles of John.   12mo.   *Biblical
       Cabinet.*   *Edinb.*, T. & T. Clark.   1837.

   Dr. Graham, of Bonn, says that "*Lücke* is impartial, learned, and
critically in earnest; yet the attentive reader soon discovers a very
decided anti-evangelical tendency.   I say anti-evangelical in our sense
of the word, for in Germany he has done much to overthrow the cold
kingdom of rationalism and unbelief."   *Graham* is severe, and a discount
may be allowed from this judgment.   Let it serve as a warning.

1390 SHEPHERD (R.)   *See No.* 1069.

I. JOHN.

1391 **APOSTOLIC INSTRUCTION,** exemplified in the First Epistle of John. [Anon.] 12mo. *Lond.*, 1840.
Upon two chapters only, but thoroughly good, and full of sweetness and light.

1392 **BINNING** (HUGH. 1627—1653). Fellowship with God , or Twenty-eight Sermons on 1 John I and II, 1—3. In his *Works*, vol. II (*See No.* 1197). Reprinted in 18mo. by Religious Tract Society. 1833.
Milk for babes, and meat for men ; calls to backsliders, and comforts for mourners. " There is no speaking," says Durham, " after Mr. Binning ; truly he had the tongue of the learned, and knew how to speak a word in season."

1393 **CALVIN** (JOHN). Commentaries upon the First Epistle of John, and upon the Epistle of Jude. Catholic Epistles. Reprint of C.T.S. edition. $3.50. Eerdmans.

1394 **CANDLISH** (ROBERT, D.D.) First Epistle of John, expounded. Complete one-volume edition. $5.95. Zondervan.
We set great store by these lectures. A man hardly needs anything beyond Candlish. He is devout, candid, prudent, and forcible.

1395 **COTTON** (JOHN, B.D., *Pastor of Boston, N.E.* 1585—1652). Commentary upon the First Epistle of John. Folio. *Lond.*, 1656.
Calamy puts his imprimatur upon this book, and speaks of the author's name as " deservedly precious among the saints of God." In doctrine and experience he is a noble teacher.

1396 **GRAHAM** (W.) The Spirit of Love. Commentary on 1 John. Sm. 8vo. *Lond.*, 1857.
Graham is sound and vigorous, and does not mince matters in dealing with semi-sceptics ; hence he brings upon himself violent reviews from opponents. *The Literary Churchman* denounces his book as containing "controversy without argument, criticism without proof, citation without reference, a show of scholarship without the fruits of it, and denunciation without decorum." To say the least of it, this review is far too severe.

1397 HANDCOCK (W. J.) Exposition of 1 John. Cr. 8vo. *Lond.*, Hamilton, Adams & Co. 1861.
The author has carefully studied the original, and has his own ideas as to its meaning ; but either he has not the power of communicating them, or else we are slow of apprehension. Very frequently we are at a loss to know what he means.

1398 **HARDY** (Nathaniel, D.D. 1618—1670). First Epistle of John unfolded and applied. 2 vols. 4to. 1656-59.
              Reprinted in *Nichol's Commentaries.* Cr.
     4to.   *Lond.,* Nisbet. 1865.

The Editor of Nichol's Edition says, " This Exposition is only a fragment. It was intended to consist of five parts, corresponding generally with the five chapters of the Epistle ; but only two of them were accomplished. In matter, the sermons are purely evangelical ; in spirit, they are earnest and affectionate ; in manner, they are eloquent and impressive." This is rather too ardent a commendation.

1399 **MORGAN** (James, D.D., *Belfast*). Exposition of 1 John. 8vo.   *Edinb.,* T. & T. Clark. 1866. S. 4/6.

Dr. Candlish says that this is a work " of great practical interest and value," and that had it appeared at an earlier date, " he might have abstained from issuing " his own Lectures on this Epistle. We are glad to possess both works.

1400 NEANDER (J. A. W.) First Epistle of John explained. Translated by Mrs. Conant. Sm. 8vo. *New York,* 1852.

Mrs. Conant in her preface says : " The treasures of genius and learning which enrich his more scientific works, here seem vivified by a new element, and melt, under the fervor of his inner spiritual life, into a glowing stream of eloquent practical instruction."

1401 PATTERSON (A. S., D.D.) Commentary on 1 John. 18mo. 1842. *See No.* 1292.

1402 **PIERCE** (Samuel Eyles). Exposition of 1 John, in Ninety-three Sermons. 2 vols., 8vo. *Lond.,* 1835.

This devout author was highly Calvinistic, but withal full of spiritual power and unction. He loved the deep things of God, and wrote upon them in a gracious manner.

1403 **STOCK** (John, M.A., *of Finchingfield*). Exposition of 1 John. 8vo. 10/- *Lond.,* Rivingtons. 1865.

Written by a well-instructed man of God. For spiritual teaching the work is second to none. Dr. Candlish prized it greatly.

1404 **COX** (Samuel). St. John's Letter to Kyria, and St. John's Letter to Caius. *See No.* 1309.

1405 **JONES** (W., D.D.) *See No.* 1311.

JUDE.

1406 BICKERSTETH (E.) *See No.* 1386.

1407 GARDINER (F., M.A.) The Last of the Epistles. Commentary on Jude. Cr. 8vo. *Boston, U.S.* 1856.
An interesting, straightforward, instructive commentary.

1408 **JENKYN** (WILLIAM. 1612—1685). Exposition of Jude.
2 vols., 4to., 1652, folio, 1656, Rev. J. Sherman's reprint, imp. 8vo. 1839. *See No.* 1251.
Earnest and popular, but very full, and profoundly learned. A treasure-house of good things.

1409 **LUTHER.** *See No.* 1372.

1410 McGILVRAY (WALTER). Lectures on Jude. 8vo. *Glasg.,* 1855. *Scarce.*
Vigorous, popular addresses by a Free Church divine.

1411 **MANTON** (THOMAS, D.D.) Commentary on Jude. 4to. *Lond.,* 1658.
Manton at first gave up all idea of printing this book on Jude, when he found that Jenkyn had taken up the subject; but he afterwards changed his mind. He tells us: " I consulted with my reverend brother's book, and when I found any point at large discussed by him, I either omitted it or mentioned it very briefly; so that his labours will be necessary to supply the weaknesses of mine." Manton's work is most commendable.

1412 MUIR (WILLIAM, D.D.) Discourses on Jude. 8vo. *Glasg.,* 1822.
Sermons which do not rise above mediocrity.

1413 OTES (SAMUEL, *the elder*). Explanation of Jude in forty-one Sermons. Folio. *Lond.,* 1633.
Of the conforming Puritan style, full of quaintnesses and singularities of learning. A book by no means to be despised.

1414 PERKINS (WILLIAM, D.D.) Exposition of Jude. 4to. 1606.
Perkins was regarded by his cotemporaries as a paragon of learning, but his writings fail to interest the generality of readers.

1415 TURNBULL (RICHARD, M.A.) Exposition of Jude. *See No.* 1367.

1416 **WILLET** (ANDREW). A Catholicon ; gathered out of the Catholike Epistle of Jude. Folio. *Lond.,* 1614.
This book is in the Museum, but we cannot procure a copy.

THE REVELATION.

The works upon REVELATION are so extremely numerous (Darling's list contains 52 columns), and the views entertained are so many, so different, and so speculative, that after completing our List we resolved not to occupy our space with it, but merely to mention a few works of repute. As for the lucubrations upon parts of the book, they lie at the booksellers' "thick as leaves in Vallambrosa." Numbers of these prophecyings have been disproved by the lapse of time, and others will in due season share their fate. The following remarks may help the student, and at the same time prove the difficulty of making a selection.

Davidson distinguishes a fourfold manner of apprehending Apocalyptic Prophecy.

1. *Preterists.* The prophecies contained in the Apocalypse were fulfilled with the destruction of Jerusalem and the fall of heathen Rome. This is the view of *Bossuet, Grotius, Hammond, Wetstein, Eichhorn, Ewald, De Wette, Lücke,* and others, among whom is the American expositor, *Moses Stuart.*

2. *Continuists.* The Apocalyptic prophecies are predictive of progressive history, being partly fulfilled, partly unfulfilled. Thus *Mede, Brightman, Isaac Newton, Woodhouse, Cunningham, Birks, Elliott* (and many Germans).

3. *Simple Futurists.* According to these, only the first three chapters relate to the historical present of the Seer, all else having reference to the absolute future of the Lord's Appearing. Thus, *Burgh, Maitland, Benjamin Newton, Todd,* and others.

4. *Extreme Futurists.* Even the first three chapters of Revelation are a prophecy relative to the absolute future of Christ's Coming—being a prediction of the condition of the Jews after the first Resurrection. *Kelly,* and some Irish authors.

1417 BENGEL (JOHN ALBERT). Introduction to his Exposition of the Apocalypse, with his preface to that work, and the greatest part of the conclusion of it, and also his marginal notes on the text, which are a summary of the whole Exposition. Translated from the High Dutch, by John Robertson, M.D. 8vo. *Lond.,* 1757.

This great author was rather too precise in his dates. The end of the forty-two months was settled for the 21st of May, 1810, and the destruction of the beast for June 18th, 1836. When so princely an expositor maunders in this fashion it should act as a caution to less able men.

1418 BONAR (H., D.D.) Light and Truth, vol. V. (*See No. 6.*)

1419 BRIGHTMAN (THOMAS). The Revelation of St. John. Thick 8vo. *Leyden,* 1644. 4to. *Amsterdam,* 1611. [See Nos. 649 and 775.]

Brightman's admirers called him "the English Prophet," and this work they styled the "Apocalypse of the Apocalypse;" but it survives only as a noteworthy monument of the failure of the most learned to expound the mysteries of this book. *Elliott* says "his Commentary is one of great vigour both in thought and language, and deservedly one of the most popular with the Protestant Churches of the time."

1420 BURGH [or, DE BURGH] (WILLIAM, M.A.)   An Exposition
      of the Revelation.   12mo.   *Dublin*, 1857.
Good in its own line.

1421 COWPER (WILLIAM, *of Galloway.* 1566—1619).   Pathmos;
      or, a Commentary on the Revelation.   4to.   *Lond.*, 1619;
      and in *Works*, folio, 1629.
The simple piety and vigorous style of *Cowper* have preserved his
old-fashioned work, and will preserve it.

1422 CRADOCK (SAMUEL, B.D.   1620—1760).   Exposition.   8vo.   1696.
Dr. Doddridge and *Job Orton* were very fond of this old author.   We are not.

1423 CUMMING (J.)   Apocalyptic Sketches.   2 vols., 12mo.
Here the views of *Elliott* are admirably popularized.

1424 DAUBUZ (CHARLES.   1670—1740).   A Perpetual Commentary
      on the Revelation.   Abridged by Peter Lancaster, A.M.   4to.
      Lond., 1730.
Subsequent writers have drawn much from this work; we have heard
it highly commended by competent judges.   There is also a larger
unabridged edition, which we have not seen.   This is said to be still
more valuable.

1425 DURHAM (JAMES.   1622—1658).   A Learned and Complete
      Commentary.   4to.   *Glasg.*, 1788.   Original edition, folio, 1658.
After all that has been written, it would not be easy to find a more
sensible and instructive work than this old-fashioned exposition.   We
cannot accept its interpretations of the mysteries, but the mystery of the
gospel fills it with sweet savour.

1426 **ELLIOTT** (C. B., A.M.   *Died* 1875).   Horæ Apoc-
      alypticæ; or, a Commentary on the Apocalypse, critical
      and historical.   4 vols. 8vo., *Lond.*, Seeleys.   1862.
The standard work on the subject.

1427 GARRATT (SAMUEL, M.A.)   Commentary.   8vo.   7/6.   *Lond.*,
      Seeleys.   1866.
This author mainly follows *Elliott*, but differs as he proceeds.   He is
an esteemed author.

1428 FULLER (ANDREW.   1754—1815).   Expository Discourses.
      2 vols., 8vo.   1815.   Also in *Works*.
Fuller is too judicious to run into speculations.   The work is both
condensed and clear.   *Fuller* called *Faber* "the Fortune-teller of the
Church," and there are others who deserve the name.

1429 GLASGOW (JAMES, D.D.)   Apocalypse Translated and Ex-
      pounded.   8vo.   *Edinb.*, T. & T. Clark.   1862.
We do not care much for the translation, and think some of the
interpretations speculative and forced; yet the work is important.

1430 HENGSTENBERG (E. W., D.D.) The Revelation expounded for those who search the Scriptures. Translated by Patrick Fairbairn, D.D. 2 vols., 8vo. *Edinb.*, 1851-52. *Scarce.*
Highly esteemed by the best judges.

1431 MEDE (JOSEPH, B.D., 1586—1638). A Key to the Apocalypse; [a Translation of Mede's *Clavis Apocalyptica.* By R. Bransby Cooper, Esq.] 8vo. *Lond.*, 1833.
There are several other works on the Apocalypse by this author, who, says *Elliott,* " was looked upon and written of as a man almost inspired for the solution of the Apocalyptic mysteries. Yet I think his success was at first over-estimated as an Apocalyptic expositor."

1432 NEWTON (BENJAMIN WILLS.) Thoughts on the Apocalypse. 8vo. *Lond.*, 1853.
Of the Futurist School. Condensed and instructive.

1433 ROGERS (GEORGE, *Principal of the " Pastors' College."*) Lectures on the Book of Revelation. 4 vols., 12mo. 1844-51.
Not half so well known as it ought to be : a mass of judicious remarks. We do not subscribe to the author's system of interpretation, but his expositions always command our respect.

1434 STUART (MOSES). A Commentary on the Apocalypse. 2 vols., royal 8vo. *Lond.*, 1845; 1 vol. 8vo. *Edinb.*, 1847; 1 vol. 8vo., *Lond.*, W. Tegg and Co. 1850.
Stuart rejects the historical interpretations generally given ; but his textual criticism and his preliminary disquisitions are very helpful. This work has laid us under great obligations.

1435 VAUGHAN (C. J., D.D.) Lectures on the Revelation. 2 vols. Fcap. 8vo. *Lond.*, Macmillan & Co. 1875.
Does not grapple with the difficulties, but inculcates the lessons of the book. A sensible course.

1436 WILLIAMS (ISAAC). The Apocalypse, with Notes and Reflections. Cr. 8vo. *Lond.*, Rivingtons. 1873.
Considering the High Church School to which he belongs, this author is marvellously rich in exposition. The whole is tinged with the mediæval spirit.

1437 WOODHOUSE (JOHN CHAPPEL, D.D., *Dean of Lichfield.* 1751—1834). Translation, with Notes. Roy. 8vo. 1805.
Bishop Hurd says, " This is the best book of the kind I have seen." We give no opinion, for we are too much puzzled with these Apocalyptic books, and are glad to write

FINIS.

NOW AVAILABLE
FROM SOLID GROUND

FROM THE PULPIT

TO THE

PALM-BRANCH

A MEMORIAL OF

CHARLES H. SPURGEON

Many will be happy to know this long-unobtainable volume on Spurgeon is to be available again. I have collected such books for years but not yet owned this rare book. May the recovery of Spurgeon's memory lead many to the devotion to Christ which so marked his life!"   **- Rev. Iain H. Murray**

"Collectors of Spurgeonalia will be delighted to have access to this once inaccessible volume. More importantly, because of the funerary contents, it will provoke reflection on the life and ministry of a choice servant of God, which may in turn prove to be of profound assistance to us as we assess the substance, faithfulness and intensity of our own Christian life and service."   **– Dr. Ligon Duncan**

"Spurgeon lovers, and what Christian minister is not, will find great satisfaction in this volume. That even after his misrepresentation by his peers, Spurgeon generated such amazing response even in his death bears testimony to the power and depth of his influence. This volume shows that the power of the gospel is pervasive in every area of life and pursued with faithfulness will change the landscape of culture and Christian ministry."   **- Dr. Tom Nettles**

"When a book of such rare quality is republished it must be read, not just for the sake of reading it, but for the purpose of the enormous spiritual enrichment it will give to anyone who take the time to get into it's wealth of content. To read this gem will leave the reader moved to worship the source of all truth, God Himself."   **- Pastor Martin Holdt**

Other Solid Ground Titles

In addition to the book in your hand, Solid Ground is honored to offer other uncovered treasure, many for the first time in more than a century:

NOTES ON GALATIANS by J. Gresham Machen

EXPOSITION OF THE BAPTIST CATECHISM by Benjamin Beddome

PAUL THE PREACHER: Sermons from Acts by John Eadie

THE COMMUNICANT'S COMPANION by Matthew Henry

THE CHILD AT HOME by John S.C. Abbott

THE LIFE OF JESUS CHRIST FOR THE YOUNG by Richard Newton

THE KING'S HIGHWAY: 10 Commandments for the Young by Richard Newton

HEROES OF THE REFORMATION by Richard Newton

FEED MY LAMBS: Lectures to Children on Vital Subjects by John Todd

LET THE CANNON BLAZE AWAY by Joseph P. Thompson

THE STILL HOUR: Communion with God in Prayer by Austin Phelps

COLLECTED WORKS of James Henley Thornwell (4 vols.)

CALVINISM IN HISTORY by Nathaniel S. McFetridge

OPENING SCRIPTURE: Hermeneutical Manual by Patrick Fairbairn

THE ASSURANCE OF FAITH by Louis Berkhof

THE PASTOR IN THE SICK ROOM by John D. Wells

THE BUNYAN OF BROOKLYN: Life & Sermons of I.S. Spencer

THE NATIONAL PREACHER: Sermons from 2nd Great Awakening

FIRST THINGS: First Lessons God Taught Mankind Gardiner Spring

BIBLICAL & THEOLOGICAL STUDIES by 1912 Faculty of Princeton

THE POWER OF GOD UNTO SALVATION by B.B. Warfield

THE LORD OF GLORY by B.B. Warfield

A GENTLEMAN & A SCHOLAR: Memoir of J.P. Boyce by J. Broadus

SERMONS TO THE NATURAL MAN by W.G.T. Shedd

SERMONS TO THE SPIRITUAL MAN by W.G.T. Shedd

HOMILETICS AND PASTORAL THEOLOGY by W.G.T. Shedd

A PASTOR'S SKETCHES 1 & 2 by Ichabod S. Spencer

THE PREACHER AND HIS MODELS by James Stalker

IMAGO CHRISTI: The Example of Jesus Christ by James Stalker

LECTURES ON THE HISTORY OF PREACHING by J. A. Broadus

THE SHORTER CATECHISM ILLUSTRATED by John Whitecross

THE CHURCH MEMBER'S GUIDE by John Angell James

THE SUNDAY SCHOOL TEACHER'S GUIDE by John A. James

CHRIST IN SONG: Hymns of Immanuel from All Ages by Philip Schaff

DEVOTIONAL LIFE OF THE S.S. TEACHER by J.R. Miller

Call us Toll Free at 1-877-666-9469

Send us an e-mail at sgcb@charter.net

Visit us on line at solid-ground-books.com

Uncovering Buried Treasure to the Glory of God